LIBYA AND THE WEST

WHAT EVERYONE NEEDS TO KNOW®

LIBYA AND THE WEST
WHAT EVERYONE NEEDS TO KNOW®

PETER L. HAHN

OXFORD
UNIVERSITY PRESS

Oxford University Press is a department of the University of Oxford.
It furthers the University's objective of excellence in research, scholarship,
and education by publishing worldwide. Oxford is a registered trade mark of
Oxford University Press in the UK and certain other countries.

"What Everyone Needs to Know" is a registered trademark of
Oxford University Press.

Published in the United States of America by Oxford University Press
198 Madison Avenue, New York, NY 10016, United States of America.

© Oxford University Press 2025

All rights reserved. No part of this publication may be reproduced, stored in
a retrieval system, transmitted, used for text and data mining, or used for training
artificial intelligence, in any form or by any means, without the prior permission in
writing of Oxford University Press, or as expressly permitted by law, by license or
under terms agreed with the appropriate reprographics rights organization. Inquiries
concerning reproduction outside the scope of the above should be sent
to the Rights Department, Oxford University Press, at the address above.

You must not circulate this work in any other form
and you must impose this same condition on any acquirer

Library of Congress Cataloging-in-Publication Data
Names: Hahn, Peter L., author.
Title: Libya and the West : what everyone needs to know / Peter L. Hahn.
Description: New York, NY : Oxford University Press, 2025. | Includes
bibliographical references and index.
Identifiers: LCCN 2024044918 (print) | LCCN 2024044919 (ebook) |
ISBN 9780190223021 (hardback) | ISBN 9780190223038 (paperback) |
ISBN 9780190223052 (epub) | ISBN 9780197805008
Subjects: LCSH: Libya—History. | Libya—Foreign relations—Western
countries. | Western countries—Foreign relations—Libya.
Classification: LCC DT224 .H34 2025 (print) | LCC DT224 (ebook) | DDC
961.2—dc23/eng/20241231
LC record available at https://lccn.loc.gov/2024044918
LC ebook record available at https://lccn.loc.gov/2024044919

DOI: 10.1093/wentk/9780190223021.001.0001

Paperback printed by Sheridan Books, Inc., United States of America
Hardback printed by Bridgeport National Bindery, Inc., United States of America

To my grandchildren

William, Rachel, Thomas, Savannah, Caleb, and Miles
and perhaps others yet unknown

Jewels in "the crown of the aged"

CONTENTS

ROSTER OF MAPS	XV
ACKNOWLEDGMENTS	XVII

Introduction	**1**

1 The Italian Colonization of Libya in the Era of the World Wars — 6

Was Italy the first Western power to become involved in Libya?	*6*
Why did the United States engage in warfare in Libya in the early nineteenth century?	*6*
When and why did Italy become a colonial power?	*9*
When and why did Italy take a colonial interest in Libya in particular?	*10*
How did Italy prepare diplomatically to colonize Libya?	*10*
What triggered the outbreak of the Italian–Ottoman War of 1911–1912?	*11*
What were the international consequences of the Italian–Ottoman War?	*13*
How did Libyans react to the Italian invasion?	*14*
How did Libya factor into the military dynamics of World War I?	*15*
What was the nature of Italian rule in Libya in the aftermath of World War I?	*17*
Why did Italy intensify its military operations in Libya in 1923?	*19*

viii Contents

How did Italy conquer Libya in 1923–1931?	20
What type of government did Italy impose on Libya?	22
Why did Italy refer to Libya as "the Fourth Shore"?	23
What was Italy's overall approach to developing Libya as a colony?	24
How did native Italian settlers figure into Italy's plans to colonize the "Fourth Shore"?	25
How did Italy's settlement schemes change after the defeat of the Senussi resistance in 1931?	26
What was the intention and impact of Mussolini's 1937 visit to Libya?	27
What was the impact of Italian colonial rule on the people of Libya?	28
What were Italy's plans for expanding its imperial presence in Africa beyond Libya?	31
How did Britain and France respond to the Italian conquest of Libya?	32
How did Britain and France respond to Italian expansionism elsewhere?	32
How did World War II affect Italy's colonial position in Libya?	34
What was the strategic significance of Libya to the European powers that fought World War II?	34
What were the views of Libyans toward World War II?	37
Did Libyans participate in the war as combatants?	38
What was the impact of World War II on the people of Libya?	39

2 From Colony to Monarchy to Revolution: Libya, 1943–1969   41

What happened in Libya after the expulsion of Italian and German military forces from North Africa in 1943?	41
How did the victorious Allies sort out Libya's permanent status in the aftermath of World War II?	43
How did the Italian Peace Treaty of 1947 address the issue of Libya?	46
What diplomatic initiatives did the Great Powers take after the Italian Peace Treaty?	47
How did strategic factors shape Western thinking about Libya?	47
How did the United Nations handle the Italian colonies issue?	49

What challenges did Libyans face during the period of Great Power
and UN deliberations about their future?   51

How did Libya advance toward statehood under the auspices of the
UN Commissioner?   52

What type of political order emerged in Libya under King Idris?   54

What foreign policies did the independent Kingdom of Libya pursue?   55

How did Libya's pro-Western orientation influence its relations with
other Arab states?   57

How did the discovery of oil shape Libya's development as an
independent state?   58

In what ways did the oil wealth change Libya's internal
socioeconomic order?   60

To what degree did the socioeconomic instability of the 1960s
contribute to political unrest?   62

What was the effect of the Arab–Israeli War of June 1967 on Libya's
political orientation?   64

What were the origins of the Libyan revolution of 1969?   65

Who was Muammar al-Qaddafi, and how was he able to seize
power from King Idris in 1969?   66

3 Libya under Muammar al-Qaddafi   69

What steps did Muammar al-Qaddafi and his confederates take to
consolidate power in Libya?   69

How did the Western powers view the Libyan coup?   70

What type of government did the Revolutionary Command Council
establish?   72

How did the Libyan domestic political order evolve under Qaddafi's
leadership in the 1970s?   75

What economic reforms did Qaddafi implement?   79

Was there domestic opposition to Qaddafi's rule?   81

What policy did Qaddafi pursue toward the Great Powers engaged in
the Cold War?   82

What policies did Western powers initially pursue toward Qaddafi's
regime?   84

x **Contents**

How did Qaddafi manage Libya's oil industry and the Western firms
that dominated it?   87

What was Qaddafi's policy toward pan-Arab unification?   90

What was Qaddafi's policy toward Israel?   94

Why did Libya engage in international terrorism to achieve its
foreign policy objectives?   95

What policies did Qaddafi pursue in Africa?   97

How did French–Libyan relations evolve in the 1970s and 1980s?   101

How did Italian–Libyan relations evolve in the 1970s?   101

How did US–Libyan relations evolve in the 1970s?   102

How did Qaddafi reach out directly to the American people?   104

Why did US and French relations with Libya reach a crisis in 1980?   105

4 Qaddafi and the West in the 1980s and 1990s   108

What was the political situation within Libya in the 1980s?   108

What was the economic situation within Libya in the 1980s?   109

Why did Western powers and Libya clash again in Chad in the 1980s?   110

What approach did the Ronald Reagan administration follow
toward Libya?   112

What triggered the military incident between US and Libyan
warplanes in the Gulf of Sidra in 1981?   114

What was the impact of the air engagement on US–Libyan relations?   115

How did the Western European powers view Libya in the early 1980s?   117

Why did the United Kingdom sever diplomatic relations with Libya
in 1984?   118

Why did US–Libyan relations deteriorate in the mid-1980s?   118

How did US security strategy toward terrorism evolve in the 1980s?   121

How did the United States react to the surge in terrorism by Libya in
particular?   121

What was the impact of these policies on US relations with Libya?   123

How did the European powers view the escalation of US pressure
on Libya?   125

Did the European powers support the US airstrikes on Libya in April 1986?	*126*
How did US–Libyan relations develop in the late 1980s?	*129*
Was Libya complicit in the bombing of civilian airliners in 1988–1989?	*131*
How did the international community handle evidence of Libyan complicity in the Lockerbie bombing?	*131*
To what extent did Western powers worry about Libyan development of nuclear weapons?	*132*
How did Qaddafi's foreign conflicts shape his people's perceptions of him in the 1990s?	*134*
Did Qaddafi face threats of internal rebellion?	*136*

5 The Rapprochement between Qaddafi and the West, Early 2000s **139**

How was the controversy over the Lockerbie bombing resolved?	*139*
Did Qaddafi otherwise moderate his foreign policy?	*141*
What verdict did the Scottish court reach in the Lockerbie trial?	*143*
Was Megrahi actually guilty?	*144*
What effect did the Lockerbie trial have on Libya's relations with Western powers?	*145*
What was the impact of 9/11 on the US–Libyan relationship?	*147*
How did the 9/11 breakthrough contribute to the settlement of the Lockerbie issue?	*148*
How did France respond to the Lockerbie settlement?	*148*
On what terms did the United Nations lift its sanctions against Libya?	*149*
When did Libya decide to renounce its weapons of mass destruction programs?	*150*
Why did Libya decide to renounce its weapons of mass destruction programs?	*152*
Did the US and British invasion of Iraq in March 2003 influence Qaddafi's decision to renounce WMD?	*153*
How did Libya and Western powers follow up on the WMD deal?	*154*
How did French–Libyan relations evolve after sanctions were lifted?	*155*

xii **Contents**

What was the nature of Italy's relationship with Libya?	156
Why did the United States restore diplomatic relations with Libya?	157
What was Qaddafi's international reputation after diplomatic relations were normalized?	158
What type of domestic leader did Qaddafi become in the early 2000s?	160

6 The Libyan Revolution of 2011 — 163

What were the long-term origins of the Libyan revolution of 2011?	163
What were the immediate triggers of the Libyan uprising?	164
Did US policies trigger the Arab Spring uprisings?	166
How did Qaddafi react to the protests?	168
What was the result of Qaddafi's decision to suppress the demonstrations with force?	170
Why did the Libyan opposition form the National Transition Council?	171
How did Western governments view the uprising in Libya?	172
To what extent did human rights concerns motivate the Western powers to act against Qaddafi?	175
What action did the UN Security Council take against Qaddafi's regime?	176
How did Western policy toward Qaddafi evolve in March 2011?	177
What action did the UN Security Council take in March 2011?	180
What military action did Western powers take under the Security Council resolutions?	181
How did the Western powers justify their military assaults?	183
What was the impact of the Western intervention on the civil war in Libya?	185
Did the Allies try to overthrow or kill Qaddafi with their airstrikes?	186
Why did NATO become involved in air operations against Libya?	188
Were efforts made to end the fighting via diplomacy?	190
How did the rebels ultimately prevail?	191
What happened to Qaddafi?	192
How did Qaddafi's legacy shape the political situation in Libya?	194
Could the Western intervention in Libya be deemed a long-term success?	196

Contents xiii

7 Civil War, Foreign Meddling, and Political Deadlock: Libya since 2011 — **200**

What steps were taken to establish a stable government after the downfall of Qaddafi? — *200*

How did the Western powers view the new government of Libya? — *202*

What were the origins of the deadly attack on the US consulate in Benghazi on September 11, 2012? — *203*

Why did the Benghazi attack become a prominent issue in US domestic politics? — *205*

How well did the elected government of Libya stabilize and administer the country? — *206*

How did the Western powers try to stabilize Libya after the Benghazi raid? — *208*

Why did the elected government of Libya decline in 2014? — *209*

What triggered the start of full-scale civil war? — *211*

Why did Muslim-majority states become involved in the Libyan civil war? — *212*

How did the Western powers assess the Libyan civil war? — *213*

What kind of threat did the Islamic State in Iraq and Syria pose in Libya? — *214*

How did the Western powers respond to the rise of ISIS in Libya? — *215*

Why did the United Nations fail to resolve the civil war? — *217*

How did the civil war shape patterns of human migration in Libya? — *219*

How did European powers attempt to resolve the political deadlock in Libya? — *221*

Did US policy in Libya change under President Donald J. Trump? — *222*

Why did the Libyan civil war resume in 2019? — *224*

How did the Western powers react to Haftar's offensive on Tripoli? — *224*

How did non-Western powers react to Haftar's offensive? — *226*

What was the outcome of the battle for Tripoli? — *227*

Was the United Nations able to broker a postwar settlement? — *228*

NOTES	231
BIBLIOGRAPHY	255
INDEX	267

ROSTER OF MAPS

Map 1	Geography and Regions of Modern Libya	*4*
Map 2	Ethnography of Modern Libya	*18*
Map 3	Oilfields and Petroleum Infrastructure of Modern Libya	*58*
Map 4	Qaddafi's Libya	*76*
Map 5	Coalition No Fly Zones and Strike Locations during the 2011 Intervention	*184*
Map 6	Zones of Control in the Aftermath of the Libyan Civil War, 2022	*229*

ACKNOWLEDGMENTS

I am grateful to several colleagues who contributed to this publication. During the preliminary phase of my labor, graduate research associates Jonathon R. Dreeze and Elizabeth Kerr and undergraduate associate Emily Lada assisted in identifying and organizing sources. During the final phase of work, graduate research associate Edward Kunz tracked down obscure materials, verified facts, proofread text, and compiled illustrations. I am grateful to the Department of History at Ohio State University for appointing such fabulous research assistants to aid in my endeavor.

Several accomplished scholars offered expert insight and advice on the scope and quality of this manuscript. My Ohio State University colleagues Jane Hathaway and Nate Rosenstein helped me understand Libya from the ancient through early modern eras. My professional colleagues Nathan J. Citino, Douglas Little, and Robert J. McMahon read the entire manuscript in draft form and provided valuable insights on how to deepen, sharpen, and improve it. Feedback from several anonymous peer reviewers recruited by Oxford University Press helped me correct errors and polish my narrative and analysis.

It has been a pleasure to work with the fine editorial team at Oxford University Press. I have benefited significantly from the seasoned insights of Executive Editor Nancy Toff, who recruited me to write the book. Project Editors Chelsea Hogue and Meredith Taylor were instrumental in shepherding the manuscript to publication. I am indebted to project managers Kavitha Yuvaraj and Ganga Balaji, copy editor Annie Woy, and indexer Thomas Vecchio for their careful contributions to the publication.

Over the years that I worked on this book, I relied on the support of my family. My wife Cathy, our children, and their spouses encouraged my research and writing. Since 2018, I have found joy in the births of grandchildren. Arriving into a world of international conflict, climate crisis, and pandemic, the grandkids have generated love, laughter, and dreams. I dedicate this book to them, in the hope that they—and every member of their generation in every land—enjoy long lives featuring family bonds, community harmony, environmental integrity, and universal peace.

Peter L. Hahn
Columbus, Ohio
August 20, 2024

INTRODUCTION

Libya has intrigued me for decades. As a professional historian of US diplomacy, I have conducted research on the dynamics of World War II in the Middle East, the rise of US power and associated decline of British imperial influence in Egypt and other Arab states, US policy toward the Arab–Israeli conflict, the surge of anti-Western terrorism in the 1980s and 1990s, and the US reactions to the Arab Spring uprisings of 2010–2011. In all these research inquiries, Libya appeared as a player, at times occupying the field of view of officials in Washington, at other times lurking in the shadows.

Libya was the base from which Italian and German armies threatened the Suez Canal during World War II. Its transition to independence was a subject of debate between East and West that contributed to Cold War tensions in the late 1940s. Under Muammar al-Qaddafi, who ruled the country from 1969 to 2011, Libya fomented violent resistance to Israel and engaged in low-intensity, irregular warfare with the United States. During and after the Arab Spring, Libya experienced popular protests, Western armed intervention, and debilitating civil war, leaving the United States struggling to shape Libya's development without being drawn into its fights.

Because Libya kept appearing in so many of my research inquiries, I conceptualized a book on US–Libyan relations. When an editor at Oxford University Press encouraged me to widen my focus to include such other Western powers as Italy, Great Britain, and France, I jumped at the opportunity to place US relations with Libya in a broad, multinational context. This book thus provides an analytical overview of the policies of Italy, Great Britain, France, and the United States toward Libya from the nineteenth century to the modern day.

When I embarked upon this study, I expected to find that the position of dominant Western power vis-á-vis Libya transitioned from Italy to Britain to the United States while France vied for influence. I soon discovered, however, that the story of Libya and the West was more dynamic than a simple tale of an Italian era giving way to British and US moments. I found that all four Western powers were simultaneously involved in Libya, jockeying against each other for influence and power. There were moments when the four powers coordinated policies, such as when they used military means to break the back of the Qaddafi regime in 2011. More often, though, they competed, such as when Britain and the United States joined forces to demolish Italian (and German) power in North Africa during World War II, and when the European states collectively stonewalled President Ronald Reagan's policies to resist Qaddafi's practice of terrorism in the 1980s. The four Western powers disagreed on the appropriate tempo for normalizing relations with Qaddafi in the early 2000s, while France and Italy competed against each other for influence in Tripoli in the post-Qaddafi 2010s. Regarding Libya, "the West" proved to be less unified than I had expected at the outset.

Research for this book revealed that Western officials typically elevated their security and economic needs in Libya over their own democratic ideals. Prior to World War II, Italy imposed a colonial regime in Libya to project military power, extract wealth, and acquire land for settlement by Italian citizens. After the world war, the four Western powers considered Libya important to such regional security interests as the containment of Soviet influence during the Cold War, confinement of Islamic extremism after the Cold War, and limitations on migrations of sub-Saharan peoples to southern Europe in the early twenty-first century. Furthermore, the Western powers assigned substantial economic and strategic worth to Libya's oil, which was closer, cheaper, and "cleaner" (less sulfurous) than that available in other Arab states or Iran. To protect these vital interests, Western leaders supported authoritarian Libyan leaders and implemented diplomatic policies that were deleterious to the development of democracy in Libya.

Libya plays a central role in this book. The Italian colonization of the North African coastline incorporated three regions that had developed distinctive identities over many centuries: Cyrenaica in the east (about half of the country), Tripolitania (or Tripoli) in the northwest (about one-sixth), and the Fezzan in the southwest (about one-third). These regions were shaped by physical geography. Coastal rainfall enabled civilizational development in Tripolitania and Cyrenaica, but their 1,100-mile Mediterranean coastline exposed them to foreign incursions. The Sahara Desert encompassed some 90 percent of the country, impeding inland economic and social development until modern times. The Sirtica, an extension of the Sahara that cuts a 300-mile path to the Gulf of Sidra in north-central Libya, isolated Tripolitania and Cyrenaica from each other and thereby caused the development of separate histories and identities. Such legacies proved hard to overcome even after the formation of the unified State of Libya in 1951 and the development of modern infrastructure and communications linking the regions.

Although I am not a specialist in the history of Libya per se, I strove to cast modern Libya in a central role. I sought to reveal what its leaders believed, declared, and practiced and to determine the impact of Libyan government policy (as well as Western interventions) on the Libyan people. Among political leaders, Qaddafi easily ranked as the most significant individual in shaping Libya's history. Taking power in a coup in 1969 and ruling as an authoritarian for 42 years, Qaddafi was assertive, bold, adventurous, provocative, ruthless, violent,

4 LIBYA AND THE WEST

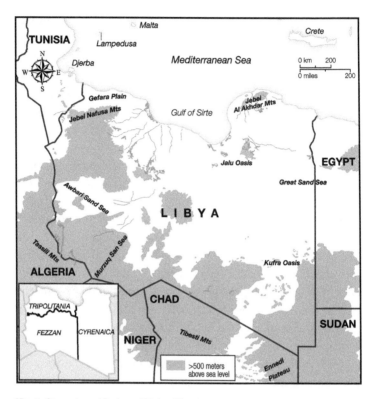

Map 1 Geography and Regions of Modern Libya

and flamboyant. Constantly seeking to advance revolutionary change at home, he cast an imposing shadow over his people. Constantly seeking to resist foreign colonialism, exploitation, dominance, and pro-Zionism, he routinely needled the four Western powers. Catalyzed by armed intervention by the Western powers, Qaddafi's sudden downfall in 2011 left a vacuum of power conducive to civil war, cultural splintering, territorial partition, and political deadlock. Although the words and actions of the leaders of Libya were readily discoverable, I struggled to find individual "voices" of the common people and thus relied on aggregated data to record their collective experiences. The people of Libya experienced considerable violence and tragedy over the past 140 years. Libya was poor before the discovery of oil there in 1959; thereafter, the enormous wealth generated by oil production was neither distributed equitably nor used effectively to elevate the quality of life of the masses. Divided by regional and tribal identities and fates of geography, victimized by their own leaders, and alternatively exploited or neglected by foreign powers, the Libyan people were no strangers to disunity, poverty, repression, warfare, and agony.

The evidence presented in this book was drawn from US and European primary and secondary sources and a smattering of Libyan sources in translation. Because Arabic is not among my three research languages, and because political and security concerns prevented me from visiting Libya during the years I worked on this book, I defer to scholars with competence in Arabic to fill in any gaps in my work, and I sincerely hope that conditions in Libya soon become favorable to historical research by native and visiting scholars.[1]

1

THE ITALIAN COLONIZATION OF LIBYA IN THE ERA OF THE WORLD WARS

Was Italy the first Western power to become involved in Libya?

Several Western powers had become involved in North Africa over the centuries prior to the emergence of Italy as a unified nation-state because the local rulers of Morocco, Algiers, Tunis, and Tripoli (known collectively as the Barbary States) exacted financial tributes from maritime nations for the privilege of sending ships through the Mediterranean unharmed. Those who refused to pay risked having their ships fall victim to piracy, with their crews held captive until ransoms were paid. European powers occasionally and ineffectively resisted the corsairs: Spanish forces occupied Tripoli in 1510, only to be expelled by the Ottoman navy in 1551. More typically, European powers paid the financial tributes on the calculation that doing so was cheaper than the alternatives of losing ships and crews or contesting the pirates with military force. Beginning in 1640, Britain, France, and Holland negotiated a series of treaties with Tunis and Algiers that secured freedom of the seas in exchange for financial payments, but the expectations of the Barbary rulers grew over time.[1]

Why did the United States engage in warfare in Libya in the early nineteenth century?

US independence from the British Empire removed the security against Barbary piracy that colonial American shippers had enjoyed under the tributes paid by London. In the 1780s and 1790s, therefore, the new US government negotiated treaties with the Barbary States that exchanged payment of nearly $1 million by the United States for protection from harm for the scores of US commercial vessels that plied the Mediterranean annually. Lacking naval power, Presidents George Washington (1789–1797) and John Adams (1797–1801) reasoned that paying tributes was essential to protect US commerce. By contrast, as secretary of state (1790–1793) and vice president (1797–1801) Thomas Jefferson reasoned that making concessions drained precious financial resources and stoked growing demands by the Barbary States. While vice president, Jefferson informed President Adams that "it would be best to effect a peace through the medium of war."[2]

Inaugurated as president in March 1801, Jefferson resolved to resist the practices of the Barbary States. Feeling empowered by the construction of the first six ships of the US Navy—for which Congress had allocated funds in 1794—Jefferson promptly refused a demand by Yusef Pasha Karamanli of Tripoli for $225,000. Two months later, Yusef declared war on the United States, announcing it by cutting down the flagpole at the US consulate. The conflict quickly escalated into armed hostilities that lasted until 1805.

In that so-called First Barbary War, the US Navy, operating in partnership with the navies of Sweden and Sicily and local mercenaries, engaged in episodic naval and land battles against Yusef. Disaster struck US forces in 1803, when the USS *Philadelphia* ran aground in Tripoli harbor and Yusef's fighters captured and enslaved its 300 sailors. (US soldiers and marines, in a daring operation, were at least able to set the ship afire to prevent it from being captured by the enemy.) Its forces and its budgets stretched thin, the US Navy prepared to besiege Tripoli in hope of rescuing the captured crewmen—with limited confidence in its own success. Feeling threatened, however, Yusef sued for peace in 1805, leading to a settlement in which he released the US captives in exchange for a ransom payment of $60,000.[3]

The tribute system remained in place, leading to the Second Barbary War—between the United States and Algiers—in 1812–1815. At the start of the War of 1812 between the United States and Britain, the Dey of Algiers, Hajj Ali, declared war on the United States and seized a US commercial ship and its crew, prompted to do so by the British as a means of distracting the leaders and weakening the economy of their transatlantic adversary. US President James Madison was unable to battle the Algerians or pay ransom for the captive crewmen while fighting the British. Soon after the Anglo–US war ended in 1815, by contrast, Madison dispatched a US Navy expedition that captured Algerian ships, took hundreds of prisoners, and poised to invade the capital of Algiers. Such exercises of US naval power—as well as a British–Dutch shelling of Algiers—convinced Dey Omar to settle. US diplomats negotiated treaties—not only with Algiers but also with Tunis and Tripoli—providing for exchange of all prisoners of war, release of all captives, and an end to the tribute system.[4]

Emboldened by the successes of the United States, European powers soon revoked their acceptance of the tribute system. Having abolished slavery in its empire in 1807, Britain pressured the Ottomans to end their trans-Saharan slave trade and, by anchoring warships off the coast of Algiers in 1817, compelled Algiers to stop its practice of enslaving Christians. The end of the Napoleonic Wars in 1815 enabled European powers to redirect their military might toward the Barbary States and thereby resist their demands. France's occupation of Algeria in 1830 marked a massive shift in the balance of power between Europe and North Africa.

As the first US armed intervention in the Mediterranean region, the Barbary Wars shaped the broad contours of US–Libyan relations. Despite such setbacks as the loss of the USS *Philadelphia*, the American people took significant pride in their military accomplishments, remembering the wars as a

Italian Colonization of Libya **9**

heroic triumph of a Christian republic over Islamic tyranny and piracy. For the people of the territories that became known as Libya, by contrast, the episode displayed US interference, hubris, and hostility.[5]

When and why did Italy become a colonial power?

Soon after its unification as a modern state in 1861, Italy became eager to participate in the "scramble for Africa," the late nineteenth-century competitive surge by European powers to seize colonial possessions on the continent to their south. Led by such groups as the Italian Geographic Society, expansionists asserted that an African empire would demonstrate Italy's standing as a great power and provide space for the country's expanding population. "To emigrate is servile," the imperialism advocate Senator Nobili Vitelleschi asserted in 1902, "but to conquer colonies is a worthy task of a free and noble people."[6]

The scramble for Africa was touched off by the Berlin Conference of 1884–1885. Attended by 13 European powers and the United States, the conference produced treaties that carved Africa into European colonies. Before the conference, European powers controlled about 20 percent of Africa in colonies along its seacoasts. By 1902, European powers colonized 90 percent (some 10 million square miles) of the African continent.

Having attended the Berlin conference, Italy initially joined the scramble by establishing colonies on the so-called Horn of Africa (the peninsula in northeast Africa that extends into the Red Sea, the Gulf of Aden, and the Indian Ocean), where maritime traffic had grown considerably since the opening of the Suez Canal in 1869. Italy established various commercial interests in coastal areas of the Horn beginning in the 1870s. In 1889, it declared colonial control of Eritrea and part of Somalia, winning legal recognition from the king of Ethiopia as well as other European powers.

10 LIBYA AND THE WEST

When it tried to expand its domain by invading Ethiopia in 1896, however, Italy suffered a humiliating defeat by Ethiopian forces at the Battle of Adowa. That setback brought down the government of Prime Minister Francesco Crispi. It also taught other Italian leaders the risks of conducting imperial military operations at the end of supply lines longer than 3,000 miles.

When and why did Italy take a colonial interest in Libya in particular?

In the early 1880s, Italian expansionists eyed Libya as a potential target for expansion for several reasons. Libya was available, the only portion of the Ottoman Empire in Africa not seized by a European power. Italy calculated that the Ottomans might be incapable of defending Libya given their decentralized governance there. Libya's proximity to Italy—only 300 miles directly across the Mediterranean—made the task of controlling it seem more feasible than occupying other unclaimed spaces on the continent, a lesson accentuated by Italy's military defeat in Ethiopia in 1896.

On a strategic level, Libya promised to become a gateway to the African continent and a perch on the edge of the Middle East. By controlling the north and south shores of the Mediterranean, Italy could exert power over crucial maritime trade routes. Expansionism among other colonial powers created pressure on Italy to act quickly before the opportunity passed. France's 1881 seizure of Tunisia, which Italy had also coveted; the British penetrations of Egypt (1882) and Sudan (1899); and Ottoman efforts to expand south from Libya to the Sahara and Lake Chad made the Italian acquisition of Libya seem more valuable and more urgent to the government in Rome.

How did Italy prepare diplomatically to colonize Libya?

Over the course of three decades, starting in the 1880s, Italian statesmen laid the groundwork for Italy's colonization of

Libya. In the 1880s, they promoted Italian commercial expansion in the Libyan provinces, achieving a highly visible presence in the steamship, railroad, and banking industries by the early twentieth century. As he pursued ambitious schemes in East Africa in the early 1890s, Prime Minister Crispi secured the tacit consent of Britain, Germany, and Austria-Hungary that Italy could make political and military claims in Libya in the future.

In 1900, Italy and France negotiated a secret agreement providing that France could penetrate Morocco, and that Italy could expand into Libya. In 1904, France seized its target, thereby implicitly signaling that it would respect an Italian thrust into north-central Africa. Italy signed similar treaties with Britain, Germany, Austria-Hungary, and Russia in 1902–1909 that assured those states' recognition of eventual Italian expansion into Libya.

The actual French move into Morocco provoked German resistance that escalated into an international crisis in 1906–1911. Several major powers met in two conferences to address the controversies, forestalling an immediate outbreak of a French–German war but also laying further groundwork for the eruption of World War I in 1914. In the short term, some Italian expansionists favored action in Libya while the great powers were distracted by the crisis.

What triggered the outbreak of the Italian–Ottoman War of 1911–1912?

Political change within the Ottoman Empire instigated an Italian plot to capture formal control of Libya. In 1908–1909, the so-called Young Turks, a political reform movement in the Turkish heartland of the empire, revolted against the absolute power of the Sultan Abdul Hamid II, forcing him to abdicate and establishing a constitutional monarchy with an elected parliament. The development encouraged the fragmentation of the empire, especially in southeastern Europe, which

12 LIBYA AND THE WEST

convinced Italian expansionists that an opportunity beckoned in Libya.

The sense of opportunity was accompanied by two simultaneous concerns. First, an initiative by the Young Turks to firm up imperial holdings and to integrate the peoples of Libya in the new electoral order portended that the opportunity to colonize Libya might not last. Young Turk expressions of concern about Italian commercial activities in Libya were taken as harbingers of trouble. Second, the assumed lust for land among other European imperial powers fed Italian fears that a rival might seize Libya first. Rumors of massive land purchases in Libya by German speculators, while exaggerated, fed the growing Italian ardor for action.

On September 28, 1911, Italian Prime Minister Giovanni Giolitti fomented a crisis with the Ottoman Empire that enabled him to invade Libya. Claiming that the Ottomans had armed Arab tribes and thereby threatened Italian business interests, Giolitti issued an ultimatum with a 24-hour deadline that the Ottomans concede to Italy the right to send troops to protect its business interests. When the Ottomans rejected these terms, Italy declared war on their empire.

On October 3, Italian forces invaded Libya and occupied the coastal cities of Tripoli, Derna, Tobruk, and Benghazi. The government in Rome pretentiously announced to its new subjects that "Italy is your father because it married Tripolitania, which is your mother." Unable to resist effectively along the coast, Ottoman forces retreated to the interior, where they rallied local tribes into an alliance by appealing to their pan-Islamic sensitivities to resist a foreign invader from Christendom. The Italians' prewar assumption that Libyans would welcome them as liberators proved woefully inaccurate. On November 5, 1911, Italy's King Victor Emmanuel claimed Tripolitania and Cyrenaica as part of his realm, but the Turkish-Arab resistance prevented Italian incursion into the hinterlands in the winter of 1911–1912.[7]

Italy launched broader military operations to secure all Libya in 1912. The Italian Navy occupied the Dodecanese Islands and used bases there to disrupt communications and supply lines from Turkey to Libya. In July–October, the Italian Army launched a broad ground offensive that penetrated Tripolitania, Cyrenaica, and the Fezzan.

Facing dire threats in the First Balkans War that erupted in early October 1912, Ottoman leaders surrendered in Libya. In the Treaty of Lausanne (also known as the Treaty of Ouchy), signed on October 18, the Ottomans transferred Tripoli and Cyrenaica to Italy in exchange for an end to hostilities and an Italian pledge (which remained unfulfilled) to abandon the Dodecanese.

What were the international consequences of the Italian–Ottoman War?

The Italian–Ottoman War hastened the demise of the Ottoman Empire. It demonstrated Ottoman military weakness relative to European powers and encouraged independence movements in the Balkans. Defeat impelled Ottoman rulers to develop a partnership with Germany that eventually led to their joining the Central Powers in World War I.

In Italy, the victory over the Ottomans stoked a wave of nationalism and militarism that encouraged an assertive foreign policy for three decades. Italy would establish colonial domination over Libya with profound and enduring consequences for its people and their history. The colonial position that Italy gained in Libya would prove to be important in the dynamics of both World War I and World War II.

Britain and France tacitly approved the Italian occupation of Libya. In 1912, Britain recognized that Italy could control Kufra, a barren district in southeastern Libya whose boundaries had remained undefined in the late Ottoman era.

14 LIBYA AND THE WEST

How did Libyans react to the Italian invasion?

Generally, Libyans contested Italy's invasion. The Ottomans encouraged mass resistance by portraying the attack as an assault against pan-Islamic interests. Turkish officers became affiliated with Arab tribes who slowed the Italian incursion in 1911.

In Tripolitania, tribal chiefs secured Ottoman weapons and offered stiff resistance to Italian forces, denying them control of inland territory. Four major tribal leaders declared the existence of a political state independent from Italian rule, although in-fighting among them prevented the state from becoming viable. Determined to protect Muslim interests and to preserve their political and cultural independence, Amazigh tribes in the Fezzan prevented consolidation of Italian authority in that region. In Cyrenaica, leaders of the Senussi, a religious order that had promoted nationalist, populist unity since the nineteenth century, encouraged their many followers to take up arms against the Italians and denied the invaders a secure foothold in that province. By 1913, some 31,000 Libyans, evenly divided between Cyrenaica and Tripolitania, engaged in armed resistance to Italy.

Local opposition to Italian rule persisted even after the Ottoman surrender of Libya to Italy in October 1912. Italy miscalculated when it agreed to recognize in the Treaty of Lausanne the Ottoman sultan's religious authority in Libya, because Libyans—impervious to Italian notions that religious and political power operated in separate spheres—continued thereafter to ascribe to the sultan political authority as well. In violation of the 1912 treaty, the Ottomans provided covert material support and military advice to the Libyan forces resisting the Italians.

In 1914, the Senussi launched offensives against Italian military units, touching off the Italian–Senussi War of 1914–1917. Even before Italy entered World War I on the Allied side in 1915, the Senussi forced a partial retreat of Italian units from the

Fezzan in 1914, and, in 1915, they ambushed and demolished Italian units transiting the Sirtica Desert and captured their considerable military supplies.

Persistent quarrels between leading Libyans limited their ability to resist Italian power. Arguments ensued, for example, between the prominent Tripolitanian nationalist Ramadan al-Suwayhli and the Senussi of Cyrenaica over questions of political authority and relations with the Ottomans and the British. In 1916, competition over tax collection even triggered a gun battle between the two factions. While the engagement ended quickly, it sowed mutual resentment that lasted for decades.

A relatively small number of Libyans collaborated with Italian authorities. Businessmen and civil administrators were recruited with material incentives to cooperate with prewar enterprises. Once hostilities began, Italian authorities recruited several thousand Libyan combatants to their imperial cause by exploiting certain tribal rivalries and using economic aid and weapons to win the political cooperation of various tribal chiefs.

How did Libya factor into the military dynamics of World War I?

World War I erupted in the summer of 1914 between the Allies (primarily Britain, France, and Russia) and the Central Powers (primarily Germany, Austria-Hungary, and the Ottoman Empire). Although hostilities originated in Europe, the conflagration spread worldwide because imperial and ideological rivalries and colonial conflicts had intensified among the belligerents during the preceding decades.

Libya became involved in the war after Italy joined the Allies in 1915. The Ottoman Empire and Germany offered military advice and material support to the Libyan forces battling Italy. Hoping to undermine the British position in Egypt and disrupt Allied shipping on the Suez Canal, the Ottomans encouraged the Senussi to invade western Egypt in concert with an Ottoman assault from the east. Under the command of Sayed Ahmed al-Sharif, who was advised by Turkish military officers and supplied by both Germany and the Ottomans, Senussi cavalry units invaded Egypt in November 1915 and captured the coastal town of El Salloum. Fearful that Senussi ideology might permeate the Egyptian people and thereby compromise British security, British imperial forces launched a series of counterattacks in December 1915–March 1916 that forced the Senussi to abandon the northern theater.

Anglo–Senussi hostilities continued until 1917 in southwestern Egypt. There, Senussi fighters occupied a series of oases, forcing the British to divert troops from other duties to defend the area. In late 1916, British units launched offensive operations against the Senussi positions, achieving the withdrawal of the Senussi from Egypt by March 1917. His reputation diminished by military defeat, al-Sharif fled into exile in Turkey.

Libya's internal political status remained precarious through the armistice of the world war in November 1918. Sayed Mohammed Idris, al-Sharif's cousin and successor as leader of the Senussi, negotiated a deal with Italy and Britain in 1917 that gained him status as emir of inland Cyrenaica in exchange for his suppression of armed resistance to Italian forces and his respect for British control of Egypt. Other regions of Libya, however, remained in a state of rebellion, and Italian military forces were isolated in coastal enclaves and constantly in danger of attack. The truce between Idris and Italy did not address the postwar status of Libya or Italy's intentions there.

At the end of the war, Italy entered a dispute with the British and French over the spoils of victory. In the secret Treaty of London of April 1915, Italy had agreed to join the Allies at war if they would recognize postwar Italian claims to territory in the Balkans. While the treaty made no provision for Italian claims in Africa, it specified that if Britain and France seized German colonies on that continent after the war then Italy would also be entitled to new claims there. At the Paris Peace Conference of 1919, accordingly, France transferred a portion of Chad, which it had colonized in 1900, to Italian Libya and Britain ceded land to Italian Somaliland. Having dreamed of vast acquisitions in Africa, however, Italian leaders were generally unhappy that they had not gained significantly larger spoils.

What was the nature of Italian rule in Libya in the aftermath of World War I?

Italy's colonial aspirations in Libya persisted after World War I despite political instability within the government in Rome and war weariness among the Italian people. Colonial officials, buoyed by the Allied military victory and carried along by prewar momentum, officially established administrative regimes over the regions of Tripolitania, Cyrenaica, and the Fezzan. Despite its aspirations, however, Italy essentially negotiated a series of uneasy truces with Libyan leaders that failed to produce long-term peace or stability.

In early 1919, Italian military officers declared an intention to conquer Tripolitania by defeating the tribal forces that had besieged them along the coast since 1915. The Italian Army dispatched 70,000 soldiers from Europe, equipped with armor and airplanes, and publicly vowed to crush the local tribes. The Army hesitated to act, however, calculating that the threat of force might compel tribal obedience. But Tripolitanian leaders such as Suwayhli, the nationalist, and Sulaiman Baruni, an Amazigh chief, refused to submit and instead threatened to launch attacks unless Italy made political concessions including adoption of political self-determination as espoused by US President Woodrow Wilson.

Italy resolved these tensions in June 1919 by issuing a so-called Fundamental Law that granted Tripolitania limited self-government at the local and provincial levels and recognized Tripolitanians as citizens of Italy, in exchange for disarmament of the local tribes. Perhaps the most liberal colonial policy enacted after World War I by a European power, the law enabled Italy

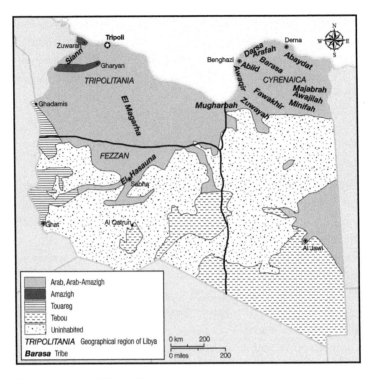

Map 2 Ethnography of Modern Libya

to reduce its armed force and avoid a potentially difficult military campaign, but it failed to establish political stability. Instead, intense rivalries developed among various tribal leaders and between tribes favoring their own autonomy and nationalists seeking to establish a republic. On a few occasions, Tripolitanian factions voiced collective proposals to achieve independence from Italy, such as a joint declaration by Suwayhli and Baruni to establish a republic based in Misrata in 1919, but authorities in Rome firmly resisted all such moves. The murder of Suwayhli by a political rival and the exile of Baruni amid a wave of popular discontent left the province devoid of experienced native leaders.

In Cyrenaica, Italy attempted to achieve a stable political order through diplomacy. In a second Fundamental Law, enacted in October 1919, Rome granted Cyrenaicans a provincial parliament, Italian citizenship, and certain economic benefits. Some 100 Cyrenaican chiefs, however, issued a collective declaration rejecting the Fundamental Law on the grounds that it would violate their sovereignty. Italian governing authorities negotiated a compromise with Sayed Mohammed Idris, whom they had recognized as emir over interior lands in 1917. The Rajma Agreement of October 1920 formally named Idris emir of major interior oases; assured Italian financial subsidies for Idris, his family, and his security forces; established an elected parliament to govern the region in partnership with Italian officials; and committed Idris to disarm anti-Italy fighters. Under this deal, an elected parliament, dominated by Senussi allies of Idris, met at Benghazi in April 1921, and a brief period of stability began. Tensions grew, however, when first Idris and then mixed Italian–Senussi patrols proved unable to disarm certain tribal fighters.

The political situation inside Libya reached a breaking point in 1922. Tripolitania remained internally fragmented although uniformly hostile to any semblance of Italian control. Cyrenaica's stability was limited by the persistence of armed tribal forces. In February, Italian Governor Giuseppe Volpi launched a military offensive against Tripolitanian forces, winning a series of victories along the coast. To reinvigorate their resistance, Tripolitanian leaders offered in April to recognize Idris as emir over their region as well as Cyrenaica. Cautious about violating his agreements with Rome and suspicious that the offer from Tripolitania was an inauthentic expedient, Idris hesitated to accept it. When fascists took control of the Italian government in October, Idris accepted the Tripolitanian recognition, but within a month, citing ill health and probably fearing capture by the Italians, he fled into exile in Egypt.

Why did Italy intensify its military operations in Libya in 1923?

Political change within Italy in 1921–1922 spawned an intensification of Italian military action in Libya. Deadlock among

20 LIBYA AND THE WEST

various political parties and postwar economic stagnation created an opportunity for Benito Mussolini, a combat veteran who had become an extreme conservative during the world war, to organize groups of like-minded citizens to agitate for control of the country. A powerful orator, Mussolini inspired these forces (called the *fasci di combattimento* or "fighting bands") to use intimidation and violence to suppress socialists, unionists, and other political rivals and, eventually, to demand national power. In October 1922, fascist militants marched on Rome, and Mussolini convinced King Victor Emmanuel III to name him prime minister. In that office, Mussolini expressed an ideology favoring a militant colonial policy as a path to national greatness and power, and he viewed Volpi's 1922 offensive in Libya as a model action. By 1923, Mussolini consolidated authoritarian control over the Italian government, enabling him to wage an aggressive military campaign in Libya.

Italy gained international legitimacy for its colonialism in Libya in the Lausanne Treaty of 1923. While drafted primarily to end the state of war between the Ottoman Empire and the Allied powers, the treaty defined the borders of the Republic of Turkey as the successor state to the Ottoman Empire and it clarified that Turkey relinquished control over the Arab lands that the Ottomans had dominated for centuries. In Article 22 of the treaty, Turkey explicitly renounced its sovereignty over Libya. That proviso affirmed international recognition of Italy's protectorate in Libya.

How did Italy conquer Libya in 1923–1931?

With the enthused support of Mussolini in Rome, Italian officials in Libya waged a relentless, thorough military campaign that gradually overwhelmed indigenous resistance to Italian sovereignty over Libya. Building on the success of his offensive against Tripolitanians in early 1922 and encouraged by Mussolini's seizure of power in Rome in October, Governor General Volpi continued offensive action against Tripolitanian militias in late 1922 and early 1923. By 1924, Italian troops occupied a swath of coastal territory that encompassed some 80 percent of Tripolitania's 500,000 native residents and pacified that territory sufficiently to launch grandiose economic development schemes. Although the native peoples in the unoccupied remainder of Tripolitania and the Fezzan offered no organized resistance, Italian authorities eventually determined to conquer those lands as well to ensure the long-term security of the colony. Under the command of Colonel Rodolfo Graziani, Italian units occupied southern Tripolitania by 1927 and the Fezzan by 1930.

Cyrenaica presented a more complicated and deadly challenge for Italian forces, leading to the so-called Second Italian–Senussi War of 1923–1931. Appointed in early 1923 as the first fascist governor of Libya, General Luigi Bongiovanni resolved to crush the Senussi militias in the eastern province. Exploiting the absence of Idris, who had gone into exile in late 1922, Bongiovanni launched a surprise offensive in March 1923 that overran Senussi armed camps in the coastal region. Within weeks, he seized Benghazi and overran Agedabia (where the Senussi had operated an administrative apparatus). By 1924, Italian soldiers had subdued Senussi fighters in the coastal region through a campaign of similar military raids. To exert political control, Italian authorities nullified the earlier diplomatic agreements with the Senussi and disbanded the Senussi-dominated parliament in Benghazi.

In the hill country south of the coastal zone, Senussi resistance persisted for years. Sheikh Umar al Mukhtar inspired Senussi loyalists to fight against Italian occupation as a means of preserving their culture and nomadic lifestyle. Citing the Christianity of Italian forces as well as the Eritrean soldiers pressed into serving Italy's cause, Mukhtar urged his followers to fight to protect Islam. Organized into small, nimble forces and operating on familiar terrain and with the support of local peoples, Senussi militias ambushed Italian troops, raided their bases, sabotaged their supply lines, and waged other forms of low-intensity warfare. When not attacking, the fighters melted into the population, posing as shepherds. Although the Senussi were able to field only about 1,000 fighters against some 20,000 Italian and colonial troops arrayed against them, they offered resistance vastly disproportional to their size.

Graziani, whose conquests in western Libya had made him a national hero at home and earned him promotion to general, was assigned command of Italian units arrayed against the Senussi in 1929. Given that his predecessors in that theater had been unable to achieve a knock-out military victory, Graziani waged a brutal war of attrition, noting that because "the olive branch" of negotiation had failed he would employ "the canes and the axe." Graziani ordered air power and armored vehicles to attack oases and settlements suspected of sheltering the resistance (reportedly using mustard gas in violation of international law). He imprisoned tens of thousands of nomadic tribesmen in concentration camps along the coast, ordered the summary execution of thousands of natives who communicated or met with enemy combatants, poisoned wells and slaughtered herds, and erected a 300-kilometer barbed wire fence along the border with Egypt to cut the enemy's supply line. "The way forward has been made clear," Governor General Marshal Pietro Badoglio commented privately in 1930, "and we have to follow it to the end, even if the entire population of Cyrenaica has to perish."[8]

By 1931, these tactics gravely weakened Senussi fighting ability. In September, Italian forces captured Sheikh Mukhtar, and, as a political message to the Senussi, they hanged him before a forced assembly of 20,000 Cyrenaicans. Mukhtar's death signaled the end of effective local resistance to Italian power, which emerged supreme throughout Libya.

What type of government did Italy impose on Libya?

After it militarily subdued Libya, Italy imposed a formal colonial apparatus on the country. In 1934, the government in

Rome declared the existence of a single colony, which was divided into four provinces—Tripoli, Misrata, Benghazi, and Derna—covering the territory of the former regions of Tripolitania and Cyrenaica, plus a special military district in the Fezzan. Rome appointed an executive officer, called the "governor general" initially and the "first consul" after 1937, who named Italian expatriates to administrative and managerial positions throughout the territory. While the governors established an advisory council including token Arab Libyan representatives, they also dismantled the traditional tribal councils and projected the power of the Italian state to the local level. In 1939, Libya was declared to be fully a part of metropolitan Italy—its nineteenth province—although its native inhabitants were not given legal equality.[9]

Why did Italy refer to Libya as "the Fourth Shore"?

The Mussolini regime used *la Quarta Sponda* ("the Fourth Shore") as a rhetorical flourish to evoke a sense of connection between Libya and the Italian homeland. Based on the notion that Italy dominated the eastern shore of the Tyrrhenian Sea and the western shore of the Adriatic Sea and aspired to control the eastern shore of the Adriatic in the Balkan states, the Fourth Shore trope signaled Mussolini's grandiose ambitions to emerge as the dominant imperial power of the central Mediterranean. "Civilization, in fact, is what Italy is creating on the Fourth Shore of our sea," Mussolini declared in 1934, "western civilization in general and fascist civilization in particular." Fascist officials issued propaganda linking the colonization of Libya to the conquests of the ancient Roman Empire, including a late 1930s postage stamp that depicted a mosque, a palm tree, and a plow with the slogan *ritornando dove già fummo* ("returning where we once were").[10]

24 LIBYA AND THE WEST

What was Italy's overall approach to developing Libya as a colony?

Italy invested considerable resources in developing and modernizing Cyrenaica and Tripolitania starting even before the Senussi resistance was repressed in 1931. (Virtually no development initiatives were launched in the military district in the Fezzan.)

Colonial officials launched an urban development initiative in the 1920s, concentrating first on Tripolitania, given its early pacification. By the 1930s, Tripoli boasted such attractions as European architecture, access to nearby Roman ruins that evoked the grandeur of the ancient empire, a trade fair, and a motor racing track that drew tens of thousands of tourists annually.

In the 1930s, Italian authorities promoted massive initiatives to establish a modern infrastructure across the territory. Transportation projects included railroads, ports and harbors, commercial air and ferry routes from Italy, and a vast paved highway system. The centerpiece of the road network was the *strada litoranea* (coastal highway), a 1,100-mile east–west highway that opened in 1937 to considerable fanfare. By crossing the 420-mile-wide Sirtica Desert, which had divided Cyrenaica and Tripolitania since the dawn of civilization, the *strada litoranea* was intended to unify the two provinces physically as well as politically and culturally. Air Marshal Italo Balbo, the Governor General of Libya in 1934–1940 who directed the project, claimed that the highway demonstrated the "pride and glory of Imperial Italy" by reviving the engineering genius of the Roman Empire. Italian military officials also justified the highway on national security grounds, noting that it would enable them quickly to concentrate military units to defend against threats from French Tunisia or British Egypt—or perhaps to exploit expansionist opportunities in either location.[11]

Other aspects of the infrastructure also gained considerable attention. Authorities drilled new water wells (and repaired others, some dating to the era of the Roman Empire), built viaducts, purified drinking water, and established a complex irrigation system in agricultural areas. Modern medical care, public education, and sanitation systems were introduced. In hope of improving the climate by foresting the coastal plains, Italian authorities planted some 1 million shade trees per year in the 1930s. To promote self-sufficiency, in the same decade, they planted some 7.5 million fruit and olive trees and 27 million grapevines, and they replenished herds of sheep, camels, and horses from some 100,000 to 1.9 million head.

How did native Italian settlers figure into Italy's plans to colonize the "Fourth Shore"?

Even before they completely defeated Libyan armed resistance, Italian authorities implemented schemes to designate Libyan territory for settlement by Italians. Between 1914 and 1929, Italy seized 180,000 acres of land, some as confiscations from armed rebels and the rest under a decree authorizing the state's takeover of uncultivated land. Initially, some 75,000 acres were sold cheaply to northern Italian prospectors who established large estates and employed local laborers to plant fields and orchards. Most of these enterprises struggled to become profitable in the arid desert climate.

In the late 1920s, Mussolini directed a more systematic scheme that required developers to settle Italians on the Libyan lands. The fascist leader was concerned with overcrowding among Italian peasant farmers and unemployment among Italian workers, dynamics that were aggravated by the US restrictions on immigration from Italy imposed in the 1920s. Thus, he directed a propaganda campaign encouraging "soldiers of the soil" and "legionaries of labor" to colonize Libya under the slogan "Believe, Obey, Fight."[12]

Inspired by Mussolini, Governor Emilio de Bono seized an additional 100,000 acres and sold it to developers on the condition that they settle Italian families on agricultural plots. But this second wave of development faced massive obstacles. Through 1931, the Senussi rebellion forced developers in Cyrenaica to divert resources to security barriers and personnel. The Great Depression that afflicted capitalist economies worldwide starting in 1929 reverberated through the Italian operations in all regions of Libya. While discovery of untapped aquifers improved irrigation capacity in the late 1920s, an early 1930s drought exacerbated the naturally arid conditions that challenged agricultural enterprise.

How did Italy's settlement schemes change after the defeat of the Senussi resistance in 1931?

The repression of the Senussi enabled Italy to hatch an ambitious settlement plan. Governor General Balbo implemented a massive scheme to thoroughly Italianize as well as modernize Libya.

Balbo's most dramatic act of colonization was an operation in 1938–1940 that imported tens of thousands of Italian settlers to take up residence in newly constructed agricultural communities—an operation reputed to have been the largest organized act of migration in human history. Balbo's administration established a state-owned corporation, the Libyan Colonization Society, which designated some 300 square miles of land for this enterprise, prepared it for agriculture by draining marshes and constructing irrigation works, divided it into nearly 2,000 farms of 37–124 acres, built roads connecting the farms to small town centers (each center including shops, a post office, and a church), and paid some 30,000 local laborers to construct stark but spacious concrete farmhouses and to till and plant farm fields. Landless Italian farm families were then selected to become settlers through a competitive screening process that favored households of eight or more members who were healthy, literate, and loyal to fascism. Balbo's goal was to implant in Libya "a predominantly Italian population with deep and firm roots."[13]

The settlement operation was launched dramatically in October 1938. A single convoy of ships, departing Italy amid a crescendo of pomp and celebration, transported some 20,000 settlers to Libya. Promptly occupying a brand-new small farm, each settler family found a kitchen stocked with food, a cow and a mule feeding in a barn, and planted fields. Settler families were entitled to purchase their farms on favorable financing terms and were obligated to occupy their plots indefinitely. Towns and roads were splashed with banners and posters declaring such slogans as "Let every colonist be a soldier under the command of the Duce." Other waves of settlement followed: by 1940, some 110,000 Italians resided in Libya (slightly more than 10 percent of the territory's population), and Italian leaders planned to increase that number to 500,000 by the 1960s.[14]

Italian authorities justified this massive land grab on several bases. Settlement in Libya relieved the social pressure of the home country's burgeoning population of rural, landless peasants. Harvests in Libya would help the country achieve agricultural self-sufficiency, the importance of which increased as international colonial tensions in northeast Africa escalated after 1935. The Italianization of Libya would solidify Rome's central Mediterranean empire. The development of military units among the Italian men of Libya would enhance Italy's strategic and tactical military assets in Africa and perhaps set the stage for Italian expansion elsewhere on the continent. The rapid consolidation of Italian power and presence in Libya, the fascists hoped, would earn international legitimacy and respect.

What was the intention and impact of Mussolini's 1937 visit to Libya?

In March 1937, Mussolini orchestrated a visit to Libya staged with elaborate pageantry and political theater designed to extol the virtues of fascist colonialism. The dictator was welcomed

28 LIBYA AND THE WEST

by brass bands and cheering masses at every stop during a 10-day visit that centered on the dedication of the *strada litoranea*. In a series of speeches, Mussolini developed the themes of Italian glory and the beneficence of imperialism. Italian influence "transformed and beautified" the cities of Libya, he declared, and in rural areas "the virile Italians . . . awoke a land that had been sleeping for centuries."[15]

Special attention was given to creating an impression of widespread Arab admiration. Reporters heard shouts of "Allah protect the Duce" from rooftops and "Viva Mussolini" from minarets, while Libyan children lined processional routes waving Italian flags. At Tripoli, the Amazigh Chief Yusuf Cherbisc presented Mussolini with a ceremonial sword, a token of high honor. Mussolini led a procession of mounted Arab troops outfitted in traditional garb and began routinely referring to Libyans as "Italian Muslims." While some Libyans sincerely accepted Italian authority, most who participated in the spectacles surrounding Mussolini's visit were motivated by self-preservation rather than genuine respect.[16]

What was the impact of Italian colonial rule on the people of Libya?

Italian colonization produced limited benefits but many hardships for the native Libyans. Among the benefits were access to modern healthcare and education, new technologies, and rising wages. Thousands of Libyans were employed in the civil service and the manual labor force that served Italian settlement. Offering further vocational opportunity, the Italian military created a Libyan Division in 1935 that provided opportunity to 9,000 Libyan soldiers who fought in 22 engagements during the 1936 conquest of Ethiopia (and suffered some 3,000 casualties). Governor General Balbo professed to see potential for Libyans to become "Italian Muslims" with rights of citizenship, and he boasted that Italian treatment of Libyans was more enlightened than the French rule of Algerians.[17]

The hardships, by contrast, were considerable. The Italian military campaigns against the Senussi left the people of Cyrenaica and Senussi followers elsewhere demoralized and dispirited, and it demolished their educated elite and middle class. Italian tactics of attrition stunted population growth in Libya for a generation and left many people homeless and landless, their herds depleted by 90 percent and their traditional livelihoods badly constricted. The top-down authority of the Italian colonial regime demolished ancient customs of tribal leadership. Italian officials proscribed the Senussi as a political or cultural organization, suppressed its leaders, and dismantled its lodges. In the military district of the Fezzan, traditional tribal councils were replaced by administrators appointed by the colonial regime.

The land seizures that enabled the massive waves of Italian settlement compromised the interests of the Libyan people. Nomadic traditions were rendered difficult or impossible by the establishment of the agricultural communities. Italians tended to designate the most fertile and verdant lands for themselves and to leave comparatively desolate parcels to the locals. Italian authorities made belated and modest efforts to include Libyans in some of the largesse of the agricultural development, including limited opportunities to settle in planned communities and a concentrated effort to replenish the animal herds that had been decimated during the Senussi war. Libyans tended not to prosper in the planned settlements, however, perhaps because they were segregated on inferior tracts. Even the restoration of the animal herds to robust levels by the late 1930s did little to mitigate their deep-seated resentment at the arrival of the Italians in the first place.

Libyans took little comfort in Italian expressions of tolerance for their Islamic religion. Colonial administrators refrained from pressuring Libyans to convert to Christianity (in stark contrast to French evangelization in Algeria, Tunisia, and Syria); recognized the authority of Islamic *sharia* courts in such matters as familial relations, inheritance, and religious

30 LIBYA AND THE WEST

practice; refurbished or constructed mosques; and allowed Muslims to practice their faith (except for the ongoing ban of the Senussi). After his visit to Libya in 1937, Mussolini declared himself a "Protector of Islam" in the hope of earning the goodwill of Muslims everywhere, to the advantage of Italian imperial interests. Yet such gestures did nothing to endear Muslims of Libya to Italian rule.[18]

In contrast to the religious tolerance, Libyans were relegated to an inferior social status. Segregation was widely practiced in social relationships. The colonial government built 120 elementary schools for Libyan children, but those facilities were inferior to schools for Italian children, and they provided basic education for workers rather than a foundation for secondary education (which was available to Italians only). Libyans were officially admitted to various professions, but they were prohibited from supervising Italians. Libyan laborers were paid lower wages than Italian laborers performing the same work.

Nor did Libyans enjoy political equality. Once Libya was formally incorporated as Italy's nineteenth province in 1939, Libyans were allowed to apply for "special Italian citizenship," but that status was awarded only to those who were fluent in Italian or who had provided heroic military or civil service, and the political rights granted were valid in Libya only and not Italy proper. Like the Italians, Libyans were expected and compelled to obey every command issued under Mussolini's authority. As Italy became associated with Nazi Germany, Italian fascism became racialized, with Libyans cast as an inferior, dark-skinned "other," worthy of domination.[19]

Throughout the 1920s and 1930s, and especially during the Balbo era, Italy spent lavishly on its Libyan colony, far more than what other European powers spent on their African colonies. But the vast bulk of the expenditures benefited Italian nationals rather than native Libyans. By 1940, substantial communities of Libyan exiles had formed in Egypt (the largest, with some 14,000), Syria, Sudan, Chad, Algeria, and Morocco. In exile, these Libyans formed various fraternal and social organizations, perhaps most prominently the Executive Committee of Tripolitanian and Cyrenaican Communities, formed in Damascus in 1928, that gradually generated a sense of political unity, identity, and activism. They also absorbed the ideology of anticolonialism from the nascent pan-Arab nationalist movement in Egypt and Syria.[20]

What were Italy's plans for expanding its imperial presence in Africa beyond Libya?

As he gained popularity at home and consolidated control of Libya, Mussolini entertained grandiose ambitions to establish an expansive empire in Africa. In 1935, military forces in Italian Somaliland, which Italy had seized in the 1880s together with neighboring Eritrea, encroached into Ethiopia (the kingdom that had defeated an Italian invasion in 1896). Mussolini used the resulting border clashes to justify a second invasion of Ethiopia, this one ending in Italian victory in 1936. The government in Rome declared the formation of Italian East Africa comprising its territory in Eritrea, Somaliland, and Ethiopia.

In this context, Balbo demonstrated ambitions to use Libya as a launching point for imperial expansion throughout north and east Africa. He pondered the possibilities of expanding into French Chad and Anglo-Egyptian Sudan in hope of establishing a corridor linking Libya to East Africa. A skilled aviator, Balbo personally conducted overflights of borderlands in both Chad and Sudan, calculating that even small acquisitions in either direction would set precedents for eventual acquisition of the entire colonies. Concerned by the possibility that Britain would close the Suez Canal to Italian naval vessels during the war in Ethiopia, Balbo laid plans to invade Egypt and even massed troops on the border. Italian propaganda suggested that Rome eyed Saudi Arabia, Yemen, and British Aden as potential areas of expansion.

Although he blocked Balbo's plans to attack the British in Egypt in 1935, Mussolini shared his vision of a massive

32 LIBYA AND THE WEST

trans-African empire. The fascist leader imagined becoming an Atlantic power by reaching beyond Chad into Cameroon, the former German colony seized by Britain and France at the end of World War I. At his most fanciful, Mussolini dreamed of someday controlling even Gibraltar and the Suez Canal.

How did Britain and France respond to the Italian conquest of Libya?

Britain and France tolerated Italy's military conquest and colonization of Libya. Having ceded Kufra to Italian Libya in 1912, the British posed no objection when Italian troops occupied the district while attacking Senussi fighters in 1931. Following several months of jockeying for possession of land in the uncharted borderlands between Libya and Sudan, Britain and Egypt agreed in June 1934 to cede the Saraa Triangle, a portion of northwest Sudan that contained oases along a traditional east–west trade route. The settlement averted a potential military clash between the two European powers.

France similarly appeased Mussolini's expansionist desires in Africa in hopes of aligning him against Nazi Germany. In an agreement signed by Mussolini and French Foreign Minister Pierre Laval in January 1935, France yielded to Libya the so-called Aouzou Strip, 44,000 square miles of northern Chad. Although Italy promptly occupied the territory, France later claimed that its parliament had never ratified the agreement and thus the strip remained part of Chad—setting the stage for conflict along the Libya–Chad border in future decades.[21]

How did Britain and France respond to Italian expansionism elsewhere?

France initially turned a blind eye to Italian expansion in east Africa. In other agreements between Laval and Mussolini signed in January 1935, France conceded small portions of French Somaliland to Italian East Africa and pledged not to interfere with Italian expansion into Ethiopia, thereby encouraging the Italian invasion of that kingdom later in that year.

By contrast, Britain faced a difficult dilemma regarding potential Italian thrusts beyond Libya. On the one hand, the Italian invasion of Ethiopia damaged the collective security provisions of the League of Nations charter, surrounded Egypt and its vital Suez Canal with Italian military power, and raised the prospect of Italian encroachments into British Somaliland. On the other hand, British strategists considered Germany and Japan to pose greater strategic dangers than Italy, and they realized that military conflict with Italy in the Eastern Mediterranean or Middle East would deplete their military capabilities needed more in other theaters.

After making a brief, principled stand against Italian expansion, British officials quickly changed gears and appeased Mussolini. When the League of Nations debated the invasion of Ethiopia in October 1935, Britain voted in favor of economic sanctions on Italy, and, by December, it reinforced its naval and air force units in Egypt and Malta. An Anglo–Italian war scare ensued, during which Balbo dispatched troops in Libya to the Egyptian frontier. Worried about the global strategic consequences, the British government decided to avoid war with Italy by doing nothing to impede the Italian conquest of Ethiopia (such as closing the Suez Canal to Italian ships). Germany's reoccupation of the Rhineland in March 1936, which stoked tensions between London and Berlin, affirmed in British minds the wisdom of placating Mussolini, however problematic his aggression in East Africa. In July, Britain voted to end League of Nations sanctions on Italy and the Anglo–Italian war scare subsided. The next month, by contrast, Britain prudently signed a 20-year defense treaty with Egypt that strengthened Britain's ability to defend Egypt against German or Italian encroachment.

By the end of the 1930s, the Franco–British policy of appeasing Mussolini faltered. Anglo–Italian agreements signed in 1937–1938 to mitigate tensions in East Africa, in Britain's estimation, failed to ease tensions or deter Mussolini

34 LIBYA AND THE WEST

from intervening in the Spanish Civil War or seeking political expansionism in Arabia. Reports that Governor Balbo personally flew reconnaissance missions over Sudan and along the border between Italian East Africa and British East Africa aggravated London's concerns with Italy's grand designs.

Although France continued to hope that it could align Italy as a counterweight to Germany, it also came to worry profoundly about Italian designs on Tunisia and Chad and evidence of a growing German political presence in Libya. Gradually, Mussolini came to perceive British and French appeasement policies as evidence of their weakness, which enhanced his admiration of German power and led him to align with Berlin.

How did World War II affect Italy's colonial position in Libya?

World War II had dramatic consequences for Italian rule in Libya. The war in Europe erupted in September 1939, when Germany and the Soviet Union conquered Poland, and Britain and France reacted by declaring war on Germany. In 1940–1941, Germany gained the upper hand in Europe by overrunning Belgium, the Netherlands, Luxembourg, France, Denmark, Norway, and Balkan states including Greece; bombing and threatening to invade the British Isles; and launching a massive invasion of the Soviet Union. Having become a formal ally of German Führer Adolf Hitler in May 1939, Mussolini collaborated with German offensives in Europe and North Africa. Ultimately, the triumph of the Allied powers (primarily Britain, the Free French, and, after 1941, the Soviet Union and the United States) over the Axis powers (primarily Germany, Italy, and Japan) effectively spelled the end of the Italian colonization of Libya.

What was the strategic significance of Libya to the European powers that fought World War II?

From his dominant position in Libya, Mussolini saw the war as an opportunity to conquer British and French colonial possessions in North Africa. Determined to protect the Suez Canal and other strategic assets to the east, British leaders resolved to defend Egypt if not defeat Italian power in Libya. Hitler saw the Mediterranean region as a sideshow to his major objective of conquering continental Europe. He deferred to Mussolini to constrict British shipping routes and to pin down or deplete British forces in Egypt before the planned (but ultimately postponed) German invasion of the British Isles in late 1940.

Hostilities erupted in Libya soon after Italy declared war on Britain in June 1940. Battles swept back and forth across the country for three years. Fighting was concentrated along the coastal plain of Cyrenaica, where highly mobile units, operating on a landscape that was generally flat and devoid of natural barriers, engaged in massive tank and aerial battles that were dynamic, dramatic, and destructive.

Following several border skirmishes, Italian forces in Libya invaded Egypt in September 1940, occupying the coastal town of Sidi Barani. Intent on demonstrating Italian military might and winning colonial spoils, Mussolini declined an offer from Hitler to send German troops to assist in this endeavor. Although badly outnumbered, a British imperial force under General Archibald Wavell counterattacked in December, using superior tank warfare tactics to rout the Italians. The British took some 130,000 prisoners and occupied Tobruk and Benghazi, in Libya, by February 1941.

The German invasion of the Balkan states in early 1941 confronted British strategists with a dilemma. On the one hand, there was reason to press the attack across Libya to smash Italian armies before they could be reinforced by more-capable German troops and to gain airbases that could be used to protect Allied shipping across the Mediterranean. On the other hand, there was fear that a German conquest of Greece would expose Egypt to German assault. The government in London elected to dispatch available forces to Greece for a desperate attempt to deny that country to the Germans. This

36 LIBYA AND THE WEST

British gamble failed miserably; Germany both dispatched armored divisions to Libya under the command of the talented General Erwin Rommel in February 1941 and conquered Greece in April. Having canceled his planned invasion of the British Isles, Hitler shifted his focus to occupying Egypt and destroying or capturing British forces there.[22]

Deploying the "Afrika Korps," Rommel immediately exploited the British pause in Libya by launching an offensive that sent British forces into retreat from most of Cyrenaica (Tobruk excepted) by April 1941. Rommel repelled two thrusts by British forces to relieve their besieged comrades at Tobruk in May and June 1941. Intent on safeguarding resources for his imminent invasion of the Soviet Union, however, Hitler declined to exploit his occupation of Greece or Rommel's successes by attacking such Western assets as Malta, Cyprus, Syria, or the Suez Canal. After Germany's reserves were depleted by its invasion of Russia in late 1941, a British force broke through the Tobruk siege lines and rescued the garrison in November. But the British failed to reach their second objective, which was to trap Rommel's armies. Casualties mounted on both sides.

After replenishing his troops, Rommel launched a major offensive in January 1942 aimed at capturing the Suez Canal. The German and Italian forces under his command captured Tobruk in June and pressed across the Egyptian frontier as far east as El Alamein, Egypt, only 60 miles from Alexandria. That advance put Britain in grave risk of losing Egypt; indeed, Mussolini flew to Libya to prepare to lead a victory parade in Alexandria astride a white horse. But the British army rallied at El Alamein to stop the German offensive in July. In November, after British naval and air power viciously attacked Rommel's maritime supply lines, General Bernard Montgomery launched a successful counteroffensive. As Rommel retreated from Egypt, US and British armies landed in Algeria and Morocco, convincing the German general to withdraw his units to Tunisia, where he would attempt a last stand for the Axis powers on the African continent. Ironically, British forces advanced across Libya on the *strada litoranea* that Balbo had built five years earlier to defend the colony, doing so even before the government in Rome had retired its construction debt.

As German and Italian forces concentrated in Tunisia in early 1943, Mussolini officially declared that he had seized that colony from France and annexed it to Libya. That step, however, would prove to be the last gasp of the Italian empire in North Africa. US and British forces squeezed the German and Italian armies between punishing attacks from the west and east, respectively. Free French forces based in Chad occupied the Fezzan in January. His situation untenable, Rommel began withdrawing German and Italian combat forces from Tunisia in February. In May, Allied forces occupied Tunis and Bizerte, capturing some 250,000 enemy soldiers and marking the end of hostilities in North Africa. Libya became strategically valuable to the Allies after Britain established military airfields at al-Adem (near Tobruk) and Castel Benito (near Tripoli) and the United States seized Mellaha Field (near Tripoli), all of which became significant in combat operations and supply lines across the Mediterranean.[23]

What were the views of Libyans toward World War II?

As World War II erupted in Europe, tribal and Senussi leaders in Libya and in exile considered the possibilities for exploiting the war to promote independence from Italian colonialism. In October 1939, Cyrenaican and Tripolitanian leaders met in Alexandria, Egypt, where they agreed to recognize Idris, the exiled Senussi emir, as their common political leader and to form a joint advisory committee. The committee proved unable to overcome the historic and cultural divisions between the two provinces, however, and thus failed to form a national identity. While accepting Idris as a political leader, for instance, the Tripolitanians remained reluctant to recognize his Senussi identity as representative of all Libyans.

38 LIBYA AND THE WEST

Once Italy and Britain exchanged declarations of war in June 1940, the Cyrenaicans and Tripolitanians in Egypt also quarreled over basic strategic questions. Idris and other Cyrenaicans calculated that a political-military partnership with Britain offered the best path to independence from Italy, while the more Anglophobic Tripolitanians feared that supporting Britain would expose Libyans to reprisals if the Axis prevailed (as many expected it to do). Disagreement also emerged at an August 1940 conference in Cairo. A Cyrenaican majority authorized Idris as "Senussi Amir" to cooperate with Britain and seek British support for a "provisional Senussi government." The Tripolitanians protested that Idris should demand complete independence of Libya, and they objected to the privileging of the Senussi identity.[24]

Did Libyans participate in the war as combatants?

Libyans participated as combatants on both sides of the war that raged in their country. As typical of European colonial regimes, Italy recruited native Libyans to serve in uniform from the earliest years of its occupation. Recruited mostly from coastal areas, especially Tripolitania, such Libyans were initially assigned to Italian military units. After the start of World War II, Italian authorities established separate Libyan units, under the command of Italian officers. The First Libyan Infantry Division was raised and attached to Italy's Tenth Army, and the Second Libyan Infantry Division was designated as the Thirteenth Corps of Italy's Fifth Army. Libyan units serving Italy were well-trained, motivated, and loyal, and they performed as well as Italian units in combat.

A colonial power facing manpower shortages, Britain also raised a fighting force of Libyan exiles. Negotiations between Emir Idris and General Wavell in late 1940 resulted in the establishment of four Libyan combat battalions and one administrative unit known alternatively as the Libyan Arab

Force and the Senussi Army, all under British command. Early recruits were exiled Cyrenaican veterans of the Italian–Senussi War, eventually augmented with Tripolitanians who had been taken prisoner while wearing the Italian uniform and who were persuaded to switch sides. General Wavell reported that the Libyans served with distinction in various campaigns. Noncombatants in Cyrenaica also aided the British by assisting escaped prisoners, providing intelligence, and offering provision to raiding parties and reconnaissance patrols—all at substantial risk of Italian and German reprisals. In January 1942, British Foreign Secretary Anthony Eden publicly recognized the contributions of the Libyan forces to Britain's objectives and declared that "His Majesty's Government are determined that at the end of the war the Senussis in Cyrenaica will in no circumstances again fall under Italian domination."[25]

What was the impact of World War II on the people of Libya?

The three years of hostilities inflicted considerable pain and dislocation on the Libyan people and their land. The intense Anglo–German/Italian hostilities along the coastal plains laid waste to cities, farms, and homes, especially in Cyrenaica, which changed hands three times. In Tobruk, which was conquered thrice and besieged for seven months, virtually every building was demolished or damaged and 130 shipwrecks clogged the harbor. Benghazi was devastated by more than 1,000 air raids, and other towns like Bardiya and Derna were damaged heavily. Water systems, the electricity grid, and other key infrastructure components were left dysfunctional, and the presence of minefields made all forms of transportation hazardous. Many townspeople fled to rural hillsides and caves to escape harm.

The war ended the economic development policies that Italy had pursued in the 1930s. The mass colonization drives were suspended, and all Italian settlers were evacuated in

40   LIBYA AND THE WEST

1942. Their departure left their gleaming white planned communities vacant and forlorn, and it seriously diminished agricultural productivity, aggravating food shortages. The end of active hostilities in 1943 left Libya in a condition of poverty, physical destruction, and political uncertainty.

2

FROM COLONY TO MONARCHY TO REVOLUTION

LIBYA, 1943–1969

What happened in Libya after the expulsion of Italian and German military forces from North Africa in 1943?

British and Free French authorities administered the three Libyan provinces as occupied Italian colonies. The British established the British Military Administration (BMA) in Tripolitania and Cyrenaica, divided the two provinces into several administrative districts, and appointed military officers to govern them. Free French forces in Chad occupied the Fezzan, whose Tuareg tribes had long interested the French because they militantly resisted both Italian and French colonial efforts. Citing such international laws as the Hague Convention, the European powers announced that they would respect the inherent Italian sovereignty and private property in Libya pending a postwar political process to clarify its permanent status. "Britain had inherited from Italy three territories that had few natural resources," the scholar Scott L. Bills noted, "and an uneducated, pastoral population . . . headed for economic ruin."[1]

As the coastal territories were secured against German and Italian resurgence, BMA officers concentrated on relief and reconstruction, especially in war-ravaged Cyrenaica. Among their top priorities were emergency distribution of food, removal of landmines and other volatile hazards, reestablishment of a healthcare system to address outbreaks of smallpox and other infectious diseases, and restoration of the physical infrastructure. Because of personnel shortages in the British military, the BMA appointed Libyans to low-level civil service posts and to a police force that maintained law and order, and it relied on Italian nurses and a handful of other civil service professionals who remained behind after the Axis armies departed. France met its comparatively milder challenge of administering the less populated and more remote Fezzan with a small military administration based in Sabha that relied on local tribes to ensure order. The overarching stability provided by the occupation forces enabled Libyans to reunite families, reclaim some confiscated lands, restore herds, resume trades, and otherwise return to a peaceful and routine existence. The repatriation of tens of thousands of exiles from Egypt and elsewhere fed optimism about the future.

While grateful for the Allied expulsion of the Italians and emergency relief and reconstruction, the peoples of Libya expressed an emerging desire to gain independence from European control. They voiced concern with the reluctance of the Allies immediately to contest the legal sovereignty of Italy and with Britain's reliance on any number of Italian administrators. They protested when the French attached some of their staff officers in the Fezzan to command structures based in Algeria and Tunisia, a step that seemed to signal French imperial ambitions in that region.

British officials deliberated whether to continue to rely on Sayed Muhammed Idris, the Senussi leader who, from exile in Egypt, had organized Libyans to assist British military operations against the Axis armies. Some British leaders doubted Idris's abilities to govern postwar Libya: Brigadier Duncan C. Cumming called him "a childless hypochondriac with acute political instinct but few of the attributes of an administrator." Others such as Brigadier R. D. H. Arundell, however, considered Idris "intelligent, reasonable, loyal, and dignified, and [he] should prove at least a reasonably satisfactory figure-head." In the end, the government in London decided to count on Idris to meet their immediate occupation needs.[2]

British officials transitioned the Libyan Arab Force that had fought with the British Army in Egypt to become the core of the new Libyan police force. Idris visited Cyrenaica in 1944, receiving a heroic welcome from the local tribes and towns. He returned in 1946 to accept knighthood from the British Crown for his wartime collaboration, receiving another heroic welcome by a resplendent British military honor guard in a ceremony designed to affirm the bonds of British friendliness. But Idris refused a British invitation to return permanently while Libya's political status remained undefined, on the calculation that such a step would connote tacit complicity with foreign control of the country.

How did the victorious Allies sort out Libya's permanent status in the aftermath of World War II?

Even before negotiating a peace treaty with Italy, the "Big Three" Allies (the United States, Britain, and the Soviet Union) addressed the question of Libya's political future. Most British officials, citing Foreign Minister Anthony Eden's 1942 pledge that Britain would oppose the restoration of Italian control to Cyrenaica, made clear that they strongly opposed Italian restoration in any African lands. Yet, by war's end, some British officials reasoned that they should consider a role for Italy in administering Libya, both in recognition of the new, antifascist political order emerging in occupied Italy and in support of their own broad plans to stabilize Italy as a friendly, pro-Western state in the postwar period.

The United States shaped a policy toward Libya in the late war period. President Franklin D. Roosevelt generally had deferred consideration of colonial issues until the Axis was defeated. He also promoted a general vision of establishing trusteeships under the authority of the emerging United Nations Organization to govern League of Nations mandates

44 LIBYA AND THE WEST

and colonies seized from enemy nations, a concept affirmed by British Prime Minister Winston Churchill and Soviet Premier Joseph Stalin during the Yalta Conference in February 1945. Like the British, US State Department officials developed conflicting thoughts about Libya's future. Some officials embraced Eden's pledge and applied it to all Libya, on the rationale that Italian restoration would violate the Atlantic Charter and provoke violent resistance by the Libyan people. But others thought that Britain might accept a postwar role in Cyrenaica only and thus did not rule out an Italian role in administering postwar Tripolitania.

The Allies briefly discussed the Italian colonies during their victors' conference at Potsdam, Germany, in July 1945. Citing the agreement that Roosevelt had brokered at Yalta, Stalin proposed the establishment of trusteeships in the Italian colonies and suggested even that the Soviet Union manage one of the Libyan provinces or join Britain and the United States in a collective trusteeship over all three provinces. Determined to contain Soviet influence, US and British officials resisted these proposals on the argument that securing a peace treaty must precede discussion of colonial issues given that the treaty would establish the legal basis for stripping the colonies from Italy. Stalin relented, and the three powers assigned the tasks of negotiating a peace treaty and then deciding the fate of colonies to the Council of Foreign Ministers (CFM), the foreign ministers of Britain, the United States, the Soviet Union, China, and France who were scheduled to meet regularly to discuss the major international issues of the postwar era.[3]

In 1945–1948, the CFM thoroughly discussed the Italian colonies, sensing that their decisions would prove momentous in shaping Great Power diplomacy toward colonized peoples worldwide. Regarding Libya, they debated what form trusteeship might take and which power would lead it, whether Italy could play an administrative role, and what impact the colonial questions might have on Italy's political disposition or willingness to sign a peace treaty. "No other colonial issue was discussed, with such energy, or with such a variety of differing proposals for ultimate disposition," Bills observed. "And having attracted so much attention from the big powers, no other colonial issue proved so intractable in the early cold war years."[4]

As the debates ensued, Libyans—monitoring the emergent independence of Syria, Lebanon, Jordan, and Iraq—expressed growing demands for political independence from foreign control and strenuous objections to restoration of Italian imperialism. Italy's postwar leaders claimed, by contrast, that the colony was necessary for Italy to achieve prosperity and that it had predated the rise of fascism and thus did not need to be purged from Italian control.

After extensive and dynamic discussions, the CFM deadlocked on the critical issues in Libya. Hoping to bolster the prestige of the new international body, US Secretary of State James Byrnes proposed that the United Nations establish a sole trusteeship over all three provinces and grant a unified Libya its independence after 10 years. Predicting that the United Nations would lack the wherewithal to administer trusteeships, British Foreign Secretary Ernest Bevin advocated for separate trusteeships over the three Libyan provinces to be managed by national powers, with Britain maintaining Cyrenaica. Soviet Minister V. I. Molotov endorsed the British approach, insisting that the Soviets would administer Tripolitania while Britain and France managed Cyrenaica and the Fezzan, respectively. French Foreign Minister Georges Bidault sought to protect France's quest to restore its own North African colonies against both the principle of forced decolonization and the prospect of Libyan independence stoking nationalism within the neighboring French colonies. Thus, he ardently suggested that Italy had been a beneficent colonizer and should enjoy an opportunity to reclaim its possessions in Libya. These discussions became increasingly contentious as the wartime Alliance disintegrated amid the broad array of global political issues that generated the Cold War.[5]

46 LIBYA AND THE WEST

How did the Italian Peace Treaty of 1947 address the issue of Libya?

As it deadlocked over the actual administration of Italian colonies, the CFM also negotiated comprehensive peace treaties with the European states that had aligned with the Axis. The negotiations on a treaty with Italy became contentious as the Western Allies and the Soviet Union disagreed on specific issues regarding Italy's government and borders and as Cold War tensions escalated. Despite these obstacles, the Allies were able to finalize an Italian Peace Treaty, signed on February 10, 1947, that clarified the legal status of Italy's African colonies.

The victorious powers enforced their earlier consensus that Italy must relinquish its colonies. The Treaty stipulated that "Italy renounces all right and title to the Italian territorial possessions in Africa, i.e. Libya, Eritrea and Italian Somaliland." The treaty further specified that the United States, Britain, France, and the Soviet Union would jointly decide the permanent status of the territories "in the light of the wishes and welfare of the inhabitants and the interests of peace and security, taking into consideration the views of other interested Governments." If the four Great Powers failed to resolve the issues within 12 months, they pledged to refer the matter to the United Nations General Assembly for a decision.[6]

Although Britain succeeded in its quest to deny the Soviet Union a stake in North Africa, the terms of the Italian peace treaty left all parties unsatisfied. None of the dominant powers gained assurances for its interests in the eastern Mediterranean. Italy swallowed the loss of legal sovereignty and immediately demanded an administrative role in any trusteeships that took shape. Enamored by pan-Arab nationalism that had grown in response to developments in Palestine and elsewhere, Libyans were grateful for the clear renunciation of Italian sovereignty but remained fearful of lingering imperial impulses among the Western powers.[7]

What diplomatic initiatives did the Great Powers take after the Italian Peace Treaty?

As prescribed by the treaty, the United States, Britain, France, and the Soviet Union thoroughly investigated the conditions within the Italian colonies and conducted negotiations about their permanent political status. A joint team of investigators visited the colonies to discern the capabilities and desires of the local peoples for self-governance. The four powers reached a consensus that Libya was not ready for self-government as its people strongly desired. The intensification of Cold War tensions throughout Europe and Asia, however, undermined the trust and willingness to compromise that the wartime Allies needed to reach an agreement about establishing some collective trusteeship or other solution. As mandated by the peace treaty, the four powers thus referred the issue to the UN General Assembly.

How did strategic factors shape Western thinking about Libya?

As the Cold War escalated in the late 1940s, the United States and Britain ascribed considerable national security value to the eastern Mediterranean. Encouraged by their legacy of wartime cooperation against the Axis, officials of these two states consulted closely on anti-Soviet security issues. Evidence of Soviet expansion into the Middle East and knowledge of Britain's declining abilities to exert authority there convinced US officials to project power into the region. The US Truman Doctrine of 1947, the joint Anglo–American attempt to establish a Middle East Command security system in Egypt in 1950, and the incorporation of Greece and Turkey into the North Atlantic Treaty Organization (NATO) in 1952 revealed a pattern of growth in US commitments to protect the eastern Mediterranean from Soviet encroachments. To undergird such security systems, Pentagon planners envisioned a network of airbases extending from Morocco to Libya and Saudi Arabia and came to favor a British presence in Libya to reach

48 **LIBYA AND THE WEST**

that objective. Sixty US diplomats who gathered at Tangiers in October 1950 recognized that North Africa "is of considerable strategic importance since it commands the southern approaches to Europe and the western approaches to the Near East. . . . It is probable that the area would play the same role in any future war as it played in the last war."[8]

British officials shared these security interests. The Foreign Office considered British airbases near Tripoli and Tobruk as "undoubtedly the best aircraft carrier in Africa," given their vitality to the maintenance of secure sea routes on the Mediterranean and given the growing likelihood that Britain might be forced to relinquish bases in Palestine and Egypt. To preserve these assets, British officials nurtured a close relationship with Idris, who returned from exile in Egypt in 1947, assumed authority as emir of Cyrenaica, and imposed a royalist constitution over that province in 1949. On the model of their partnerships with monarchies in Egypt, Jordan, and Iraq, British officials began to realize the strategic value of promoting Idris as a conservative king of an independent Libya who would be compliant with their security interests. They were further motivated by the realization among Western diplomats that, under UN protocols, only an independent state—and not a UN trusteeship—could grant base rights to a foreign power.[9]

In this context, US security strategists took an enduring interest in an airbase near Tripoli, Libya. Constructed by Italy in 1923, Mellaha Air Base was captured by the British army in January 1943 and transferred to US Army Air Forces, which used it to launch bombers against Italy and southern Germany. At the end of World War II, the US Air Transport Command designated the base as a vital link in military air supply routes and renamed it Wheelus Field (in honor of an officer who had been killed in the war). The Pentagon deactivated the base in May 1947, but reactivated it in June 1948, when the Berlin Crisis portended hostilities against the Soviet Union. After the outbreak of the Korean War in June 1950, US Air Force traffic at the base increased, and, by late 1950, the US Strategic Air

Command used the base for bombers poised to attack the Soviet Union in the event of another world war. The United States legally justified its occupation of the base by securing permission from Britain, under the latter's international authority to administer Libya as occupied territory.

France viewed developments in Libya with increasing alarm. Recalling how British and US leaders had rejected the French imperial position in Syria and Lebanon during World War II, Foreign Minister Georges Bidault strongly opposed British dominance in Libya because it would imperil French colonial interests in northwestern Africa. French leaders identified strategic value in their own occupation of the Fezzan, which offered a layer of protection for French territories in northwestern and central Africa and more direct transit routes between those territories.[10]

How did the United Nations handle the Italian colonies issue?

The UN General Assembly took up the issue of Italian colonies in early 1949. Discussion soon centered on a plan suggested by British Foreign Secretary Ernest Bevin and Italian Foreign Minister Carlo Sforza stipulating that Libya would gain independence in 10 years, and that, during the transition, it would be administered as three separate UN trusteeships, with Britain in control of Cyrenaica; France, of the Fezzan; and Italy, of Tripolitania (after a two-year transfer of authority from the British military administration there). The United States and other Western powers signaled support for this resolution on the grounds that it would enhance Western strategic interests in the Mediterranean by ensuring that the Libyan provinces were developed in a favorable direction.

As the proposal progressed through subcommittee votes, however, a considerable backlash formed against it within Libya, Arab countries, and other developing states. Tens of thousands of Libyans participated in mass demonstrations, and their tribal and political leaders denounced the delay of statehood and, especially, the reimposition of Italian authority. Protestors in Libya and other Arab states burned the flags of Italy, Britain, and the United States and cheered the Soviet Union for criticizing the proposal. Arab delegates to the United Nations lobbied heartily against the resolution, appealing especially to Latin American states to abandon their usual deference to US influence and affinity for Italy.

When the General Assembly voted on the resolution in mid-May, the measure failed to garner the two-thirds affirmative support needed for passage under UN rules. The decisive vote came on a measure regarding the disposition of Tripolitania to Italian supervision, which gained 33 votes in favor to 17 opposed with 8 abstentions, just shy of a two-thirds majority. The decisive "no" vote was cast by the Haitian delegate, Emile Saint-Lot, for whom a street in Tripoli was later named. Once the measure failed, a variety of amendments were attached to the main resolution, which was defeated on May 17 by a tally of 14 "yes" and 37 "no" votes with 7 abstentions.

In the aftermath of this defeat, the Western powers yielded to a move among other UN members promptly to grant Libya independence, leading to the passage, on November 21, 1949, of UN General Assembly Resolution 289. By a unanimous vote of 49–0 (with 9 abstentions), the assembly directed that the three Libyan provinces would gain independence as a unified state no later than January 1, 1952. To prepare the country, the United Nations would appoint a commissioner who would assist a national assembly of Libyans in drafting a constitution and who would administer the territories in consultation with a 10-member council composed of four Libyan representatives (one from each province and one to speak for minorities) and delegates from six states (Egypt, Pakistan, Britain, the United States, France, and Italy). "The United Kingdom of Libya was an accidental state," the scholar Dirk J. Vandewalle observed, "created by, and at the behest of, Great Power interests and agreed to by the local provinces who feared other alternatives."[11]

What challenges did Libyans face during the period of Great Power and UN deliberations about their future?

Libyans faced monumental problems during the late 1940s. Economic and social challenges were astounding. The economy continued to suffer from wartime dislocations and destruction. At $35 per year, per capita income was the lowest in the Arab world. People survived on meager diets, fashioned clothing and shoes from discarded military uniforms and tires, and earned small profits by selling scrap metal scavenged from wrecked military vehicles. The country remained resource-poor, with vast stretches of desert, periodic droughts, deficient water resources, limited agriculture, and virtually no industry. (Oil had not yet been discovered.) Ninety percent of the country's 1 million residents were illiterate; the population lacked trained professionals, managers, teachers, and technicians; and a high birth rate was offset by an infant mortality rate of 50 percent.

Libya continued to face traditional political schisms defined by the established identities of the three provinces. Residents of Cyrenaica and the Fezzan demonstrated political and social loyalty to their tribes. Sayid Muhammed Idris commanded respect as the dominant political and cultural leader of Cyrenaica, while the Sayf al-Nasr tribe was paramount in the Fezzan. While considering familial ties significant, Tripolitanians assigned some loyalty to modern political parties organized around ideology and ideas. Threatening the old order in all three provinces, a growing number of young adults were attracted to pan-Arab nationalist ideology advocated by political upstarts in Iraq, Syria, and Egypt and galvanized by the opposition of the Arab masses to the emergence of Israel in 1947–1948.

Libyans began to form political parties, but that process accentuated conflict rather than building consensus among political activists. The Cyrenaican National Front formed to demand the independence of that province under

52 LIBYA AND THE WEST

Idris's authority. A Tripolitanian National United Front also materialized, but it gave priority to independence of a united Libya rather than an emirate under Idris. A conference between the two groups in January 1947 deadlocked over these competing goals. Other movements to build national unity, such as the formation of the Libyan Liberation Committee by Bashir al-Sadawi, also sputtered. Even after the announcement of the Bevin-Sforza plan provoked massive street protests in Tripoli and elsewhere, Libyan political elites failed to form a unified political organization to represent their people to the United Nations or the Great Powers.[12]

How did Libya advance toward statehood under the auspices of the UN Commissioner?

Appointed as Commissioner in Libya during his long career as a League of Nations and United Nations official, Adrian Pelt of the Netherlands presided over an orderly, peaceful, and efficient transition of Libya to independence. He began by appointing the 10-member advisory council and then established the Committee of Twenty-One, consisting exclusively of Libyan nationals (seven from each of the three provinces), to debate the framework of the new state.

Disagreements developed within the Committee of Twenty-One. Tripolitanians, whose province was the most populous, favored a unified state with representation proportional to population. Delegates from Cyrenaica and the Fezzan, eager to protect the cohesiveness knit by the Senussi and the stature of Idris, favored a federal state with representation equally divided among the three regions. The United States and Britain encouraged Commissioner Pelt to promote a federal state because it seemed most likely to protect their rights to military bases in Tripolitania and Cyrenaica. The Committee of Twenty-One agreed only to select representatives to a new National Constituent Assembly of Libya (NCAL) that would be empowered to decide essential issues and write a constitution. Throughout this process, Pelt relied on a small number of Libyan elites rather than determining the will of the people through a mass democratic process.[13]

The NCAL, composed of 60 delegates drawn equally from the three provinces, convened in November 1950 and promptly decided several crucial issues. A resolution unanimously passed on December 2 stipulated that "Libya is to be an independent, sovereign state, that the form of the state is to be federal and just," that "the government is to be a constitutional monarchical representative democracy," and that Sayed Mohammed Idris would be crowned as "King of Libya."[14]

A committee of the NCAL then wrote a constitution for "the United Kingdom of Libya" that established a hereditary monarchy; a bicameral parliament consisting of an elected House of Representatives and a partially elected and partially appointed Senate; a ministerial cabinet; a national judiciary; and three provincial governments centered in Benghazi, Tripoli, and Sebha. The constitution recognized that "Islam is the religion of the State," defined citizenship, provided that the capital would alternate between Benghazi and Tripoli, and otherwise established the framework of the new state. Key provisions privileged royal power over democratic tendencies. The king would be entrusted to exercise national sovereignty, and he "shall be inviolable" and "shall be exempt from all responsibility"—that is, above the law. The king would have the authority to decree laws and adjourn parliament. Even the various civil rights that were enshrined were made subject to suspension by law.[15]

The constitution was ratified in October 1951. Even before that official action, British officials began to transfer authority from their military administrative regimes to the provincial governments enumerated under the constitution. On December 24, 1951, Idris declared Libyan independence and formally adopted the title King Idris I.

54 LIBYA AND THE WEST

What type of political order emerged in Libya under King Idris?

During its first decade of independence, Libya emerged as an undemocratic, fragmented, and unstable state. An early political crisis affirmed the monarchical foundation of the state. In the very first democratic elections, held on February 19, 1952, the National Congress Party (NCP) of Tripolitania attempted to win enough parliamentary seats to amend the constitution to modify the federal system that the party disliked. When the NCP secured only 20 percent of the 35 seats it campaigned for, its advocates charged the authorities with electoral fraud, sparking street protests and police suppression resulting in 17 deaths and 300 arrests. Soon after the election, the press was restricted, political parties were outlawed, and Bashir al-Sadawi, the head of the NCP, was exiled. Thereafter, quadrennial elections became highly arranged affairs in which a royalist elite with oligarchic tendencies essentially decided who would hold office.

Libya also failed to achieve national political unity or identity. Libyans remained strongly attached to tribal and provincial loyalties. The three provincial regimes established under the constitution exercised considerable administrative authority, competing with various national interests and duplicating the efforts of the state. Gaining office through elite patronage and thus lacking popular mandates, government ministers tended to be ineffective, and governments turned over frequently. Two prime ministers resigned during the first three years of independence. King Idris's lack of a male heir also called into question the viability of the hereditary monarchy.

King Idris also displayed limitations as a monarch. While he never practiced brutal despotism, he failed to achieve widespread credibility and his original popularity waned as he proved unable to solve the complexities of the modern state. His inherent sense of favoritism toward Cyrenaica and his practice of isolating himself in a palace near Tobruk alienated those loyal to the other two provinces. A quarrel within his own family over royalist perks and succession to the throne touched off a prolonged crisis in 1954, after members of the extended family assassinated the king's closest confidante. Idris exiled several princes and placed tight restrictions on or stripped royal privileges from several relatives. Childless, the king designated his brother as heir in 1953, but that brother, lacking political experience or charisma, died in 1955. In pursuit of a male heir, the 65-year-old king took a second, 38-year-old wife (under Islamic laws allowing multiple marriages) in 1955, but that marriage also failed to produce an heir. Idris named a 28-year-old nephew, Hasan al-Rida, as crown prince, but did little to prepare him to be king or the people of Libya to accept his authority. The nation's confidence in the hereditary monarchy waned.

What foreign policies did the independent Kingdom of Libya pursue?

King Idris steered Libya into a firmly pro-Western orientation. A lifelong Anglophile, he secretly negotiated a 20-year mutual defense treaty with Britain, announcing it publicly in 1953. The treaty authorized the British military to continue to occupy facilities and training grounds in the northeastern coastal region of the country, and it pledged Britain to defend Libya against external aggression. The government in London also provided economic aid and technical assistance much needed by the kingdom to become financially viable.[16]

King Idris allowed the United States to retain Wheelus Field. The US Department of Defense eagerly sought to secure the legal right to control the base, given the escalation of the Cold War. Even before Libyan independence, US officials and King Idris negotiated a draft base rights treaty, although disagreements over financial and legal terms prolonged negotiations until 1954. Once US officials offered a $40 million aid package—an annual royalty of $4 million in 1954–1960 and $1 million thereafter, plus additional economic and

56 LIBYA AND THE WEST

food aid—as an incentive, Libya ratified the treaty in October 1954. Scheduled to endure until 1970, the treaty provided the United States unrestricted access to Wheelus Field and such other benefits as the legal right of extraterritoriality for US personnel. After ratification, the US government elevated its legation in Tripoli to an embassy, and the US Air Force quickly established various command, bomber, and fighter wings at Wheelus Field. By the early 1960s, Wheelus Field had grown to some 27,000 acres housing more than 10,000 US personnel.[17]

Libyan relations with Italy and France were more mixed. With the former, Libya signed a deal in 1956 that provided $8 million in economic aid from Italy and ensured the property rights of Italian nationals remaining in Libya. The two states also developed interlocking trade arrangements whose value soared from 23 billion lire in 1960 to 407 billion lire in 1972. Despite the legal assurances, however, most Italian settlers sold their property and departed, and the Italian population in Libya declined from 40,000 to 20,000 in 1945–1970. Among Libyan nationalists, moreover, there remained a reservoir of resentment toward the Italian colonial legacy, and Italy's insistence that the funds provided were economic aid and not any form of compensation for past colonial deprivations did nothing to soothe the nationalists' sentiments.[18]

Libya's relationship with France was strained. Having been denied a formal trusteeship in the Fezzan, France abstained when the United Nations voted for Libyan independence and remained in possession of airbases in its occupation zone. King Idris refused to grant France long-term base rights like he granted to Britain and the United States. Tensions increased during the Algerian War for Independence of 1952–1962, because Algerian rebels against French imperial control secured covert arms supply from Egypt via transit routes through the Fezzan. France sought permanent base rights to interdict those supply lines, but Libya refused. Instead, the two powers signed a deal in 1955 that provided for the withdrawal of all French military personnel from the Fezzan by 1956, although it permitted French civilians to operate airfields there.

Consistent with its global disposition, Libya maintained a distant relationship with the Soviet Union. Viewing Libya as pro-Western, Moscow vetoed its membership in the United Nations in 1952–1955. As part of a diplomatic deal through which Libya and 14 other powers were admitted to the United Nations in 1955, Libya diplomatically recognized the Soviet Union. But, in deference to its close ties with the West, Libya did not pursue interaction with Moscow, and it declined a Soviet offer of economic aid.

How did Libya's pro-Western orientation influence its relations with other Arab states?

Libya's pro-Western orientation aggravated its relationships with other Arab powers. Soon after it secured admission to the League of Arab States in 1953, Libya found itself at odds with other members, most notably Egypt, where Colonel Gamal Abdel Nasser had taken power in an anti-Western and antimonarchical revolution in 1952.

Nasser, who forced Britain to agree in 1954 to withdraw its army from Egypt and who campaigned to expel imperial influence from across the region, strongly criticized Idris's defense and military base agreements with the Western powers. Tensions escalated sharply after 1955 because of political clashes across the region. In 1955, a populist protest movement forced King Hussein of Jordan to begin repudiating his military alliance with Britain. In 1956, Britain and France attempted to overthrow Nasser through an ill-conceived military invasion coordinated with Israel; Nasser survived the assault and emerged as the hero of the masses across the Arab world. In 1958, nationalist army officers in Iraq overthrew that country's pro-British monarchy in a bloody coup. Badly shaken by these developments, especially those in Iraq, Idris became even more dependent on the US and British forces within his country as his ultimate defense against the actual and implied Egyptian threats.

How did the discovery of oil shape Libya's development as an independent state?

The discovery of oil in Libya in 1959 resulted in dramatic changes to the country's internal economic and political systems and eventually empowered it to take a more assertive role in international affairs. For better or worse, the discovery proved to be a major turning point in Libyan history.

In the early 1950s, Western oil companies took an active interest in exploring potential oilfields in North Africa. That

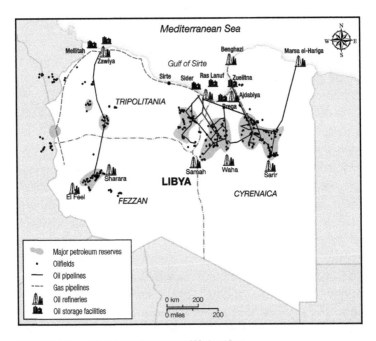

Map 3 Oilfields and Petroleum Infrastructure of Modern Libya

region offered several advantages over the oilfields of Iran and the Arabian Peninsula that had been established before and during World War II. Given the growing Western dependence on oil for security and economic reasons, there was a general desire to diversify and increase its sources. Libya was some 700 nautical miles closer than Saudi Arabia and nearly 4,000 nautical miles closer than Iran to oil-thirsty Western Europe, which was rebuilding its industrial base from wartime devastation. Transportation from North Africa was not vulnerable to shipping delays caused by political turmoil at such chokepoints as the Straits of Hormuz and the Suez Canal, concerns over which grew during the political turmoil in Iran and Egypt in the early and mid-1950s. The British and US firms that had built the oil infrastructure of Iran and the eastern Arab states viewed Libya, ruled by a pro-Western monarch and safeguarded by Western military bases, as an attractive location to explore for oil.[19]

Beginning in 1955, the Kingdom of Libya facilitated oil exploration by Western firms by offering exclusive concessions to prospect on designated pieces of land in exchange for a 50 percent share of any eventual revenues. By 1957, the so-called seven sisters (major, international oil corporations) as well as a small number of independent US firms engaged in exploration. In June 1959, the Esso Corporation became the first firm to discover a major concentration of petroleum in the Zaltan field, about 100 miles from the coast in the Sirtica Desert of Cyrenaica. Several other corporations soon found pay dirt as well. Esso opened the first coastal port as Marsa al-Burayqah (also known as Marsa el-Brega) for the export of its oil in 1961, and four other companies opened ports by 1968. To the delight of the oil companies, Libyan crude oil proved to be of both high quality and voluminous quantity. The oil bonanza produced phenomenal wealth for the corporations and for the historically impoverished desert kingdom, which equally shared an annual revenue stream that started at $6 million in 1961 and reached a stupendous $1.2 billion in 1969.[20]

Libya's Petroleum Law of 1955 was carefully designed to incentivize rapid development of oil resources on terms favorable to Libya. King Idris's government realized that it needed to offer generous terms to attract oil firms that were preoccupied in established markets to the east. Such terms of the law as low entry fees and relatively generous potential royalties attracted large and small oil firms. Other features of the law—such as limits to the geographical size and chronological endurance of concessions—incentivized companies to explore immediately rather than sit on untapped acreage. The law generated dynamic activity and rapid development of Libya's oil industry. Within a decade of the proven discovery of oil in 1959, nearly 40 large and small firms operating through more than 130 concessions were producing 2.6 million barrels per day. As an indication of growing dependence on North African oil, Europe imported 21 percent of its oil from Libya and Algeria in 1964, up from 5 percent in 1960.[21]

As Libyan oil began reaching markets in the early 1960s, the Idris regime amended the 1955 Petroleum Law to extract greater shares of revenues. By mid-decade, companies were required to relinquish at least 50 percent of revenues as rent to Libya. Companies grumbled, but they were forced to comply by the competitive environment in Libya and the government's threat to cancel concessions and redistribute opportunities to other firms waiting in the wings. Emulated by other oil-producing states, Libya's legislation diminished the power and influence of Western oil firms across the Middle East.[22]

In what ways did the oil wealth change Libya's internal socioeconomic order?

While the sudden infusion of oil wealth offered the potential to lift the people of Libya from their historic poverty, during the 1960s it seemed to aggravate rather than resolve social and political tensions within the kingdom.

King Idris attempted to steer the country into healthy growth and development. By a fate of nature, most of the oilfields lay within the Cyrenaica, whose elites, citing the federalism of the constitution, tried to secure the largesse for themselves. Sensitive to the suspicions common in Tripolitania and the Fezzan that he favored his native province, King Idris took bold action to distribute the wealth nationally. In 1963, he revised the constitution, abolishing the federal system in favor of a unitary state subdivided into 10 new administrative districts. The king also promoted the adoption in 1963 of a Five-Year Plan to devote oil revenues to the reform and modernization of the economy, public health, education, housing, and communications.

The Libyan government tried to advance the interest of Libyans employed by the international oil firms. The Libyan Labor Law of 1957 encouraged oil firms to hire Libyan workers and required the firms to pay Libyans a minimum wage, provide working and living conditions that met government safety standards, and extend to Libyan workers the same benefits given to foreign workers. Although Western firms protested these regulations, they were compelled to abide by them by the late 1950s.[23]

Despite efforts by the king and certain civil officials, however, problems mounted. Oil wealth tended to remain concentrated in the hands of elites, generating resentment among the masses who lingered in poverty amid new pockets of opulence. In a country of 1.8 million citizens, only about 8,000 Libyans gained stable jobs in the oil industry, and foreigners filled the high-salary technical positions. Common people hungry for steady paychecks migrated in large numbers from agricultural and undeveloped areas to the oilfields and coastal terminal towns, where they were greeted by shantytowns, malnutrition, and disease while they were cut off from their familial and tribal support networks. Rapid growth also became problematic in Tripoli and Benghazi, whose populations increased by 67 percent and 100 percent, respectively, in

62 LIBYA AND THE WEST

1954–1964. A shortage of educated and experienced government officials—as well as the depth and complexity of the social challenges—starkly limited the effectiveness of the Five-Year Plan of 1963–1968 and a follow-up plan launched in 1969. The government devoted oil wealth to construction of sparkling new school buildings, but there were few qualified Libyan teachers to staff them. The regime imported teachers from Egypt, most of whom inculcated Nasserite ideology and ideas into their students.

Organized labor in Libya became more radical and activist in the 1960s, despite a concerted effort by the US State Department and liberal US unions to encourage anticommunist, pro-Western unions. As the Libyan unions were radicalized, they pressured the Western oil firms for better pay and working conditions. The Idris regime, with US backing, used police power to break strikes and otherwise suppress the unions. In response, the unions became antiroyalist, feeding growing public discontent with the regime.[24]

To what degree did the socioeconomic instability of the 1960s contribute to political unrest?

The socioeconomic challenges besetting Libya stimulated popular discontent with the government. The growing disgruntlement was facilitated by a political environment susceptible to pan-Arab nationalism fomented throughout the 1960s by Egypt's Nasser. A proponent of neutralism in the Cold War, Nasser promoted the diminution of Western imperial assets and influence in the Middle East and the development of pan-Arab political strength. He sharply criticized King Idris for allowing the United States and Britain to occupy military bases in Libya and otherwise supporting the West. Pan-Arab nationalism also rallied around opposition to Israel that mounted steadily during the 1960s.

Political unrest suddenly erupted in Libya in January 1964, when King Idris declined to attend the Cairo Summit of Arab

Colony to Monarchy to Revolution 63

leaders, called by Nasser to discuss how to bolster Jordan and Syria in their conflict with Israel over water rights. The king claimed reasons of health, although intense pressure from Britain and the United States to defy Nasser's leadership likely encouraged his decision. In any event, young adults in Benghazi launched street demonstrations to protest the king's decision. The authorities suppressed the demonstration with force, killing two protesters, but that action merely sparked a wave of copycat protests in other cities and near the Western military bases and compelled Prime Minister Muhieddin al-Fikini to resign.

Tensions built steadily in subsequent months. When Nasser demanded assurances that the United States and Britain would not use their Libyan bases to defend Israel against Arab states, public outcries among Libyans forced the parliament, in defiance of royal demands, to insist on early termination of the base rights of both powers. The British, realizing that their facilities had lost strategic value and political credibility since the Suez War of 1956, abandoned their two major bases near Tripoli and Benghazi in 1966–1967, maintaining possession of an airfield at al Adem and a garrison at Tobruk, both used to train Libyan soldiers. The United States remained in control of Wheelus Field and asked Libyan authorities to renew the base agreement beyond its scheduled expiration in 1970.

King Idris steadily lost influence and confidence during these years of unrest. His declaration of a unitary state in 1963 did little to win him support outside of Cyrenaica. Parliament's defiance of his authority in the argument over the Western military bases undermined his authority, especially after he threatened (in a bluff, it turned out) to abdicate. Idris clearly lacked charisma in the eyes of his countrymen smitten by Nasser's political charm, and, as the king grew older and frailer, he isolated himself in his remote palace in northeast Cyrenaica, becoming psychologically distant from his people. Key sectors of the population, such as educated urbanites and professional army officers, lost faith in their king. The absence

64 LIBYA AND THE WEST

of a male heir stoked popular fears that power soon would pass to the al-Shalhi family, which had provided several key advisors to the king but lacked popular support.

What was the effect of the Arab–Israeli War of June 1967 on Libya's political orientation?

In a context of mounting threats of a pan-Arab military attack, Israel launched a brief but intense war against Egypt, Jordan, and Syria on June 5, 1967. In six days of fighting, Israel demolished the air forces of the three Arab states, mauled their armies, and seized huge swaths of their territory by occupying the Sinai Peninsula, Gaza Strip, West Bank, and Golan Heights. News of the dramatic Israeli victory triggered a volcanic eruption of nationalist passions across the Arab states. Eager to find scapegoats for his debilitating battlefield defeat, Nasser charged, falsely, that the United States and Britain had colluded with Israel in its attack, and specifically that US and British warplanes based in Libya had participated in air raids on Egypt.

Masses of enraged Libyans promptly took to the streets of Tripoli, Benghazi, and other cities to protest their government's alleged complicity in the Israeli assault. Mobs violently assaulted the country's small Jewish population, killing 130, and attacked the British and US embassies and the offices of Western oil companies. Rioters ransacked the first floor of the US embassy in Benghazi, while two dozen US Foreign Service officers and military soldiers locked themselves in a second-floor vault, burning classified documents and demolishing code machines while awaiting rescue by a British armored car. So tense were conditions that the US government organized an emergency evacuation of some 6,000 US citizens. Oilfield and dock workers went on strike, shutting down the oil export business for about a month.[25]

The Libyan masses also protested their own government's detachment from the Arab front lines. An official statement declaring Libya's solidarity with the quest to liberate Palestine did not satisfy a public demand to intervene in the war. The Libyan army organized a battalion for action, but the war ended well before the troops could reach the front. Among the soldiers who began to advance toward the war zone in Egypt was 25-year-old Captain Muammar al-Qaddafi.

Gradually, the government restored order on the streets and normal life resumed. To win favor among other Arab leaders, King Idris attended the Arab Summit at Khartoum in September 1967, where the Arab leaders famously voted the so-called three noes resolutions opposing negotiations with Israel, peace with Israel, or recognition of Israel. Libya also joined the oil-rich monarchies of Saudi Arabia and Kuwait in pledging, in 1968, to provide some $280 million per year to help Egypt, Jordan, and Syria recover from the fighting. Nasser, however, continued to criticize the king's pro-Western orientation, which Idris refused to recant. At home, the king and Abdel Hamid al-Bakkush, a young attorney who became prime minister in October 1967, discussed possible liberal reforms including anticorruption and pro-efficiency measures and rapid modernization of the military. In 1968, however, Bakkush was pressured to resign after Idris decided he was promoting excessive change. The conversations about reform thus accomplished little beyond raising and then dashing expectations in the minds of the growing number of detractors from the constitutional monarchy.

What were the origins of the Libyan revolution of 1969?

The Libyan revolution of 1969 originated in a complex of factors. Libya's infusion of oil wealth during the 1960s filled the coffers of the Finance Ministry and created pockets of wealth among the country's elites, but authorities proved unable to use the wealth to build a diversified, balanced, or stable economy. The fast growth in the oil industry, moreover, disrupted familial and tribal networks and cultural identities that had provided social stability over many generations, and it created the impression that while the privileged elite thrived, the working masses remained impoverished. Despite his benign intentions, King Idris proved to be an ineffectual ruler, unable to organize an efficient government or win the patriotic loyalty of his people. Modern communications and economic intercourse exposed Libyans to competing ideologies from other countries, most notably the nationalism, neutralism, and anti-Zionism espoused by Nasser. These ideologies captured the imagination of the Libyan people as they grew despondent with their situation.

The aging of the heirless King Idris generated a succession rivalry among various Libyan elites. The nephew whom the king had named as Crown Prince Hasan was poised to assume the throne but lacked a credible mantle of authority. The al-Shalhi family, who had served as top-level confidantes of the king, secretly plotted to replace the crown prince with one of their own. Yet other elites favored finding a capable leader from among the business community or technocracy. Senior officers in the Libyan army plotted to seize power at the moment of Idris's demise. Finally, a clique of junior military officers, organized by Captain Qaddafi, watched for an opportunity to replicate the coup that Nasser had led against King Farouk in Egypt in 1952.

Stressed and fatigued by age, infirmity, and the burdens of power, King Idris departed Libya on June 12, 1969, for medical treatment and recuperation in Greece and Turkey, naming the crown prince as regent. His departure set the stage for a revolution. Idris would never return to Libya.

Who was Muammar al-Qaddafi, and how was he able to seize power from King Idris in 1969?

The son of a poor Bedouin shepherd, Qaddafi was born in a tent in the desert near Sirte in 1942. Educated in Muslim schools, he developed a personal culture based on austere adherence to Islamic law and a commitment to the rugged individualism and egalitarianism of his nomadic, desert tribe. In his youth, he became enamored with Nasser, whose ideology of nationalism, neutralism, and anti-Zionism permeated the Libyan people via Radio Cairo and reached Qaddafi through several Egyptian teachers and Nasser's popular book *Philosophy of the Revolution*. Such international events as the Palestine War of 1948–1949, the Egyptian Revolution of 1952, the Suez War of 1956, and the Iraqi revolution of 1958 had a deep impact on the youthful Qaddafi, steering him toward a determination to embrace Nasserism and channel it into his own country.

Qaddafi pursued a career in the Libyan military, the most viable path to social mobility available to him given that he lacked the elite tribal or personal connections needed to pursue other options in royalist Libya. An army career offered Qaddafi the potential to gain political influence like his idol Nasser had gained in Egypt. Qaddafi graduated from the Libyan military academy at Benghazi in 1965, despite a record of insubordination against the school's British instructors. He gained advanced military communications training in Britain under a program designed to promote Anglo–Libyan relations, but he returned home with his Anglophobia deepened by the culture of London.

While in the military academy, Qaddafi organized a secret cadre of several dozen fellow junior officers who shared his political ideology and adulation of Nasser. He called the group the Libyan Free Unionist Officers' Movement, borrowing the name from Nasser's Free Officers Movement of the early 1950s. The outcome of the 1967 Arab–Israeli War profoundly embittered the Libyan Free Officers and galvanized them to take bold action to overthrow the king and steer their country into a bright future. When Idris, while on medical leave in Greece, signed an edict to transfer power to the crown prince effective on September 2, the Free Officers decided to strike for power.

68 LIBYA AND THE WEST

The Free Officers launched their coup at 3:00 AM on September 1, 1969. Some 70 officers, in command of soldiers driving Western trucks and a few British-made Centurion tanks, occupied government and police headquarters, the national radio station, royal palaces, and other key facilities in Benghazi, Tripoli, and Baida; declared the overthrow of King Idris and the abolition of the monarchy; and arrested the crown prince and other leaders of the royalist regime. "To execute your free will, to realize your precious aspirations," the officers declared to the Libyan people, ". . . your armed forces have destroyed the reactionary, backward, and decadent regime whose putrid odor assailed one's nose and the vision of whose attributes made one's eyes tremble. With one blow from your heroic army, the idols collapsed and the graven images shattered. In one terrible moment of fate, the darkness of ages—from the rule of the Turks to the tyranny of the Italians and the era of reaction, bribery, intercession, favoritism, treason, and treachery—was dispersed. Thus, from now on, Libya is deemed a free, sovereign republic under the name of the Libyan Arab Republic."[26]

Initially, the Free Officers remained secretive, if not mysterious, probably calculating that anonymity protected their personal security. They immediately clarified that the Revolutionary Command Council, a committee of 12 officers, had launched the coup under the leadership of Colonel Saad al-Din Abu-Shuawayrib, who had been educated in the US Army's Command and General Staff College at Fort Leavenworth, Kansas, in 1964–1965. Western officials suspected, accurately, it turned out, that Shuawayrib was a mere figurehead for younger officers who hoped to earn credibility among foreign powers. Within weeks, foreign observers concluded that Qaddafi was indeed the mastermind of the new regime.[27]

3

LIBYA UNDER MUAMMAR AL-QADDAFI

What steps did Muammar al-Qaddafi and his confederates take to consolidate power in Libya?

The challenge facing the Revolutionary Command Council (RCC) of consolidating power after its September 1, 1969, coup was minimized by the unpopularity of the monarchy they overthrew. Indeed, in the immediate aftermath of the takeover, various units of the Libyan Army quickly endorsed the RCC's action, and expressions of public opinion were uniformly enthusiastic about it. The conspirators had feared resistance from Cyrenaica and the Fezzan, but none materialized. In fact, the coup was completely peaceful, with no deaths or gunfights reported.

Prudently, the members of the RCC imposed measures to suppress any opposition to the coup. They announced that counterrevolutionary movements would be "crushed ruthlessly and decisively" and took special precautions against potential challengers in the royal family. They neutralized the greatest royalist threat when they persuaded Crown Prince Hasan, in a statement broadcast on radio, to announce, "I abandon all my constitutional and legal rights to the throne" and "I request all the people to support the new regime because I support it." In an agreement arbitrated by Egypt, moreover, King Idris pledged never to return to Libya, and the new regime assured the personal safety of members of the royal family who remained in the country. The exiled ex-king took residence in Egypt, where he died in 1983.[1]

Qaddafi and his colleagues on the RCC also feared potential Western intervention in their coup, considering the strategic and economic interests that the United States and Britain had developed in Libya in partnership with the Idris regime, the legacy of Western covert operations in Iran in 1953, and the presence of 5,000 US troops at Wheelus Field, 1,200 British troops at a base near Tobruk, and the US Sixth fleet on patrol in the Mediterranean. The RCC thus broadcast a statement on September 1 offering assurances that it would protect the personal safety of foreigners, respect the property rights of foreign companies, and honor all treaties and international commitments. "It pleases us at this moment," the RCC declared, "to reassure our foreign brethren that their lives and property will be under the protection of the armed forces."[2]

How did the Western powers view the Libyan coup?

Western governments were surprised by the Libyan coup. Given the weaknesses of the Libyan monarchy and the social and economic challenges facing the country, they had anticipated a power struggle of some magnitude at the time of Idris's death, but they had not anticipated the sudden power grab conducted by Qaddafi. While certain officials in the United States and Britain contemplated intervention in Libya to restore the king, both Western powers promptly decided to accept the new regime as the legitimate authority in Libya and extended formal diplomatic recognition within a week of its takeover.

The US State Department resolutely opposed any form of intervention to preserve King Idris. Years before Qaddafi's coup, department experts had defined US objectives in Libya to include the preservation of Libya's independence and the protection of US interests there, but not loyalty to King

Idris or any specific government. Once the coup occurred, Secretary of State William P. Rogers concluded that any form of intervention would anger other Arab states and thereby dash his hopes of negotiating an Arab–Israeli peace settlement. Alone among top US officials, National Security Adviser Henry Kissinger urged action to restore King Idris, to safeguard Western oil resources and military bases. "The return to our balance of payments and the security of U.S. investments in oil are considered our primary interests," State Department officials countered. "We seek to retain our military facilities, but not at the expense of threatening our economic return. We also wish to protect European dependence on Libyan oil; it is literally the only 'irreplaceable' oil in the world, from the point of view both of quality and geographic location." US officials also calculated that they had little leverage to effect meaningful change in the political situation in Libya and that any attempts to do so would both strengthen and alienate the revolutionary regime, to the detriment of Western interests.[3]

The RCC's declarations that it sought friendly relations with all powers, that it would not disrupt the oil industry, and that it was anticommunist encouraged US officials to accommodate the new regime. While realizing that such RCC assurances might be "deliberate dissimulation, designed to reduce any threat of foreign counterrevolutionary intervention," the CIA noted that the RCC leaders "show a posture of moderation and caution. . . . No Libyan leader has mouthed the extremist slogans typical of Arab radicals. To the contrary, such themes as the protection of foreign lives and property, the fulfillment of international obligations, and the elimination of corruption and favoritism at home have been stressed."[4]

British officials essentially adopted the same approach as the Americans. Prime Minister Harold Wilson promptly rejected a request from King Idris to intervene to restore him to the throne. Foreign Secretary Michael Stewart advised that such action would be "dangerous and wrong."[5]

72 LIBYA AND THE WEST

Italy immediately resolved to accept the new regime in Libya, becoming the first non-Arab state to offer it diplomatic recognition. Foreign Minister Aldo Moro believed that pursuing a postcolonial, progressive, and respectful policy toward Arab states offered the best means to keep them out of the Soviet orbit and otherwise to promote Italy's national interests in the Mediterranean. A policy of accommodation also promised to preserve the burgeoning trade between the two states, protect Italy's access to Libyan oil, and assure the safety of Italian nationals in Libya.

Libya sent signals of friendship to other Western states. "We sincerely desire the development of continuing and friendly relations with France," Qaddafi told a journalist on October 1. "We have considered France a friendly state since it changed its policy toward the Arab world and ceased its military assistance to Israel." RCC members spoke openly of their desire to sell oil to West Germany in exchange for access to its technology.[6]

What type of government did the Revolutionary Command Council establish?

Relatively young and inexperienced in politics and government, RCC members moved slowly and deliberately in establishing their new regime. They adopted the slogan "freedom, socialism, and unity" as an organizing concept. "The people who have surged forward, broken the shackles and trodden down idols, will impose freedom, socialism and Arab unity by force on the enemies of Arabism and Islam," Qaddafi declared in an address on September 22. "Freedom, socialism, and unity are not the outcome of the first of September, nor the fruit of one day or night; they have been deeply buried in this people for centuries past." Such "exalted principles," another RCC member declared, "concern the occurrence of fundamental change in every part of the republic."[7]

The RCC initially held power behind a façade of an administrative cabinet of six civilians and two military officers (neither one a member of the RCC), headed by Prime Minister Mahmud Sulayman al-Maghrabi. A Palestinian lawyer, Maghrabi had joined the Esso oil corporation in 1966 but had been jailed by the monarchy in 1967–1969 for organizing a labor union among dock workers. Exiled in 1969, he was summoned by the RCC to return to Libya as the titular head of the government and was appointed prime minister on September 7, 1969. The next day, the RCC promoted Qaddafi to colonel and named him commander-in-chief of Libya's military. That move affirmed that Qaddafi was the actual broker of power in the regime. His dominance over the RCC and the government of Libya would grow steadily in succeeding years.

Over a period of weeks, the RCC issued a series of proclamations clarifying its intentions. The officers declared that Libya would support unified pan-Arab aspirations including the liberation of Palestine from Israeli occupation. They professed neutrality in the Cold War, opposition to colonialism, adherence to Islam, and resistance to atheistic communism. On the home front, the RCC intended to reform the country's political, social, and economic structures for the common good. It made clear that it would govern authoritatively when it abolished the national parliament, prohibited political parties and labor unions, and suppressed independent newspapers. Arabic was declared as the official language, and English was removed from official documents and road signs. The remnants of Libya's Italian settler and Jewish communities were exiled, their property was nationalized, and foreign banks were restricted.

Qaddafi aimed to harness his new regime to Islam, a major foundation of Libyan society and culture over many centuries, on terms consistent with his political ambitions. The September 1969 revolution, he declared, "stems from the eternal message of Islam and from the Holy Quran." The RCC issued edicts to suppress churches, alcohol, pornography, and other un-Islamic vestiges of Western colonial culture. Qaddafi clarified that the Sharia would become the foundation of all laws, civil, criminal, and commercial as well as religious, and that civil and religious courts would be merged. Qaddafi identified and elevated the stature of various religious leaders who affirmed his new regime on grounds of piety and who refrained from objecting to Qaddafi's declaration that he alone would retain the authority to interpret matters of religion.[8]

By contrast, Qaddafi subdued religious leaders who might challenge his authority. He quickly suppressed the Senussi on his suspicion that it harbored loyalty to the deposed monarchy or that it would defy his authority to implement his revolutionary vision. He targeted the fundamentalist Muslim Brotherhood that had been implanted in Libya by Egyptian exiles after Egypt outlawed the organization in 1949 and that had emerged as a rival to King Idris in the mid-1960s. Soon after taking power, Qaddafi quashed the Brotherhood on the grounds that it opposed Arab nationalism, Arab socialism, and Arab unity, none of which Qaddafi considered to be inconsistent with Islam. Declaring the group "an ally of the colonialists and an opponent of Arab Unity" and calling its leaders "deviant heretics" and "stray dogs," Qaddafi jailed, executed, or exiled the Brotherhood's leaders, virtually eliminating the group by the late 1970s.[9]

By the end of 1969, the RCC more explicitly displayed its authoritarianism. "No partisanship after today," Qaddafi declared in an address on October 16. "He who engages in party activities after today commits treason." After accusing the ministers of defense and the interior of plotting a coup in December, the RCC dismissed both officials and named Qaddafi as prime minister and defense minister. In mid-1970, after foiling a second reported coup by members of the royal family and a tribe in the Fezzan, RCC members took over several other ministries, gaining a majority of seats in the Cabinet.[10]

The RCC continued to gather strength in the early 1970s. It conducted more than 200 trials of former officials of the monarchy, including King Idris (in absentia), handing down five death sentences (including one against the king) and dozens of prison sentences (including five years for former Crown Prince Hasan). The RCC abolished the Senussi Order, nationalized the press, and established a single legal political party, the Arab Socialist Union. Independent parties, trade unions, and labor strikes were outlawed.

How did the Libyan domestic political order evolve under Qaddafi's leadership in the 1970s?

Qaddafi faced a daunting challenge in organizing and stabilizing the political system of Libya. When he came to power, the country had a decentralized, tribal legacy and lacked national cohesion. Nationalism had taken root in opposition to Italian colonialism, but nationalist movements remained fragmented and internally divided. King Idris had tried to build a single state but failed to overcome regional and tribal loyalties. Qaddafi essentially found the rudimentary state he inherited to be impractical, inefficient, untrustworthy, and unreliable, so he set out to replace it with something new, unconventional, and revolutionary.

After establishing his political authority in 1969–1970, Qaddafi subjected Libya's internal political structures to five stages of dynamic and sweeping reform reaching across a decade. Cognizant of his own inexperience and wary of provoking backlash, he initially took limited, cautious steps. As he gathered political stamina over the 1970s, by contrast, he demonstrated a growing determination to experiment with political reforms that would put into practice his evolving revolutionary ideology on an increasingly bold, if not outlandish, scale.

Qaddafi's first stage of reform in 1970–1973 was marked by caution and timidity. He tried to stoke nationalism and

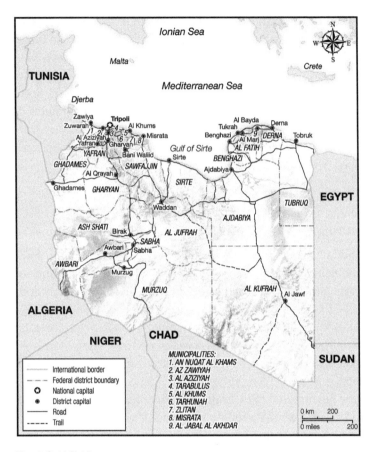

Map 4 Qaddafi's Libya

patriotism through mass rallies and other rituals, but he remained unsatisfied by the progress. He relied on the Arab Socialist Union (ASU)—the single authorized political party—to mobilize political activity in a controlled context and thereby generate mass support for state policies. Although a small number of middle-class technocrats joined it, however, the ASU neither overcame traditional tribal and regional loyalties nor inspired the masses to embrace it. To enable himself to engage in more visionary leadership and to become a more effective agent of change, Qaddafi entrusted the prime ministry and other domestic responsibilities to RCC colleagues while remaining the commander in chief of the armed services and the de facto authority in the country.

In a second wave of reform, known as the cultural or popular revolution of 1973, Qaddafi shifted his focus from mobilizing the people through top-down leadership to organizing them at the grassroots level. He called on the masses directly to elect "people's committees" that would assume administrative control of local governance by removing entrenched, inefficient bureaucrats who seemed to encumber government services. By mid-decade, more than 2,000 people's committees dominated city and town governance as well as universities, businesses, media outlets, and other local institutions. Qaddafi steered the people's committees to support such initiatives as replacing existing laws with a new legal code based on Islam, eliminating bureaucratic inertia and inefficiency, and purging political dissidents.

As the cultural revolution unfolded, Qaddafi articulated a sweeping ideological doctrine that explained his vision and goals. His so-called Third Universal Theory posited that a blend of Islam and Arab nationalism offered a compelling, superior alternative to both Western capitalism and Soviet communism as an organizing concept for Libya, for other Arab states, and, indeed, for the global order—as the universalization of Islam and a bastion of unified Arab power would prove superior to the competing US and Soviet systems. In *The Green Book*, a three-volume manifesto published in 1975–1981, Qaddafi expressed this ideological vision, identified political obstacles (which included elected parliaments and political parties), and suggested needed reforms. His overarching goal was to remove all corrupt and inefficient structures and enable the people to rule themselves via direct participation in the political process and state administrations.[11]

Publication of volume one of *The Green Book* initiated the third wave of political reform in 1976–1977. Seeking to consolidate populist rule, Qaddafi directed the people's committees to elect representatives to a new national body, the General People's Congress (GPC). In March 1977, he officially renamed Libya as the "Socialist People's Libyan Arab *Jamahiriya*." (Meaning "peopledom" or "state of the masses," according to one scholar, *Jamahiriya* connoted "a country directly governed by its citizens, without the intervention of intermediaries.") The GPC also named Qaddafi as its general secretary, affirming his ultimate authority; replaced the RCC with a new general secretariat of the GPC, empowering it to decide fundamental matters of state; and replaced the ministerial cabinet with a General People's Committee, authorizing it to run the government. Then the local people's committees were encouraged to form Basic People's Congresses to debate governance issues and submit recommendations for reform to the higher-level GPC. Infused with revolutionary ardor, Qaddafi essentially abolished the state in favor of a channeled, mass democracy while retaining ultimate authority for himself.[12]

In 1977, Qaddafi launched a fourth period of reform when he encouraged his most zealous supporters to form local "revolutionary committees" to ensure that political activities undertaken at the local level remained loyal to his revolutionary ideals. Although they were technically nongovernmental entities, the revolutionary committees within two years essentially controlled elections to the Basic People's Congresses. They also suppressed political dissent via methods including "revolutionary courts," targeted killings, and other inhumane forms of suppression.

In 1979, finally, Qaddafi directed the GPC to designate him as "Leader of the Revolution." He remained commander in chief of the armed forces but relinquished other official titles and positions. The national government was reorganized to encompass a new cabinet called the General People's Committee, in which all issues except oil production, foreign policy, and industry were entrusted to a specialized people's committee headed by a committee secretary. Qaddafi remained the country's ultimate authority and even styled himself as a messianic figure who would not only advance Libya but also reform Islam and serve as a beacon for oppressed peoples worldwide.

In practice, Qaddafi continuously launched experimental reforms that bordered on eccentric. He once required people to raise chickens as an instrument of self-sufficiency, arbitrarily banned a popular motor vehicle, nationalized savings accounts, and tried renaming months and adopting a new calendar. He denied gender equality but created symbols of female empowerment to mark the success of his revolution, like employing women, stylishly dressed and bearing machine guns, as his bodyguards. Qaddafi received official visitors in a tent—a tribute to his Bedouin roots—and he dressed ostentatiously, earning a worldwide reputation for sartorial flamboyance.

What economic reforms did Qaddafi implement?

As he reformed Libya's political order, Qaddafi implemented his vision of building socialism, in line with his original "freedom, socialism, and unity" principle. Within a month of taking power in 1969, Qaddafi defined "socialism" as "the participation of all in production . . ., the participation of each individual in producing what he consumes. Socialism is untiring collective work . . . leading us to the society of equality and justice." Socialism was "necessary to dissolve class distinctions, and to bring about the emancipation of the mass of this people from the grip of poverty." In part 2 of *The Green Book*, Qaddafi identified the lingering obstacles to pure socialism in Libya and the solutions to those problems. He revealed his ideological principles that wage labor was tantamount to slavery, that material wealth should be shared, and that private ownership beyond necessities involved exploitation of others.[13]

In the late 1970s, Qaddafi applied these principles in sweeping reforms of Libya's economy. He abolished wages

80 LIBYA AND THE WEST

in favor of collective ownership of the means of production by workers. He outlawed rent and expropriated residential rental property on the principle that a dwelling should belong to its inhabitants. People's committees assumed management of some 40,000 private shops and small companies—including most of the retail sector—and replaced them with 200 state-run mega-stores where everyone shopped from among a uniform if irregular inventory of consumer products. Private bank accounts were seized, and farms and landed estates were declared to be collectively owned. The government expropriated the endowments of Islamic societies and directed people's committees to assume control of mosques.

Aware that Libya's oilfields would someday run dry, Qaddafi channeled some of his considerable oil revenues into initiatives to diversify the country's economic infrastructure even while imposing his sweeping reforms. He sought to bolster Libya's anemic agricultural and industrial productivity, which each generated about 2 percent of gross domestic product, while reducing the dependence on oil, which accounted for 99 percent of state revenues.[14]

Under the "Three Year Economic and Social Development Plan" for 1973–1975 and "Five-Year Economic and Social Transformation Plan" for 1976–1980, Qaddafi allocated tens of billions of dollars to develop agricultural self-sufficiency and launch new industries that would outlive the oil age. He wanted to bolster the non-oil sectors of the economy so they would produce at least half of the national wealth, even while oil revenues remained robust. He set grandiose targets such as aiming to bring some 350,000 acres of land into cultivation over five years—more land than the Italian imperialists had developed over three decades. While Qaddafi invested lavishly in such schemes, they generally failed because of a shortage of technical experts and engineers, lingering bureaucratic inefficiencies, and such environmental factors as the aridity of the desert.

Was there domestic opposition to Qaddafi's rule?

The people of Libya remained generally passive toward if not modestly supportive of Qaddafi. He demonstrated charisma, stoked the people's national pride and anti-Western impulses, and spent lavishly to improve the standard of living. Flush with oil revenues, Qaddafi invested heavily in improvements to public health, social welfare, housing, and education, giving Libya one of the highest standards of living among African states. In 1969–1980, measures of life expectancy, infant mortality, and availability of healthcare improved, and per capita annual income soared by 500 percent, to $10,000.

To be sure, dissent against Qaddafi simmered and occasionally flared but proved largely ineffective. More than 100,000 technocrats, businessmen, investors, and property owners who were disadvantaged by the economic reforms fled for foreign destinations, draining Libya of their expertise but also their potential opposition. Some of them formed expatriate groups critical of Qaddafi's regime. Within the country, disgruntled citizens and nonconformists occasionally criticized the regime, while those Muslim clerics who initially approved the regime grumbled that Qaddafi's policies on direct democracy and restrictions on private property were un-Islamic. Students protested military conscription, censorship of free speech, and the imposition of people's committees in university administration. In 1975, Minister of Planning Omar Abdullah Meheishi and ASU chairman Bashir al-Hawadi, two of the RCC's original members who had tired of Qaddafi's foreign adventurism, plotted a coup but were discovered and forced to flee the country.

In sharp contrast to the peacefulness of his takeover in 1969, Qaddafi brutally suppressed these forms of dissent. He warned prominent expatriates to return home or face punishment. He ordered the arrests of dissidents and student protestors. Shortly after declaring the *Jamahiriyah* in March 1977, Qaddafi ordered the public hanging of several students who had been arrested for protesting at Al-Fateh University in Tripoli and forced other students to watch. He executed four Libyans and an Egyptian convicted of espionage as well as 22 officers implicated in the failed 1975 coup. In 1979 and 1980, Qaddafi crushed additional rebellions from within the armed forces—provoked by the resistance of the professional officer corps to the rising influence of people's militias—with heavy loss of life.

Qaddafi institutionalized the means of violent suppression in the late 1970s. He said of his revolution, "It is a moving train. Whoever stands in its way will be crushed." In 1979, he created the Revolutionary Committees Movement, which mobilized paramilitary groups across the country to intimidate dissidents, fix local elections to the People's Congress, control the media, and inform on anyone who engaged in suspicious activities. Revolutionary committees were created within the army and police to detect any anti-Qaddafi conspiracies. The revolutionary committees established an independent judicial system where accused dissidents were tried, convicted, and sentenced to prison or death, and pressures were placed on committee members to meet annual quotas for identifying suspects. Qaddafi appointed members of his family and tribe to key positions of oversight over these groups to ensure their loyalty. The rise of this apparatus of suppression had a chilling effect on dissent and rebelliousness across the country.[15]

What policy did Qaddafi pursue toward the Great Powers engaged in the Cold War?

Within months of taking power, Qaddafi defined a fervent and revolutionary vision of Libya's place in the world order that embraced the principles of anti-imperialism and neutralism in the Cold War. Qaddafi's devout anti-imperialism stemmed from his repudiation of the Italian colonial legacy, the strong Western influence over King Idris, Western and especially US support for Israel, and Anglo–French aggression against Egypt in 1956. "It is well known that the foreigner was the master in this country," Qaddafi declared on November 28, 1969. "This is one of the reasons for the revolution. . . . We will continue with the policy of clearing the country of foreigners." Inspired by Nasser, neutralism in the Cold War meant that Libya would engage with both superpowers but would refuse to support either side's ambitions in their global struggle.[16]

Qaddafi moved quickly to repudiate the military base rights the royalist government had given to Britain and the United States. "The Arab people of Libya . . . can no longer live with the foreign bases side by side," he declared publicly. "The fate of the bases in our land is already doomed for we accept no bases, no foreigner, no imperialist, and no intruders. . . . We will liberate our land from bases, the imperialist and foreign forces, whatever the cost." Britain evacuated its military bases in Libya in late March 1970.[17]

US officials briefly explored the possibility of striking a deal with the new regime to renew the base deal of 1953, but they soon realized that such a goal was unachievable. They also calculated that the acquisition of base rights in other countries and new missile technologies had reduced the strategic importance of Wheelus Field, which was used mostly for fighter pilot training. Thus, the US military conducted a phased withdrawal from Wheelus Field that honored the scheduled termination of the 1953 treaty in 1970, removing the last contingent of US soldiers on June 11. To celebrate the British and US withdrawals, Qaddafi declared March 31 and June 11, 1970, as national holidays and for years marked those dates with parades and fiery speeches.

Zealous in his anti-Westernism, Qaddafi sought support from the Soviet Union in confidence that it would not compromise his independence, neutralism, or anticommunism. The Libyan leader considered Egypt's split with the Soviet Union in the early 1970s not as a warning of the difficulties of relying on Soviet support, but as an opportunity to become a beneficiary of Soviet support to the advancement of Libyan interests.

84 LIBYA AND THE WEST

Shunning traditional arms suppliers in Britain, Qaddafi gradually purchased significant quantities of Soviet military equipment including tanks, other armored vehicles, and Scud missiles, enabling rapid growth in the size and strength of his army. Thousands of Soviet soldiers served in Libya as engineers and advisers, Libyan officers received advanced training in Moscow, and trade in industrial goods developed between the two states. In 1978, the Soviet Union announced that it would provide Libya a nuclear reactor and research center. Qaddafi also established diplomatic relations with such Soviet allies as Yugoslavia, East Germany, North Korea, and Cuba, all of which provided Libya military, law enforcement, and intelligence training.

The Libyan–Soviet partnership benefited both states. Libya gained international stature, access to military hardware and industrial goods, and a potential safeguard against bullying by Western powers. The Soviets earned considerable revenues in Western currencies as well as the opportunity to project influence in the Mediterranean theater. Yet distance remained in the relationship. Offended by the Soviets' atheism and suspicious of their intentions, Qaddafi neither sought nor affirmed Soviet declarations of support for his revolution, which he viewed as opportunistic and insincere. For their part, Soviet leaders remained somewhat reluctant to align fully with a leader they viewed as erratic and unreliable.

What policies did Western powers initially pursue toward Qaddafi's regime?

For a few years after Qaddafi took power, Western officials accommodated him in hope of achieving stable, friendly relations. As with most developing countries, they wanted to align Libya with the West and against the Soviet Union in the Cold War. They sought to secure their access to vital Libyan oil exports. Given Qaddafi's distance from the Soviet Union and professed anti-communism, they downplayed his expression of revolutionary ideals and his curtailment of Western interests and privileges in his country, calculating that accommodation of the young ruler was the best strategy.

Hoping to improve relations with Qaddafi, US officials delivered eight military transport airplanes that King Idris had purchased before the revolution. In 1972, after a delay of two years, they approved the delivery of F-5 fighter jets that also had been sold to the king. US officials initially interpreted audacious moves by Qaddafi to drive up oil prices as an unfortunate but tolerable cost of maintaining access to Libyan oil. While the nationalization of US commercial interests was slightly more distasteful, even those steps did not push US officials across a threshold into a more confrontational policy toward Libya before 1973.

Aiming to reduce its oil-driven trade deficit with Libya, France became a major arms supplier. In a deal signed in January 1970, France agreed to sell Libya 100 state-of-the-art Mirage military jets valued at some $400 million and to provide training for pilots and mechanics. To assuage security concerns among those who feared these jets might migrate into Egypt's or Syria's arsenal, France specified that the jets could not be transferred to another power nor used in any operation against France or its allies. Skeptics—including Israeli officials who chafed under an arms embargo imposed by France after the 1967 Arab–Israeli War—charged that such conditions would prove unenforceable and that the French action thus imperiled Israeli security. France delivered the jets by 1974, although the paltry training received by Libyan pilots and mechanics limited the value of this air power to symbolic status.

Despite intense anti-Italian sentiment among Qaddafi and his colleagues, Italy also pursued stable relations with Libya. Foreign Minister Moro reasoned that Italy could exert influence in the central Mediterranean and thereby contribute to the security of the Western world and that practicing an enlightened and effective foreign policy toward Libya would advance these objectives. As the international reputation of the United States became tarnished by the Vietnam War, moreover, Moro thought that maintaining some distance from Washington in policymaking would win Italy credibility among Arab powers that would redound to Italy's and the West's advantages. Moro also sought to advance more immediate objectives, especially access to Libyan oil, which comprised about one-third of Italy's oil consumption in 1970. Moro ventured to Tripoli in May 1971, to strike a deal with Qaddafi under which Italy provided Libya technical expertise on oil production and Libya provided the Italian energy firm Ente Nazionale Idrocarburi (ENI) favorable operating terms and conditions not granted to other Western powers.[18]

Moro remained committed to improving his relationship with Libya even when it was sorely tested, in 1970, by Qaddafi's expulsion of Libya's Italian community. Upon coming to power, Qaddafi deeply suspected that Italy bore responsibility for the political and economic dislocations besetting Libya, that the 1956 Italian–Libyan economic aid deal had inadequately compensated Libya for these losses, and that the 20,000 Italians residing in his country continued to enjoy privileges at the expense of his people. That the Italians resided in separate neighborhoods and attended segregated schools and churches fed this perception. In July 1970, the RCC passed two laws that unilaterally repealed the 1956 treaty, ordered Italian citizens to depart from Libya by October 7, and expropriated their property. The laws decreed similar provisions for Libya's 37,000 Jews, many of whom were Italians but some of whom were members of an indigenous Jewish community with roots dating back over two millennia.

Moro considered the RCC decrees unfortunate and inappropriate but nonetheless accepted them. He rejected calls from Italian hawks that Rome should use military force or economic sanctions to force Qaddafi to honor the 1956 treaty, arguing that military means would be "absurd and inconceivable." In a meeting with Libyan Foreign Minister Saalih Buwaysir on

July 31, Moro agreed to extract the Italian nationals and not let the incident disrupt the binational relationship, given the mutual gains from trade between the two powers. Driven by insecurity, the Italian and Jewish communities of Libya promptly complied with the Libyan laws, even exhuming their dead for repatriation. October 7 became another Libyan national holiday with a pronounced anti-Western theme: the Day of Revenge.

So determined were the Western powers to accommodate Qaddafi that they collaborated to defend Qaddafi against counterrevolutionary movements originating within their countries. In 1970–1971, US, British, and Italian intelligence officers tracked a plot among Libyan royalist exiles to infiltrate mercenaries and weapons to Libya by ship and spark an uprising against the RCC. In March 1971, Italian authorities boarded *Conquistador XIII*, a ship laden with weapons and fighters, in Trieste Harbor and arrested the crew after determining that they intended to sail to Libya and provoke an uprising. In addition to this operation, Italian authorities routinely shared with Qaddafi intelligence about potential insurrectionary activity against him.[19]

How did Qaddafi manage Libya's oil industry and the Western firms that dominated it?

Qaddafi aimed to maximize his country's oil resources to fund his revolutionary domestic agenda and gain regional and international influence. Ideally, he sought to rid his country of Western influence, especially the corporations that ran the oil extraction business, although he realized that his citizenry lacked the technical skills and expertise needed to manage the operations. Thus, he moved slowly and deliberately first to increase the revenue stream and then to impose control over the foreign firms. Western governments did not effectively resist this process because Qaddafi implemented it incrementally, careful to avoid any bold step that would provoke a strong,

88 LIBYA AND THE WEST

unified reaction. Although tensions developed between Libya and Western corporations and states, the oil continued to flow given that the West remained dependent on it and Libya remained eager to earn the Western currencies needed to finance arms purchases, consumer imports, and Qaddafi's reform agenda.

When it took power, the RCC signaled that it would not disrupt the oil concessions that King Idris had granted, consistent with the RCC's strategy of professing moderation in order to avert Western counterrevolutionary reaction. "There will be no spectacular changes in Libya's oil policy," Prime Minister Maghrabi stated publicly in late 1969. "Oil companies are welcome as long as they respect the interests of the Libyan people."[20]

Yet Maghrabi also signaled that the RCC was unhappy with the price controls imposed by the oligopoly of the seven dominant Western oil firms. Those firms set production quotas and commodity prices on their operations spanning the Middle East, which benefited their corporate interests and averted inflation in Western economies but also limited the royalties paid to local states. In 1970, Qaddafi emerged as a strident critic of this system, accurately claiming that Libyan oil exports were sold in Europe well below market value. With massive economic power derived from a diverse range of activities, the major corporations resisted Libyan demands that they increase the prices they charged Western consumers for Libyan oil. But Libyan officials did not relent, with Oil Minister Izz al-Din al-Mabruk noting that "we see no sense at all in political independence if it is not accompanied by economic liberation."[21]

In late 1970, Qaddafi decided that he could break the oligopoly by concentrating pressure on the so-called independents, the smaller venture firms that abided in the oligopoly's price and production controls even though they were not a part of the cartel. He singled out Occidental Petroleum, a relatively small US firm that derived 97 percent of its earnings from Libyan oil—and thus was vulnerable to Libyan threats of nationalization. In the so-called One September Agreement (timed to mark the first anniversary of the 1969 revolution), Occidental accepted Qaddafi's demands that it must limit production and sharply raise sale prices. Once Occidental conceded, other independents and then even the seven major firms were forced to follow suit.

Libya's success proved to be the start of a region-wide rebalancing of economic and political power across the Middle East. Encouraged by Qaddafi's audacity, Iraq, Iran, and the states of the Arabian Peninsula—even though some of these countries had pro-Western orientations—demanded similar concessions from their Western corporate partners. In the Tehran Agreement of February 1971, several major firms granted those states the terms that Libya had gained. Suddenly, the Organization of Petroleum Exporting Countries (OPEC) that had been founded in 1960 (and which Libya had joined in 1962) became influential. Collectively, these developments amounted to a momentous shift in economic power from the Western corporations to the oil-producing states. Qaddafi's leadership in that transition earned him immense, although impermanent, stature among the members of OPEC.[22]

Concluding from this episode that blustering and threats would compel Western powers to make concessions, Qaddafi pressed for more. On December 7, 1971, Libya suddenly nationalized the local assets of British Petroleum (BP), including its 50 percent share in the massive Sarir oilfield, and withdrew BP's massive cash balances from London banks. In 1972–1973, he nationalized 50 percent of the holdings of Azienda Generale Italiana Petroli (General Italian Oil Company or AGIP), a major Italian firm, and varying shares of a dozen other corporations. Several US firms were singled out for expropriation in 1973, in retaliation for US support of Israel. By the end of that year, Libya had seized all shares of all Western companies engaged in the country—some 70 percent of his country's oil structure—allowing continued Western

90 LIBYA AND THE WEST

ownership only in those cases where operations remained dependent on Western technical expertise.

Qaddafi played a major role in organizing the oil embargo that Arab members of OPEC imposed in the aftermath of the Arab–Israeli War of 1973. He intended "to deprive Europe completely of oil," he declared. "We shall ruin your industries as well as your trade with the Arab world . . . we are determined to hit America, if necessary by striking Europe." The embargo sent shockwaves through Western economies and indicated clearly that the oil-producing states, and not Western corporations, controlled the Middle East's oil enterprises.[23]

The revolution in oil production corporate configurations generated enormous profits for the Libyan government. As the per-barrel price of Middle East oil soared from $2 to $11 in 1972–1974, Libya's oil revenue quadrupled from $1.5 billion to $6 billion even though production fell to about one-half of late-1960s levels.[24]

As lucrative as it was, the oil revolution eventually generated new problems for the Libyan state. Encouraged by his success, Qaddafi tended to become even more confrontational with Western and other foreign states on issues on which they were unwilling to concede, thereby causing tensions. The abolition of Western corporate controls left the oil industry much more vulnerable to market volatility, resulting in uneven and irregular production and profit streams. The global economic recession of the late 1970s limited the overall demand for energy and further strained the Libyan economy. By 1978–1979, Libyan oil production finally leveled off at about 2 million barrels per day—about one-third less than production levels of the late 1960s.

What was Qaddafi's policy toward pan-Arab unification?

Consistent with his adulation of Gamal Abdel Nasser of Egypt, Qaddafi ardently promoted pan-Arab unity, implemented practical steps for achieving it, and rejected the notion among many Arab leaders that the vision was unachievable. Despite sustained effort, however, his vision remained unrealized, and he eventually quarreled with other Arab statesmen. In short, Qaddafi's embrace of Nasserism was belated, as Nasser had fallen out of fashion among Arab leaders by the time Qaddafi took power. "The 'Mantle of Nasser' he inherited," one scholar noted, "was decidedly tattered."[25]

Qaddafi had been mesmerized by a vision of Arab unity since his youth. At age 19, he had been arrested for participating in a rally protesting the dissolution of the United Arab Republic (UAR), the merger of Egypt and Syria that lasted from 1958 to 1961. Upon taking power in 1969, Qaddafi elevated pan-Arabism in his political rhetoric. "Arab unity is an inevitable necessity, a vital necessity," he declared on September 16. "Unity is necessary to protect the Arab people from enemies. . . . Unity is necessary to protect freedom and socialism. . . . Unity is the decisive historical reaction to the challenges of Zionism and colonialism."[26]

Given that he was enamored with Nasser, Qaddafi immediately pursued a political union with Egypt. He and Nasser discussed a unification scheme that would bolster their personal reputations and revive pan-Arab power by merging Egypt's political prestige and large population with Libya's oil wealth. They also consulted with Sudanese Prime Minister Jaafar al-Nimeiri, another admirer of Nasser who took power in a coup in 1969, and who had the potential to add land and natural resources to the new union. These negotiations ended abruptly, however, when Nasser died unexpectedly in September 1970.

Although Nasser's death, in retrospect, marked the end of any realistic chance of success, Qaddafi continued to pursue pan-Arab unification schemes on several fronts for many years. Hoping to seize Nasser's leading role, he opened negotiations with Nasser's successor Anwar al-Sadat as well as with Syrian Premier Hafez al-Assad, both of whom came to power in 1970. In 1971, the three leaders agreed to establish the Federation of

Arab Republics (FAR) on January 1, 1972, with the intention of unifying their legal systems, military forces, and foreign policies. When follow-up meetings failed to achieve unification goals beyond symbolic statements, Qaddafi pressed Sadat to form a binational union based on the model of the UAR. In 1972–1973, Sadat and Qaddafi negotiated various unification schemes but failed to reach any meaningful agreements.

Qaddafi's efforts to unify with Egypt soon stalled. Sadat realized that the Egyptian people were more secular and diverse than the Libyan people. He also mistrusted Qaddafi, who ruled Libya with a more authoritarian hand than Sadat believed he himself exercised in Egypt. Qaddafi favored immediate unification whereas Sadat preferred a more incremental and deliberative process. The two states were also mismatched; Egypt's population of 34 million dwarfed Libya's 2 million, although Libya's economic status exceeded that of oil-poor Egypt. Among the peoples of both countries, patriotic loyalty to the nation-state outweighed pan-Arab idealism.

Once unification stalled, Libyan–Egyptian relations deteriorated sharply over several issues. Qaddafi disliked Sadat's decision to expel Soviet military advisers in 1972 and thereafter reorient his country toward the United States. Sadat did not consult Qaddafi before he and Assad coordinated the combined Egyptian–Syrian attack on Israel that started the Arab–Israeli War of 1973. Affronted, Qaddafi sharply criticized Egypt's and Syria's wartime policies, including their original objectives and their eventual willingness to sign an armistice that preserved Israel. Alarmed by reports that Qaddafi had contemplated a state-sanctioned act of terrorism against a British cruise ship on the Mediterranean, Sadat accused Libya of subversive activities against his government in Cairo. The Egyptian leader concluded that Qaddafi was "100 percent mad."[27]

In succeeding years, Qaddafi remained a vocal detractor of Sadat's policy of moderation toward Israel, which US officials nurtured into a peace process that culminated in the Camp David Accords of 1978 and the Egypt–Israel peace treaty of 1979. The rising tensions between Egypt and Libya even sparked a brief round of hostilities along their border in 1977. Thousands of Egyptian workers departed from Libya as a result, which disrupted Libya's oil industry and other enterprises. Together with Syria, South Yemen, Algeria, and the Palestine Liberation Organization (PLO), Libya formed the Steadfastness and Confrontation Front in December 1977, which bitterly criticized Egypt's decision to make peace with Israel. By 1979, Qaddafi and his collaborators persuaded most Arab states to break diplomatic relations with and impose economic sanctions on Egypt. Qaddafi openly celebrated the 1981 assassination of Sadat, denouncing him as a traitor to the Arab cause.

As his relationship with Egypt deteriorated, Qaddafi proposed unification schemes to Algeria, Tunisia, Syria, and Morocco, but success eluded him. Tunisian President Habib Bourguiba not only rejected Qaddafi's overtures but also quarreled with him over ownership of oil deposits, and Bourguiba suspended diplomatic relations after accusing Qaddafi of provoking revolts within Tunisia. In 1980, Qaddafi persuaded Assad to resume unification talks in exchange for massive Libyan financial assistance, but Libya and Syria became isolated during the Iran–Iraq War that started in September 1980, when they alone among Arab states backed Iran. Qaddafi also became the target of angry and enduring criticism by Lebanese Shiites after one of their religious leaders, Imam Musa Sadr, disappeared while visiting Libya in 1978.

Nor did Qaddafi sustain his cooperative relationship with PLO chief Yasser Arafat. After the two leaders quarreled over their competing strategies to resist Israel, Qaddafi began to support radicals and extremists within the Palestinian cause, alienating Arafat. The bottom fell out of the relationship when Arafat agreed to withdraw from Lebanon in summer 1982, a move that Qaddafi criticized relentlessly as a sellout to Israel.[28]

94 LIBYA AND THE WEST

Qaddafi's dream of leading the unification of the Arab world clearly failed to materialize. His initiatives to establish pan-Arab political structures foundered on the shoals of policy disagreements, political rivalries, and backlash against Qaddafi's assertive style and subversive methods. His efforts to rally all Arab states behind his leadership and in opposition to Israel and Western power failed to prevent several Arab states from aligning with the United States, resulting in a divided community of Arab states.

What was Qaddafi's policy toward Israel?

From his earliest days in power, Qaddafi spoke fervently about armed resistance to Israel. He considered Israel to be an intolerable manifestation of Zionism, a subtle and pernicious form of European imperialism. He called on all Arab peoples to "solve the cause of Palestine with arms, men, and economy, and not by broadcasts, the press, conferences, aids, or charities." Libya's armed forces, he declared in October 1969, "will not take their fingers off the trigger until the stolen territory [Palestine] is recovered."[29]

Through the 1970s, Qaddafi emerged as the most outspoken Arab statesman on the justice of armed struggle against Israel. His frustration with US backing of Israel stoked his anti-US passions. As discussed above, Qaddafi hoped to achieve Arab unity by rallying other Arab states in vehement resistance to Israel, and Egypt's growing acceptance of Israel during the 1970s alienated Qaddafi and undermined Libyan–Egyptian amity. As discussed below, Qaddafi took the initiative to convince such African states as Chad and Uganda to sever diplomatic relations with Israel.

To minimize international backlash against his policy, Qaddafi specified in his public statements that he deplored terrorism as distinct from revolutionary struggle and that he found fault not with the Jewish people but only with the ideology of Zionism. But his behavior demonstrated a penchant for supporting violent means to challenge Israel. He began supplying the Black September extremist group, perhaps as early as 1972–1973, when it conducted the massacre of Israeli athletes at the Munich Olympic Games and the kidnapping of the Israeli ambassador to Thailand. Apparently with the support of Libya, Black September murdered two US diplomats, Ambassador Cleo Noel and Chargé d'Affaires George C. Moore, as well as Belgian Chargé d'Affaires Guy Eid in Khartoum, Sudan, in March 1973, announcing that it was punishing the United States and Belgium for their support of Israel. By the mid-1970s, Qaddafi was widely believed to be arming and training various Palestinian militias for armed struggle against Israel in theaters around the world.

Why did Libya engage in international terrorism to achieve its foreign policy objectives?

From the start of his rule, Qaddafi embraced violence by non-state actors as a legitimate means to globalize his revolution. He pursued the twin visions of establishing a radical Islamic union under his own control and battling Western imperialism around the world. His substantial oil revenues provided the financial resources needed to pursue such goals. By signing an $800 million arms deal with the Soviet Union in 1975, Qaddafi acquired weaponry that he distributed to militants and terrorists around the world. Unable to contest regional rivals or global superpowers by conventional military means, Qaddafi instigated unconventional acts of violence in pursuit of his objectives.

Qaddafi projected his principled opposition to Western colonialism in Libya into his policies toward other states in the Middle East and beyond. He envisioned leading oppressed peoples everywhere to liberation from inequality, poverty, corrupt capitalist systems, and other vestiges and manifestations of Western culture and empire. He sought to consolidate his domestic power, gain international stature, and achieve expansive revolutionary goals by developing a global counterimperialism strategy that began with a focus on the liberation of Palestine from Israeli control and broadened into a campaign to support radical movements everywhere. Unconventional forms of violence seemed to him the most effective means to these ends.

Beginning in the 1970s, Libya was widely suspected of organizing or supporting terrorism and political subversion across the Middle East. Even as he joined the pan-Arab struggle against Israel and financed Palestinian activities against the Jewish state, Qaddafi aimed to undermine the governments of such Arab neighbors as Egypt, Jordan, Lebanon, Sudan, Tunisia, and Morocco. It was widely believed that Qaddafi bolstered such leading transnational terrorists as Carlos the Jackal and Abu Nidal, and that the Libyan leader played a key role in the mass murder of Israeli athletes at the 1972 Olympic Games in Munich.

Qaddafi extended material and political support to anticolonial and militant movements around the world. His beneficiaries included antimonarchical rebels in Morocco, Muslim Moro resistance militias in the Philippines, the militant Red Army in Japan, and revolutionary movements in more than a dozen states in Africa and Asia. Omar Abdullah Mehishi, the minister of planning who rebelled against Qaddafi in 1975, later reported that Qaddafi had allocated $580 million to terrorist activities in 1976. In the late 1970s, Western intelligence officials estimated that Qaddafi organized camps in which Soviet, Cuban, Syrian, and East German personnel offered paramilitary training to some 10,000–20,000 fighters from a variety of countries. Qaddafi supported "any cause which . . . would weaken traditional Arab kingdoms or would be directed at Britain or the United States," Under Secretary of State David D. Newsom testified to the Senate Judiciary Committee in August 1980. "What we call terrorism, they call revolution."[30]

Qaddafi increasingly became a thorn in the side of Western powers during the 1970s because he emerged as a leading advocate of violent revolution against what he considered the Western imperial structure that oppressed peoples worldwide. He endorsed the revolutionary struggles of the Black Panther Party and the Nation of Islam in the United States. He was believed to support materially such revolutionary groups as the Irish Republican Army (IRA), the Red Brigades in Italy, and the Baader-Meinhof Gang in West Germany. "These [IRA] bombs which are convulsing Britain and breaking its spirit are the bombs of the Libyan people," Qaddafi said in 1976. "We have sent them to Irish revolutionaries so that the British will pay the price for their past deeds." Qaddafi was believed to have played a role in the December 1973 attack at the Rome airport that left 32 people dead and to have supplied the Red Brigade terrorists who bombed the Bologna train station in 1980, killing 84 persons.[31]

What policies did Qaddafi pursue in Africa?

Shunned increasingly by Arab statesmen, Qaddafi tried to extend his political and ideological influence into non-Arab African states. He was motivated by a vision of building a pan-Islamic entity and contesting the legacy of Western imperialism in Africa. "We are Africans," Qaddafi declared. "We are part of Africa. Africa is our continent." Qaddafi's oil wealth enabled him to intervene in other states by sending troops, supplying arms and other forms of aid, and otherwise exerting political influence. His many detractors charged that Qaddafi was merely substituting militant Libyan imperialism for the former European variety. Citing a legacy of centuries of North African trafficking in black slaves, most sub-Saharan leaders remained profoundly suspicious of Qaddafi's intentions.[32]

Qaddafi targeted Chad, his neighbor to the south, for expansionism through diplomatic and military means. He initially set his sights on the Aouzou Strip, a sliver of 42,000 square miles of desert that stretched from east to west along the Libya–Chad border. Punctuated by a few oases and inhabited by a small population of nomads belonging to the Tebu tribe, the strip rose in strategic and material value after reported discoveries of uranium and speculation about petroleum resources in the area.

Sovereignty over the strip had been contested since European colonialism had brought the Western concept of precise, legal borders to African colonies. During the imperialist heyday, France and Italy both coveted the land, although resistance by the Senussi and tribal fighters had prevented either power from controlling it. In 1935, French officials signed a treaty recognizing Italian control—although the treaty was never ratified by the French parliament. In 1940, Italian forces moved against French military units in northern Chad until the capitulation of France to Germany and the rise of the Vichy France regime officially added Chad to the Axis domain. As Axis power declined in North Africa in 1942–1943, however, Free French forces formed up in Chad, occupied the Aouzou Strip, and encroached into the Fezzan. As it gained independence, Libya argued that the 1935 treaty, though unratified, should be honored, but French military forces remained in the region, denying access to Libyan soldiers as well as to US oil prospectors. In 1955, France prevailed on King Idris to sign a treaty recognizing that the Aouzou Strip belonged to French Chad.

Chad inherited this concession when it became independent in 1960, but it proved unable to control the territory. As French troops gradually withdrew from northern Chad in 1960–1965, instability grew in the Aouzou Strip. Tensions between the northern tribes—independent-minded and Muslim in their cultural orientation—and the southern Chadians who dominated the government in N'Djamena sparked violence in 1963 and outright insurrection in 1966.

Upon taking power in 1969, Qaddafi eyed the Aouzou Strip as a target of opportunity. He viewed King Idris's 1955 concession of the territory to France as a regrettable capitulation to European imperialism by a feckless king. By forging tribal and religious connections in the borderlands of northern Chad and southern Libya, Qaddafi hoped to build a foundation for projecting power into central Africa. In 1973, therefore, he ordered Libyan troops to occupy the strip, and he formally annexed it in 1976. Chad relented, recognizing Libyan control and allowing Libya to build an airbase there in exchange for financial subsidies. French troops helped suppress the Chadian rebellion south of the Aouzou Strip.

Chad thereafter descended into a vicious civil war in which foreign powers became involved. Initially, Qaddafi channeled material support to antigovernment rebels led by Goukouni Oueddei of the Tebu tribe. In 1978, he committed airpower, tanks, and artillery to support Goukouni's fighters. By the late 1970s, some 10,000 Libyan soldiers intervened on behalf of the rebel forces and briefly imposed Libyan revolutionary principles on the areas they occupied. France sent military advisors to bolster the government of Chad and, in 1978, sent airpower and 2,500 soldiers to defeat a rebel advance on the capital. Aided by a fracture within the Chadian government, however, the rebel forces under Goukouni persisted, occupying N'Djamena (while France remained neutral) and winning control of the country in 1980.

Qaddafi struggled, however, to maintain the upper hand. Qaddafi and Goukouni negotiated a political union that promised to advance Qaddafi's ambitions, but intense opposition to the idea from neighboring states, France, and even Goukouni's own forces scotched the plan. Qaddafi also calculated that continued occupation would risk embroiling him in debilitating warfare against factions backed by the United States. He further hoped to host the Organization of African Unity meeting in 1982 and realized that his intervention had lessened the prospects of that by alienating other leaders. By the end of 1981, Libyan soldiers withdrew from central Chad to the Aouzou Strip, as opposition forces under Hissène Habré liberated the

100 LIBYA AND THE WEST

capital from rebel control. By the time he withdrew, Qaddafi's machinations there had earned the scorn of Egypt, Sudan, Tunisia, Gabon, Niger, Nigeria, Mali, and Senegal, several of which severed diplomatic relations with Libya.[33]

Qaddafi also quarreled seriously with Sudanese Prime Minister al-Nimeiri. After he survived a coup attempt by communists in 1971, Nimeiri distanced himself from the Soviet Union and gravitated toward the United States. Irritated, Qaddafi funneled aid and weapons to rebel groups inside Sudan, even training a force that raided Khartoum to overthrow Nimeiri in 1976. Narrowly surviving, Nimeiri executed about 100 captured rebels and then immediately joined a mutual defense pact with Egypt, further aggravating Libya. The Sudanese leader censured Libya's armed intervention in Chad, voicing the fear that Qaddafi might also have sights on Sudanese borderlands, and, in 1981 he tried to rally Arab leaders to expel Libya from the Arab League if not to overthrow the Libyan leader. After a bomb blast targeted the Chadian embassy in Khartoum, Nimeiri accused Libya of plotting the attack and expelled Libyan diplomats from his country. Qaddafi had "a split personality," Nimeiri observed, "both of them evil."[34]

Qaddafi was able to befriend Uganda's notorious dictator Idi Amin. Taking power in 1971, Amin tormented and murdered tens of thousands of his own people and became a pariah among most leaders of African countries. After Amin broke Uganda's diplomatic relations with Israel and publicly lauded Adolf Hitler for having tried to exterminate the Jewish people, Qaddafi rewarded him with financial aid, thus earning a share of the international opprobrium that mounted against Amin as the decade passed. In 1979, when Amin invaded Tanzania, Qaddafi dispatched troops to Uganda to help defend against a Tanzanian counteroffensive. Qaddafi withdrew his forces only when Tanzanian and Ugandan exile forces closed in on Kampala, Uganda's capital. After Amin was ousted from power, Qaddafi provided him asylum.[35]

How did French–Libyan relations evolve in the 1970s and 1980s?

Despite the tensions generated by the indirect clash in Chad, France and Libya maintained a modicum of stability in their relationship. Leaders in Paris moderated their military operations against Libya in Chad. They realized that unbridled warfare would exceed the tolerance of French public opinion, tarnish France's image among Arab peoples, and place France at risk of descending into a quagmire in Chad and of provoking Libyan terrorist strikes against French assets worldwide. Through the 1970s and early 1980s, France continued to supply weapons to Libya and remained dependent on free-flowing Libyan oil.

For its part, Libya also wanted to maintain cooperation. Qaddafi opportunistically calibrated his activities in Chad, intervening only when it appeared he could make gains at little cost, and backing down when it became clear that France would resist. He sought symbolic declarations of "unity" with the Arab peoples of northern Chad more than an actual political unification with the country. While it was feasible to make trouble in Chad for his rivals, Qaddafi seemed to reason, accepting responsibility to govern Chad would incur too many costs.[36]

How did Italian–Libyan relations evolve in the 1970s?

Heavily dependent on Libyan oil, Italy eagerly developed a close relationship with Qaddafi despite his increasingly erratic and dangerous international initiatives. On May 5, 1971, Foreign Minister Moro visited Qaddafi in Tripoli and proposed that they turn "a new page in Italo-Libyan relations." By mid-decade, the two powers negotiated a stable relationship based on mutual advantages. Italy won Libyan favor by providing access to arms, technology, and technical advice. Italian weapons, including artillery and ammunition, flowed to Libya

102 LIBYA AND THE WEST

as early as 1971. To reciprocate, Qaddafi treated AGIP gently during his oil expropriation and price hike initiatives.[37]

Meeting in Rome in February 1974, Libyan and Italian authorities signed a "framework agreement" that provided extensive economic, political, and military cooperation. Libya raised its annual target for oil sales to Italy from 23 million tons to 30 million tons. Italy pledged to sell factories and machine tools, cargo and tanker ships, and consumer goods. The two powers agreed to form joint investment partnerships, setting the stage for Libya's purchase, in 1976, of a 10 percent share of Fiat, a move that injected $415 million of much-needed cash into the troubled Italian automaker. Italy increased the arms available for Libyan purchase and agreed to consider selling advanced weapons, including missiles and submarines.

The two powers also suppressed their lingering debate on historical legacies. Libya gradually stopped pushing for reparations for the deprivations suffered under Italian colonialism. Italy dropped its claims for compensation of those Italians who were forced to abandon their property and evacuate Libya in 1970.

How did US–Libyan relations evolve in the 1970s?

Regarding oil, the United States and Libya remained engaged in symbiotic relations through the 1970s. US consumers demanded oil and preferred Libya's because of its low sulfur content, while Libya welcomed the profits from sales. US imports of Libyan oil soared from $216 million in 1973 to $2.2 billion in 1976. By 1980, Libya provided the United States about 700,000 barrels per day—about 11 percent of total US imports and 40 percent of Libyan exports—making Libya the third-largest US supplier (after Saudi Arabia and Nigeria) and making the United States the greatest Libyan market. Despite a series of quarrels across the 1970s between the Libyan government and US oil firms over contract rights and royalties, more than 50 US firms with some 2,500 staff operated in Libya in 1980.[38]

Although the oil exports flowed, overall US–Libyan relations crossed a threshold from accommodation to conflict during the 1970s. Considerable tension emerged from Qaddafi's opposition to US policy on the Arab–Israeli conflict. Angry about US support for Israel and Jordan, the Libyan government refused, in 1972, to deal with US Ambassador Joseph Palmer, prompting the State Department to recall him from Tripoli and conduct relations thereafter at the level of chargé d'affaires. Qaddafi retaliated against the US arms supply of Israel during the Arab–Israeli War of 1973 by strongly promoting the Arab oil embargo of 1973–1974. Qaddafi focused strident criticism on Egyptian President Anwar al-Sadat in the mid-1970s because he aligned his foreign policy with US objectives in the Middle East. The Carter administration supported Egypt during its July 1977 border clash with Libya, providing $200 million in military aid. Qaddafi expressed bitter anger about the US-brokered Camp David Accords of 1978, which set the stage for the Egyptian–Israeli peace treaty of the following year, because it enhanced the legitimacy of Israel.

US officials became increasingly concerned, moreover, with Libya's deepening ties to the Soviet Union. In 1974–1975, Qaddafi purchased advanced Soviet weapons, secured a pledge from Moscow to construct a 10-megawatt nuclear reactor and research center in Libya, and received Soviet Premier Alexei Kosygin in Tripoli. Some 10,000 Soviet troops arrived in Libya to train Libyan soldiers. In response, the United States curtailed weapons supply to Libya and canceled training programs for Libyan military officers in 1975. Two years later, Qaddafi paid an official visit to Moscow. In reaction to the Camp David Accords, Qaddafi threatened to join the Warsaw Pact. US officials became concerned that Libya would become a channel for Soviet influence to permeate the Mediterranean and North Africa.

Qaddafi's role in fomenting international terrorism also became a point of contention. US officials deplored Qaddafi for giving sanctuary to the perpetrators of the terrorist attack

104 LIBYA AND THE WEST

on Israeli athletes at the 1972 Olympic Games in Munich. They noted with deep concern evidence that Libyan agents had planned terrorist attacks against the Republican and Democratic conventions of 1976 and had plotted to assassinate US Ambassador to Cairo Herman Eilts because he had promoted Egyptian–US rapprochement and Egyptian–Israeli peace.

US–Libyan relations degraded rapidly in the late 1970s. In 1977, the Pentagon listed Libya as the fourth most likely country (after the Soviet Union, China, and North Korea) to become a hostile military adversary. In 1978, Carter banned the sale of all military equipment to Libya, although he authorized the sale of five Boeing 727 civilian jetliners and some 400 heavy trucks—both to incentivize Libya to affirm an international accord against hijacking as well as to balance trade. Carter canceled those sales in 1979, however, after Libya used previously purchased, US-made civilian airliners to ferry troops to a battle zone in Uganda.

How did Qaddafi reach out directly to the American people?

In a transnational application of the "people power" ideology he had pursued at home, Qaddafi attempted in the late 1970s to improve his interests in the United States by appealing directly to the American people to influence the policy of the government in Washington. He concentrated first on the citizens of Georgia and Idaho, the home states of President Carter and Senate Foreign Relations Committee Chairman Frank Church. In 1978–1979, delegations of businessmen, farmers, and other citizens of these two US states and Libya exchanged visits and engaged in conversations about common interests. "I think it is legitimate to establish genuine relations," Qaddafi told a reporter, "and we have every intention to forge them with the American people."[39]

This initiative neither became prominent nor influenced official relations between the two countries, but it did trigger an oddball affair involving Billy Carter, the eccentric younger brother of the president, that attracted widespread attention and smudged President Carter's reputation on the eve of the 1980 presidential election. Billy Carter visited Libya in 1978 and returned there in 1979 to attend celebrations marking the tenth anniversary of the Libyan Revolution. Published photographs of Billy standing next to Yasser Arafat caused considerable consternation to President Carter, which increased when the media reported in 1980 that Billy had received $220,000 from the Qaddafi regime. Billy claimed that the payment was part of a loan made in a complex business deal, although he registered quickly as an agent of the Libyan government to minimize the likelihood of a criminal prosecution for accepting the payment.

Why did US and French relations with Libya reach a crisis in 1980?

Libyan diplomatic relations with the United States and France verged toward crisis in 1980. Inspired by Iran's seizure of US diplomats as hostages in November 1979, a mob attacked and partially burned the US Embassy in Tripoli on December 2. Tensions soared the following month, when Libya backed an armed insurgency in Tunisia against President Bourguiba, with whom Qaddafi had quarreled since 1974 over oil rights along their mutual border and other policy matters. The United States airlifted armored vehicles and helicopters to Tunisia while France sent additional supplies and positioned three naval vessels in the Gulf of Gabes along the Libyan–Tunisian border. Qaddafi then instigated a mob to attack and burn the French Embassy in Tripoli and the French Consulate in Benghazi on February 4. France closed its embassy as well as the Libyan equivalent in Paris. Concerned for the safety of its diplomats, the United States closed its embassy in Tripoli on March 2, although diplomatic relations were not broken and the Libyan embassy (what Qaddafi called the "Libyan People's Bureau") in Washington remained open.

106 LIBYA AND THE WEST

Amid mounting evidence of Qaddafi's involvement in terrorism, the Carter administration labeled Libya a state sponsor of terrorism on December 22, 1979, but that action did little to curtail Qaddafi's misdeeds. In 1980, exiled Libyan dissidents were murdered, presumably by agents of Qaddafi, in Britain, Malta, Greece, and Italy. Carter expelled several diplomats from the Libyan People's Bureau in Washington after charging that they were "would-be assassins" pursuing dissidents in the United States.[40]

Tension also resulted from an escalating confrontation between US and Libyan naval and military forces in the disputed Gulf of Sidra along Libya's north coast. Under the 1958 Geneva Convention on the Territorial Sea and Contiguous Zone, a nation could declare territorial rights over seawater up to 12 miles from its coastlines, meaning that it could deny entrance to a gulf with an outlet to the sea of 24 miles or less. Because its opening from the Mediterranean was some 275 miles wide, the Gulf of Sidra was international waters, except within 12 miles of Libya's coastline. In 1973, however, in defiance of this law, Qaddafi defined 32 degrees 30 minutes north latitude, which stretched across the mouth of gulf, as a "line of death" to be broached by foreign powers at their peril.

US–Libyan conflict over this boundary issue developed in the early 1970s. As Soviet arms supply to Libya increased, the US Navy and Air Force tracked deliveries by conducting aerial overflights over the gulf. On March 21, 1973, the Libyan Arab Air Force (LAAF) fired (without effect) on an unarmed US Air Force RC-130 aerial reconnaissance plane flying 80 miles from Libya's coast. US tracking operations continued through the 1970s, despite Qaddafi's threats of military resistance. In 1980, the LAAF began making threatening gestures, such as "buzzing" US aircraft at close range and locking on radar (a preliminary step to firing antiaircraft missiles). Carter suspended the US patrols in the Gulf, out of fear that an escalation to military hostilities would complicate his efforts to resolve the Iran Hostage Crisis, undermine his Arab–Israeli peacemaking initiative, and disrupt his campaign for reelection to the White House.

The Gulf of Sidra conflict, however, festered. On October 22, 1980, the eve of the US presidential election, Qaddafi published a letter to President Carter and his Republican challenger Ronald Reagan in a paid advertisement in the *Washington Post*. He warned the United States to "keep its naval and air forces away from the Libyan Arab borders in the Mediterranean. . . . It is America that violates the Arab airspace with its warplanes" and thereby risked war with Arab states that engage in "a legitimate and Holy defence" of their territory. Reagan defeated Carter in the election, and, in 1981, US–Libyan hostilities would erupt in the Gulf of Sidra.[41]

4

QADDAFI AND THE WEST IN THE 1980S AND 1990S

What was the political situation within Libya in the 1980s?

Muammar al-Qaddafi remained the undisputed leader of Libya and enjoyed widespread, if diminishing, popularity. Many Libyans admired his ideology, his international audacity, and his record of establishing new institutions that involved citizens in aspects of governing themselves. They rallied around the flag when foreign adversaries pressured the country. Qaddafi's skillful distribution of oil-derived largesse and patronage placated many citizens despite their lack of political rights, and his imprisonment or exile of dissenters eliminated alternative leaders.

By the mid-1980s, however, flaws emerged in the political system. Government at the local level was strained by imprecise lines of authority, and the committee system of government was marred by inefficiencies. Many people tired of the relentless experimentation of the revolution, economic malaise, deprivations, and deteriorating quality of life. A growing number of Libyans became uninvolved in political matters.

Qaddafi took several steps to address growing public discontent. In 1986, he downgraded the power of the revolutionary committees (while leaving them intact to avoid the appearance of error in creating them). He implemented reforms, such as establishing cooperatives to overcome earlier prohibitions on the payment of wages for labor. He professed adherence to human rights protocols, released a small number of political prisoners, and eased restrictions on foreign travel. On balance, however, Qaddafi refrained from yielding any power to the General People's Congress (GPC). He continued to rule absolutely and to rely on trusted deputies and security services to defend his power.

The impact of Qaddafi's reforms remained limited. Public skepticism grew as a new generation—unaffiliated with the original revolution and reaching adulthood with more education—recognized the costs and the lost opportunities resulting from Qaddafi's domestic policy and foreign adventurism. Lacking any viable means to express their discontent, they withdrew from the political system.[1]

What was the economic situation within Libya in the 1980s?

Qaddafi's economic policies became problematic in the 1980s, in large part because of the impact of the revolutionary reforms he imposed earlier. Laws and regulations designed to implement his vision tended to undermine enterprise and innovation. Steps taken to distribute wealth eroded the support of elites and sapped the will of the people to work or invest.

The vast revenues generated by the oil industry proved to be ineffective at achieving long-term economic stability. Qaddafi spent much of the wealth on patronage of his trusted allies and on the purchase of foreign-made military hardware. He allocated substantial funding to large-scale agricultural and industrial projects designed to generate employment, diversify the economy, and reduce imports. For example, beginning in 1983, Qaddafi invested tens of billions of dollars in the so-called Great Man-Made River, a network of thousands of kilometers of concrete pipes with the capacity to convey 5 million tons of water per day from aquifers in the Kufra Oases to coastal agriculture, industry, and households. But these

110 LIBYA AND THE WEST

projects did little to improve Libya's economic infrastructure or the quality of its workforce, and they proved sustainable only with heavy government subsidies.

To make matters worse, Libyan oil production flagged in the 1980s. Centered in the Sirte Basin, production was slowed by such factors as overpricing, competition with other oil exporting states, depletion of several fields, aging infrastructure, and (eventually) Western sanctions. Wary of political conditions in Libya, oil firms refrained from exploring potential new oil reserves in the Kufrah, Murzuq, and Ghadames Basins. Falling oil prices curtailed the government's ability to fund various domestic and foreign initiatives.

In 1987, Qaddafi addressed this conundrum by liberalizing the economy and allowing more private decision-making, but economic problems persisted. The per capita gross national product (GNP) plateaued in 1980 at $11,706 before tumbling to $6,013 in 1990. Murmurs of complaint arose, as bread lines and black markets signaled the dereliction of the food supply via the state-run grocery stores, even while the elites in Qaddafi's government enjoyed luxury goods that were unavailable to the masses.[2]

Why did Western powers and Libya clash again in Chad in the 1980s?

After Libyan military forces withdrew from Chad in 1981, Qaddafi continued to meddle in that country's civil war. Hissène Habré took power as prime minister of Chad in 1982, but Qaddafi offered material support to armed resistance fighters in northern Chad led by Goukouni Oueddei. When the rebels advanced to the south, Libyan troops reentered the fray and fought alongside them.

Determined to contain Qaddafi's influence, France and the United States moved to strangle Qaddafi's foray. By bolstering Chad and encouraging Egypt and Sudan to contest Libya's gambit in Chad, US Secretary of State Al Haig sought to "bloody Qaddafi's nose" and "increase the flow of pine boxes back to Libya." In 1982, France sent troops to bolster the Habré regime, and the United States dispatched fighter and surveillance airplanes to airbases in Sudan from which they monitored Libyan military maneuvers. Even with such Western backing, however, the Habré regime lost control of its capital to rebel forces in August 1983. France thus essentially declared that Chad would be divided into two spheres divided by the sixteenth parallel, with the Habré government in control of the south. Qaddafi extended military and transportation infrastructure from southern Libya across northern Chad. The United States continued aerial reconnaissance missions to monitor Libyan activities until the situation stabilized.[3]

In hostilities that stretched across the 1980s, Chadian forces under Habré proved able to defeat the Libyan military in northern Chad. Armed and trained by France and the United States, the Chadian army launched a broad offensive against Libyan forces in 1986–1990. In this so-called Toyota War (named after all-terrain pick-up trucks favored by Chad's mobile units), Habré's forces liberated the country, killed some 7,500 Libyan soldiers (10 percent of Qaddafi's army), and captured Soviet-supplied military hardware worth $1.5 billion. The offensive slowed when it reached the Aouzou Strip, however, and a battlefield deadlock resulted. Because Libya's military capacity and record of aggression made it a "standing threat" to Chad, US President Ronald Reagan resolved to bolster the government in N'Djamena with security assistance and to pressure Libya to desist even while supporting a genuine diplomatic settlement.[4]

Eventually, the conflict in Chad dissipated. Qaddafi came to realize that his intervention had tarnished his international reputation, especially among African and Middle Eastern leaders who suspected that he sought power at their own expense and who viewed his interventionism with opprobrium. Sudan and Egypt remained stalwart in offering support to the French and US military forces arrayed against Libyan operations in Chad.

After Habré was ousted from power in a 1990 coup, Libya and Chad submitted the Aouzou Strip dispute to international arbitration at the International Court of Justice (ICJ), which ruled in 1994 in Chad's favor. UN troops moved into the strip to maintain peace and monitor the Libyan withdrawal and transition of authority to Chad. By the late 1990s, Libya and Chad pacified their relationship and exchanged diplomatic recognition. When an internal fight among Chadian factions erupted in 1998–2001, Libya played a mediating role in restoring stability.[5]

What approach did the Ronald Reagan administration follow toward Libya?

From the start of his presidency in 1981, President Reagan espoused a policy of firmness toward foreign states he deemed troublemakers. Having campaigned against Jimmy Carter's supposed international weakness and foreign policy miscues, Reagan set a more determined tone. "Let terrorists be aware that when the rules of international behavior are violated, our policy will be one of swift and effective retribution," he declared, just one week into his presidency, in a speech to the hostages freed by Iran. "We hear it said that we live in an era of a limit to our powers. Well, let it also be understood, there are limits to our patience."[6]

The Reagan administration viewed Libya with considerable concern. The growth of Qaddafi's partnership with the Soviet Union troubled Reagan because it signaled the failure of the hope among Western leaders of the 1970s that positive engagement with Qaddafi might lure him away from Moscow. US officials calculated that the Libyan leader's anti-Westernism and revolutionary radicalism earned him a reputation of being a threat to US interests around the world. Qaddafi's opposition to Arab–Israeli peace threatened Middle East stability. His aid to rebels in El Salvador and to the Sandinista regime in Nicaragua undermined US goals in Latin America.

Officials in Washington viewed with alarm Qaddafi's growing ties to Soviet Union in the 1980s. In April 1981, the Libyan leader visited Moscow, where he secured economic and technical aid and repeated his desire to join the Warsaw Pact. Three months later, he welcomed two Soviet naval vessels to Tripoli. From 1970 to 1985, Qaddafi spent some $20 billion on Soviet arms, and, by the early 1980s, 2,500 Soviet military advisers were stationed in Libya. His intervention in Chad seemed to advance Soviet opportunities to project political influence in northern Africa. The US Central Intelligence Agency (CIA) concluded that "Soviet objectives are served by Qaddafi's anti-Western policies."[7]

Qaddafi's support of terrorism and subversion emerged as a deep concern among Reagan administration officials. They took note in 1981, when Libya's GPC affirmed the legitimacy of national liberation movements. By the early 1980s, the US State Department estimated that Qaddafi was involved in terrorism or subversion in more than 30 countries and that he trained foreign militants at more than 10 camps in Libya. CIA director William J. Casey called terrorism Libya's "second largest export, after oil."[8]

US officials were quite troubled by evidence that Qaddafi dispatched "hit squads" to murder Libyan dissidents residing in other countries. Qaddafi created the "Mathaba [World Center] to Resist Imperialism, Racism, and Reactionary Forces" to disseminate propaganda around the globe, and he assigned political loyalists to Libya's embassies (called "people's bureaus") around the world to spread his revolutionary message. Soon, evidence surfaced that Libyan people's bureaus had become bases of operations for assassins targeting Libyan exiles who criticized Qaddafi's regime. Between 1980 and 1986, more than a dozen prominent dissidents were gunned down in mosques, hotels, restaurants, and railway stations in the United Kingdom, Italy, West Germany, Cyprus, Greece, and Egypt. Other dissidents were kidnapped or otherwise disappeared. After Libyan intelligence agents attempted to murder a Libyan

114 LIBYA AND THE WEST

exile in Colorado, Reagan closed the Libyan people's bureau in Washington in May 1981.

US officials sought to understand Qaddafi's unconventional political and personal practices by conducting psychological assessments of him. "Because of special circumstances in his childhood," a 1981 CIA assessment found, "Qaddafi absorbed, in exaggerated form, the Bedouin characteristics of naive idealism, religious fanaticism, intense pride, austerity, xenophobia, and sensitivity to slight." Qaddafi's Bedouin roots also shaped "an intense disdain for established elites . . . , a strong identification with the downtrodden," and tendencies for "rebellion against authority" and "indiscriminate support of rebel causes throughout the world." Reagan also used humor to disparage the Libyan leader in private. Upon hearing that Qaddafi occasionally dressed in women's clothing, he joked to aides that "maybe we could stop the terror by letting him into Nancy's closet."[9]

What triggered the military incident between US and Libyan warplanes in the Gulf of Sidra in 1981?

The incident originated in a dispute in the 1970s over the legal status of the Gulf of Sidra along Libya's Mediterranean coast. In contrast to President Carter's retreat from the Gulf, Reagan resolved to flex US military muscle and baited Qaddafi into a showdown. "I approved naval maneuvers in Mediterranean waters that Khadafi [Qaddafi] of Libya has declared are his territorial waters," Reagan noted in his diary on June 1, 1981. "I'm not being foolhardy but he's a madman. He has been harassing our planes out over international waters & it's time to show the other nations there Egypt, Morocco, et al that there is different management here." With fanfare, Reagan dispatched a US Navy carrier fleet into the gulf in early August, announcing in advance that the voyage would affirm the international status of the water. On August 19, two Soviet-supplied Libyan Arab Air Force (LAAF) fighter airplanes feinted attacks on the fleet and then fired a missile at a US Navy surveillance airplane. The surveillance plane evaded the missile, and two US F-14 fighters, waiting in ambush formation, shot down the two Libyan aircraft.[10]

What was the impact of the air engagement on US–Libyan relations?

A war of words immediately followed the confrontation in the Gulf. Reagan cited the incident as a sign of restored US power and resolve. "Military adventurism and subversion threaten in faraway areas of the world," he declared in a speech to the crew of the carrier USS *Constellation*, one day after the incident. "Let friend and foe alike know that America has the muscle to back up its words, and ships like this and men like you are that muscle."[11] For his part, Qaddafi boldly replied on September 1, the twelfth anniversary of the revolution, that if the United States again attacked Libya, he would retaliate against Western military assets across the Mediterranean. He also threatened to sign an alliance with the Soviet Union.

US–Libyan conflicts ensued. In August 1981, the media reported leaked information that the US government was planning a coup against Qaddafi, which the Reagan administration denied, although Qaddafi claimed to have found evidence of such US planning. US intelligence detected a threat from Qaddafi to assassinate Reagan and several members of his Cabinet to avenge the Gulf of Sidra humiliation. In mid-October, Italian police disrupted an apparent Libyan plot to assassinate US Ambassador to Rome Maxwell Rabb, who was urgently evacuated to the United States for his personal safety. In a December 1981 interview on a US television network, Qaddafi denied that he plotted to assassinate any US leaders. Reagan replied, however, that "I wouldn't believe a word [Qaddafi] says if I were you. . . . We have the evidence and he knows it."[12]

To deter Libyan attacks on US interests, Reagan enacted several restrictions on Libya by signing National Security

116 LIBYA AND THE WEST

Decision Directive (NSDD) 16 on December 10. "Any acts of violence directed by Libya or its agents against officials of the U.S., at home or abroad," he warned Qaddafi, in a letter delivered through the Belgian government, "will be regarded by the U.S. government as an armed attack upon the U.S. and will be met by every means necessary to defend this nation in accordance with Article 51 of the United Nations Charter." Reagan prohibited US citizens from traveling to Libya and advised Americans who were there to leave immediately. He urged US companies to minimize trade with Libya and encouraged them to withdraw US citizens working in Libya. Finally, the president directed the Department of the Treasury to prepare for an eventual imposition of embargoes on Libyan oil imports and on US exports to Libya, and the Department of Defense to plan appropriate military action if Libya attempted an assassination or took US citizens as hostages.[13]

In March 1982, the Reagan administration embargoed the import of Libyan crude oil and banned export to Libya of oil and gas equipment. Given that at the time the United States purchased about one-third of Libya's oil (which comprised about 5 percent of US oil imports), the embargo disrupted Libyan oil production. To retaliate, Qaddafi tried to organize another embargo by the Organization of Oil Exporting Countries (OPEC) on all oil sales to the United States, but other OPEC members demurred. Although Libya was able to develop new markets in Europe and elsewhere, a downturn in world oil prices in 1982 created financial havoc for it in international markets. In addition, the US embargo on equipment exploited Libya's dependence on US-made machinery and spare parts, the alternatives for which were in short supply and more expensive. Weaknesses in the infrastructure of Libyan oil production soon became acute, making Libya vulnerable to external pressure.

The United States and Libya also competed for regional influence. In August 1981, Libya, Ethiopia, and South Yemen signed an economic and political agreement designed to challenge

Western, primarily US, interests in the Mediterranean and the Indian Ocean. To deter the Libya–Ethiopia–South Yemen bloc from aggression, the United States sent "show-the-flag" military delegations to Sudan, Oman, and Somalia. The United States also conducted military drills in Egypt and provided military aid to Sudan, Morocco, Tunisia, and Somalia.

On balance, the confrontation with Reagan seemed to give Qaddafi pause. The Gulf of Sidra episode stirred Libyan patriotism to a degree, but the military setback in the Gulf accented his humiliation in Chad and his ostracism by other Arab leaders. Popular support waned as the largesse from the oil industry declined. In 1982 and 1983, US officials noted that Qaddafi's international mischief-making seemed relatively limited except for his ongoing intervention in Chad.

How did the Western European powers view Libya in the early 1980s?

On the one hand, European leaders eyed Qaddafi with suspicion. They protested his suspected complicity in the series of murders of Libyan exiles in Europe in 1980. Britain, Italy, and West Germany, moreover, refused Qaddafi's demand that they pay financial reparations for the physical destruction inflicted on Libya during World War II, even though Qaddafi threatened to expropriate their property if they failed to comply.

On the other hand, European powers did not confront Libya as stringently as the United States did. They cited Qaddafi's withdrawal from Chad as a responsible step forward. They cautioned that the United States exaggerated the threat that Qaddafi posed to the Europeans' vital interests. They predicted that Reagan's firmness might provoke Qaddafi to more misbehavior or drive him further into Soviet reliance all while imperiling their economic interests in Libyan oil.

In the aftermath of the 1981 Gulf of Sidra incident, the European powers opposed any political or economic sanctions on Libya. In fact, Europeans took advantage of the

118 LIBYA AND THE WEST

US oil embargo to improve their economic interests. Libyan oil exports were redirected from the US markets to Britain, Germany, Italy, Turkey, and Brazil. British imports increased by more than threefold within a year of the US embargo. Libya also integrated vertically, buying refineries and gasoline stations in Europe, Malta, and Egypt to ensure outlets for its exports.

Why did the United Kingdom sever diplomatic relations with Libya in 1984?

Britain severed relations with Libya following an episode of violence by Libyan officials in London. On April 17, Libyan dissidents conducted an anti-Qaddafi demonstration outside the Libyan people's bureau in central London. Suddenly, gunfire from within the people's bureau sprayed into the crowd, wounding 11 demonstrators and killing British police officer Yvonne Fletcher. Hoping to arrest the perpetrators, British police surrounded the people's bureau for 11 days, but Libya, rather than surrender the gunman, retaliated by surrounding the British embassy in Tripoli. Britain promptly severed diplomatic relations with Libya but ultimately honored the principle of diplomatic immunity, allowing the Libyan officials in London to exit the country with their baggage under diplomatic seal. Home Secretary Leon Brittan told Prime Minister Margaret Thatcher that "we would have to allow a murderer to go free."[14]

Why did US–Libyan relations deteriorate in the mid-1980s?

US–Libyan relations deteriorated in the mid-1980s mainly over the issue of terrorism. After relative quiescence in Libyan activities in 1982–1983, the State Department monitored a renewal of Libyan subversion in 1984–1985. A series of murders of Libyan dissidents living in Western states was suspected of being Qaddafi's handiwork, and the killing of the British police officer in London clearly was Libya's deed. US officials monitored reports of Libyan attacks against Egypt, Sudan, and Chad as well as Libyan assistance to the anti-US Sandinista regime in Nicaragua. As evidence surfaced of Libyan plots to assassinate King Hussein of Jordan, King Hassan II of Morocco, and Palestine Liberation Organization (PLO) chief Yasser Arafat, Qaddafi declared in 1985, "I will take up responsibility and begin terrorism against the Arab rulers, threaten and frighten them, and sever relations. And if I could, I would behead them one by one."[15]

The joking about Qaddafi's eccentricities or fashion choices notwithstanding, Reagan administration officials seriously viewed Qaddafi's policies and practices that menaced Western interests. Within the government in Washington, "there was a kind of social and intellectual disdain for Qaddafi, a tendency almost to twit him," the reporter Bob Woodward noted, after a discussion with a CIA officer. "But there was also the combatant's esteem" for Qaddafi given that he had power, money, and purpose.[16]

US officials concluded that undermining Qaddafi's regime through covert action was the most effective means to stem the surge in Libyan terrorism. After Qaddafi defeated a violent coup attempt by the National Front for the Salvation of Libya in May 1984, Director of Central Intelligence William Casey observed that the attempted coup "proves for the first time that Libyans are willing to die to get rid of this bastard." Within a month, an interagency task force concluded that Libyan exile groups, "if supported to a substantial degree, could soon begin an intermittent campaign of sabotage and violence which could promote further challenges to Qaddafi's authority" and that "disaffected elements in the military could be spurred to assassination attempts."[17]

In 1985, the Reagan administration discussed twin operations to overthrow Qaddafi. Under Operation Tulip, US officials hoped to collaborate with Libyan dissidents to oust Qaddafi through covert action. Operation Rose envisioned a preemptive

120 LIBYA AND THE WEST

military strike, in partnership with Egypt, to undermine the dictator. In August, the CIA reported that Egypt, Iraq, and Algeria were conspiring to bring external pressure on Libya and that "if the dissidents have supporters in the military willing to assist, we assess their chances of toppling Qadhafi at better than even." Although the Reagan administration suspended Rose as too risky, it gained the approval of the House and Senate intelligence committees to move forward with Tulip. A combination of leaks to the US media and repressive measures by Qaddafi, however, eroded the enthusiasm of Tulip's Libyan accomplices, rendering the operation infeasible.[18]

Qaddafi not only remained in power, but also seemed to escalate his terrorism in a wave of strikes in late 1985. US officials charged that Libya had supported bombings of a Northwest Orient Airlines office in Copenhagen in July, and a café near the US Embassy in Rome in September. In October, Qaddafi lionized the Palestinian terrorists who highjacked the *Achille Lauro* cruise ship off the coast of Egypt and murdered a disabled American passenger. Libya was found to have bankrolled the Abu Nidal Organization's November hijacking of Egypt Air Flight 648 that was forced to land in Malta, where the hijackers executed several Israeli and US passengers before Egyptian commandoes stormed the plane, provoking a gun battle and fire that left 60 people dead. Libya was also linked to Abu Nidal's December gunfire and grenade attacks on ticket counters in the Rome and Vienna Airports that killed 25 people, including five Americans. Although it was difficult to determine exactly who was culpable for each of these attacks, US officials associated them with Qaddafi, given his rhetoric, his international aspirations, and evidence showing connections between Libya and some 30 terrorist groups worldwide. Given Qaddafi's "connection with the massacres at the Rome & Vienna airports," Reagan noted in his diary at year's end, "we all feel we must do something yet there are problems including thousands of Americans living & working in the mad clown's country."[19]

How did US security strategy toward terrorism evolve in the 1980s?

The surge in terrorist activities attributed to Libya coincided with growing US resolve and preparation to deal firmly with the menace of terrorism in general. In NSDD 30, of April 30, 1982, Reagan took a preliminary step of setting up an administrative chain of command for monitoring, assessing, and advising on responses to terrorist attacks at home or overseas. Two years later, he approved a more proactive national policy of combating terrorism by legal, diplomatic, military, and covert means. In the top-secret NSDD 138, signed on April 3, 1984, the president directed the Department of Defense to "develop a full range of military options to combat terrorism throughout the entire terrorist threat spectrum." He ordered the CIA to develop "capabilities for the pre-emptive neutralization of anti-American terrorist groups" and to "develop a clandestine service capability, using all lawful means, for effective response overseas against terrorist acts committed against U.S. citizens, facilities, or interests." In July 1985, Reagan established a task force chaired by Vice President George H. W. Bush to coordinate antiterrorism preparations across the government. "Terrorists are waging a war, not only against the United States, but all civilized society," NSDD 179 observed. "We should undertake action in concert with other nations which share our democratic institutions to combat the menace of terrorism. We must, however, be prepared to act unilaterally when necessary."[20]

How did the United States react to the surge in terrorism by Libya in particular?

By early 1986, US officials concluded that Libya was a key instigator of international terrorism and needed to be scorned for such. "The scope and tempo of Libyan-supported terrorist activity against western targets is widening and accelerating," Reagan affirmed in NSDD 205, signed on January 8. Evidence

122 LIBYA AND THE WEST

of Libyan involvement in the Rome and Vienna attacks and other attacks was "indisputable." The president directed his administration to implement measures to stanch Libyan terrorism as well as isolate Libya politically through a "global diplomatic and public affairs campaign."[21]

Beginning in late 1985, Reagan imposed economic sanctions on Libya to impede the flow of financial resources that it used to perpetrate terrorism. In November, he blocked the import of Libyan refined oil. Under NSDD 205, the United States banned the import to or export from Libya of all commodities except publications and medicines, prohibited Americans from signing service contracts with Libya, prohibited travel between the two countries (except for journalists), denied entry to US ports of any Libyan-flagged vessel, and blocked the issuing of credits and financing to Libya (although Libyan assets in the United States were not frozen at that time). The administration determined to persuade its Allies to impose similar measures or at least pledge not to exploit new opportunities created by the US embargoes. By ending the role of Americans in operating and maintaining Libya's oilfields, these restrictions contributed to the sharp decline in Libyan oil revenues from $21 billion in 1982 to $5.4 billion in 1986.[22]

Furthermore, Reagan moved to stigmatize Qaddafi in public speaking. "These murderers could not carry out their crimes without the sanctuary and support provided by regimes such as Colonel Qadhafi's in Libya," Reagan declared publicly, regarding the Rome and Vienna airport attacks. "Qadhafi called them heroic actions, and I call them criminal outrages by an outlaw regime." When asked by a journalist to react to Qaddafi's blustering threats to send hit squads to Washington, Reagan rhetorically questioned, "How can you not take seriously a man that has proven that he is as irrational as he is on things of this kind[?] I find he's not only a barbarian, but he's flaky." Noting in April that Qaddafi "has been quite outspoken about his participation in, urging on, and supporting terrorist acts," the US president branded him "this mad dog of the Middle East."[23]

Reagan also decided to display military muscle against Libya. Because Libya's "policies and actions in support of international terrorism . . . constitute an unusual and extraordinary threat to the national security and foreign policy of the United States," the president determined in January 1986, the United States would "demonstrate resolve in a manner that reverses the perception of U.S. passivity." He ordered the Pentagon to deploy a second carrier battle group to the Mediterranean and to patrol the Gulf of Sidra as means to show US resolve, protect US citizens, position the Navy for possible military action, and create uncertainty in Libya about US intentions.[24]

What was the impact of these policies on US relations with Libya?

These US policies led to an escalating cycle of violence between the United States and Libya. Three ships from the US Sixth Fleet entered the Gulf of Sidra in late March 1986, triggering attacks by Libyan Navy ships and coastal antiaircraft batteries. In the ensuing battle, the US Navy destroyed two Libyan ships, grounded the LAAF, and demolished radar stations at the LAAF's most important antiaircraft battery at Sirte (taking care to spare the missiles there out of concern that the resulting explosions would kill or wound nearby Soviet military technicians). Some 72 Libyans were believed to have been killed, while US forces suffered zero casualties. Libya broke off the engagement—thereby avoiding even more punishing assaults in the US battle plan—although Qaddafi vowed to turn the Mediterranean into "a sea of fire" and called for attacks on US oil fields, military bases, and personnel across the Arab world.[25]

Despite Qaddafi's threats to retaliate in the Arab world, he apparently struck back with a terrorist attack in Berlin, West Germany. On April 6, a bomb demolished a discotheque in

124 LIBYA AND THE WEST

West Berlin frequented by US soldiers, killing one GI and a Turkish woman and injuring some 50 Americans and 200 others. Citing evidence of communications between the government of Libya and its people's bureau in East Berlin, Reagan publicly charged that "this monstrous brutality is but the latest act in Colonel Qadhafi's reign of terror." The evidence that Libya executed the attack "is direct; it is precise; it is irrefutable." To punish Qaddafi, deter future attacks, and degrade Libya's military capabilities, Reagan ordered the Pentagon to conduct a proportional military strike on the infrastructure Qaddafi used to engage in terrorism while sparing as much as possible civilians and those Libyans opposing Qaddafi.[26]

Nine days after the Berlin bombing, about 100 US warplanes conducted air raids against five military targets in Tripoli and Benghazi. The targets were selected based on such factors as military and political importance, psychological impact on Qaddafi, relation to Qaddafi's terrorism, isolation from civilians, and proximity to the coast (to minimize risks to US airmen). Qaddafi was present at one site and narrowly escaped injury. Libyan officials reported that the dictator's 15-month-old adopted daughter, Hanna al-Qaddafi was killed in the raid (although journalists reported years later, after the fall of the Qaddafi government, that this claim likely was a hoax). Several dozen civilians were killed by bombs that missed their targets. One US aircraft with two crewmen was lost in the operation. Rumors circulated that the United States had tried deliberately to kill Qaddafi, a charge that Reagan denied.[27]

In the days following the air raids, Libya retaliated in a series of attacks against Western interests across Europe. Libya fired two SCUD missiles at a US Coast Guard base on the Italian island of Lampedusa; both missiles missed their target and fell harmlessly into the sea. US officials suspected Libyan culpability in attempts to kill US diplomatic personnel in Sudan and South Yemen, the murders of three Western hostages in Lebanon, an attempt to plant a bomb on an Israeli airliner in

London, an attempted attack on a US officer's club in Ankara, and a bombing of an American Express office in Madrid.[28]

How did the European powers view the escalation of US pressure on Libya?

While they remained deeply concerned with Libyan-backed terrorism, West European governments viewed the US firmness toward Libya with skepticism. They reasoned that pressure or violence would make Qaddafi even more defiant and erratic. More sympathetic than the United States to the interests of the Palestinians, the European powers believed that advancing Palestinian statehood would reduce the impetus behind terrorism more effectively than suppressive measures. Several Europeans sought in principle to practice foreign policies independent of US leadership, while Italy and Greece demanded more definitive proof that Libya was involved in the terrorist attacks of late 1985.

The European powers declined to affirm the US economic sanctions imposed in early 1986 after privately calculating that sanctions would be too costly to themselves. Deputy Secretary of State John Whitehead ventured to nine European capitals in January to persuade US allies to reduce oil imports from Libya, embargo arms sales to Libya, condemn Libyan terrorism, and close Libyan people's bureaus. European leaders explained to Whitehead, however, that sanctions rarely worked to effect desired outcomes. Italy, especially, feared that that pressuring Qaddafi would undermine its ability to collect the $800 million that Libya had borrowed from Italian banks and would imperil Italy's bilateral trade with Libya valued at $7 billion per year (some 40 percent of Europe's total trade with Libya).[29]

Whitehead succeeded only in persuading several states to limit arms sales and new financial loans to Libya and to refrain from filling shortfalls in Libya's trade caused by the US total embargo. The European Community foreign ministers adopted a resolution that embargoed arms sales to countries

126 LIBYA AND THE WEST

that practiced terrorism but that did not identify Libya specifically. Upon his return to Washington, a frustrated Whitehead told reporters that President Reagan "reserved the right to come back to the military option in case the non-military, peaceful measures failed to work."[30]

Did the European powers support the US airstrikes on Libya in April 1986?

European reactions to the US airstrikes on Libya ranged from sharp criticism to sympathetic support. In hope of garnering support for the airstrikes he planned in retaliation for the Berlin bombing, Reagan dispatched Ambassador to the United Nations Vernon L. Walters to ask for support from the leaders of Britain, France, Italy, Germany, Spain, and Canada, delaying military action from April 12 to 14 to allow time for such diplomacy.

The Allies' responses were measured. While they affirmed the principle of counterterrorism, they rejected Reagan's inclination to use calibrated force on Libya because it risked provoking future Libyan attacks against targets in Europe and generating Arab and African sympathy for Qaddafi. They proposed inter-Allied consultations on the problem in lieu of an immediate resort to force. "We do not think the Sixth Fleet is the best way of fighting terrorism," Belgian Foreign Minister Leo Tindemans remarked. France later claimed that it would have favored a major operation to overthrow Qaddafi over Reagan's planned calibrated strike that seemed likely to strengthen Qaddafi. Disliking Ambassador Walters's presentation of US intentions as a fait accompli, France and Spain denied permission for US warplanes departing from Britain to overfly their territory enroute to Libya, meaning that those US aircraft would have to fly longer and riskier routes over the Atlantic and Mediterranean.[31]

To head off US military action, the foreign ministers of the European Community hastily arranged a meeting at the Hague on April 14. They publicly denounced terrorism, required the downsizing of staffs at Libya's people's bureaus, and imposed travel restrictions on Libyans entering Europe. They refrained, however, from imposing a complete embargo on trade, and they called on all powers to work toward political solutions and refrain from military action.

Breaking ranks with the European community, Britain alone supported the US military strike, granting permission for US warplanes to launch their missions from airbases in Britain. In a meeting with Walters, Prime Minister Thatcher agreed that the United States was entitled to act under the self-defense clause of the UN Charter, that the planned airstrikes were proportional to Libya's misdeeds, and that they would target the infrastructure of Libyan terrorism. Thatcher's abiding animosity for Qaddafi over Libya's murder of the British police officer and support of the Irish Republican Army contributed to her motivations, as did her enduring appreciation for Reagan's support of Britain in the Falklands War. Recent oil discoveries in the North Sea, moreover, reduced Britain's reliance on Libyan oil and thus afforded Thatcher freedom of action against Libya. Qaddafi later reciprocated Thatcher's ill will, calling her a "stupid woman" and "a rotten lackey to terrorist Reagan."[32]

The immediate reactions among European allies to the actual US airstrikes remained mixed, although they shifted slightly toward the US perspective. In the face of searing public criticism, Prime Minister Thatcher firmly defended her decision to allow US use of airbases in Britain by warning the House of Commons of the dangers of "appeasement" and of being "supine and passive" toward terrorism. Chancellor Helmut Kohl revealed that West German investigators had confirmed that Libyans had planted the Berlin disco bomb, which justified the US military action as "a preventive strike against the further escalation of terrorism." While he had advised the United States to use methods other than airstrikes, Kohl recognized that European passivity left Reagan with few options.[33]

France moved quickly to address US public criticism of its denial of permission for US overflights. Ambassador Emmanuel de Margerie explained the decision as a reaction to Ambassador Walters's fait accompli rather than a sign of appeasement of Libyan terrorism, which France had resolutely battled in Chad. "Terrorism is extremely complex, stemming from many causes," de Margerie observed. "It should be combated in such a way as to minimize the ever-present danger of a continuing spiral of violence. . . . The risk of strengthening Khadafy's [Qaddafi's] hold on Libya and of alienating moderate Arab countries are factors that cannot be ignored." Deflecting US criticism to Italy, de Margerie added that "it is certainly not French companies that keep the wheels of the Libyan oil industry turning."[34]

The strongest criticism of the US action stemmed from Italy, Spain, and Greece, which felt most vulnerable to potential Libyan reprisals. Unhappy that the United States had not allowed time for the European measures decided on April 14 to have effect, Italian Prime Minister Bettino Craxi expressed concern that the US airstrikes would cause "a further explosion of fanaticism and extremism." (Years later, Craxi's son claimed that his father had alerted Qaddafi to the impending US airstrikes, thus perhaps saving the dictator's life.) In Italy as well as Spain, Greece, and Cyprus, sizeable public demonstrations protested the US action.[35]

By early May, the Western allies were ready to close ranks, with the Europeans embracing firmer counterterrorism measures long sought by the United States. At the Group of Seven (G-7) meeting in Tokyo, the leaders of the United States, Britain, France, West Germany, Italy, Japan, and Canada issued a statement that they "strongly reaffirm our condemnation of international terrorism in all its forms, of its accomplices and of those, including governments, who sponsor or support it." Singling out Libya as a "state which is clearly involved in sponsoring or supporting international terrorism," the G-7 leaders agreed to engage in such measures as a total arms embargo against states practicing terrorism, restrictions on the diplomatic missions of such states, and cooperation in law enforcement, travel restrictions, and border controls to disrupt terrorist activities. Their statement seemed to fulfill Reagan's goal for the meeting of wanting "to get down to the nitty-gritty and get some agreement as to how we're going to deal with it [terrorism]."[36]

How did US–Libyan relations develop in the late 1980s?

US–Libyan relations remained antagonistic in the years following the US airstrikes of April 1986. Humiliated by his inability to defend against the US attack, Qaddafi became more defiant. The CIA reported in July that the Libyan leader "is tightening his personal security, seeking Soviet assistance in strengthening Libya's defense capabilities, promoting diplomatic initiatives to ease Libya's international isolation, and restructuring his terrorist support apparatus to achieve greater deniability." In an address on September 1, the seventeenth anniversary of his revolution, the Libyan leader vowed to form an army that "will spread out to all corners of the globe and destroy the American presence everywhere."[37]

For their part, US officials remained concerned by evidence that Qaddafi, after a brief pause following the airstrikes, engaged anew in terrorism planning and operations. US objectives, Reagan affirmed in August, were to deter Libyan terrorism and "enhance the chances of a positive change of leadership" in Tripoli. The United States would engage in a "multi-faceted strategy which intensifies pressures on Qadhafi [Qaddafi]. Our actions should keep Qadhafi off balance and embolden dissident Libyans by creating the impression, and to the extent possible, the reality that further U.S. actions are underway." To reach these goals, Reagan directed his government to extend international embargoes on Libya, maintain readiness to strike militarily if Libya engaged in terrorist attacks,

130 LIBYA AND THE WEST

and engage in clandestine activities to isolate Qaddafi's regime from its neighbors and its own people.[38]

The United States and Libya openly clashed on two issues in the waning weeks of the Reagan presidency. When US intelligence detected evidence that Libya was building a chemical weapons plant at Rabta, 40 miles south of Tripoli, Reagan warned publicly of the danger of a terrorist state developing weapons of mass destruction. He leaned on such allies as West Germany and Japan to embargo exports of equipment needed to operate the facility. Reagan also refused to rule out military action against the plant, although its defense by Soviet-supplied surface-to-air missiles rendered such an option daunting. Qaddafi's explanation that the plant was pharmaceutical and his offer to allow a one-time international inspection were viewed with skepticism by the United States, especially after Libya reportedly used chemical weapons in Chad. In the wake of an international conference in Paris, in January 1989, where 140 nations agreed to condemn the use of chemical weapons in principle but could not agree to establish prohibitions or deterrents to their manufacture, Libya reportedly suspended the production at Rabta. In 1990, however, it was believed by Western officials to have resumed production of poison gas at Rabta shortly before a fire of suspicious origins destroyed the facility. West Germany denied Libya's accusation that it covertly started the fire.[39]

The Rabta issue might have provoked the final US–Libyan military incident of the 1980s. On January 4, 1989, two Libyan MiG-23s approached two US Navy Tomcat jets on routine patrol some 600 miles north of Libya. Concluding that the Libyans displayed hostile intent based on their flying maneuvers and display of weaponry, the Tomcats preemptively shot down both MiGs. Western officials speculated that Qaddafi might have sent the aircraft to attack the aircraft carrier USS *John F. Kennedy* out of fear that the US fleet was poised to bomb the plant at Rabta. In seeking UN Security Council condemnation of the United States, Qaddafi claimed that his aircraft were unarmed, but US officials released videos showing that both MiGs indeed were armed. The Security Council declined to act.[40]

Was Libya complicit in the bombing of civilian airliners in 1988–1989?

Yes, Libya carried out the bombings of two civilian airliners. On December 21, 1988, Pan Am Flight 103, flying from London to New York, was destroyed by a bomb in the airspace over Lockerbie, Scotland, killing 259 passengers and crew and 11 people on the ground. Western investigators seeking to identify the perpetrators initially focused on Iran, on a suspicion that it was motivated to avenge the accidental downing of an Iranian civilian airliner by the US Navy five months earlier. Forensic evidence, however, eventually led authorities to link the Lockerbie bombing to Libya, on the motive of avenging the air raid ordered by Reagan in 1986. The investigation turned in October 1990, when investigators discovered in the wreckage a computer chip linked to Qaddafi's intelligence service.

In addition, France's Union de Transports Aériens (UTA) Flight 772, flying from N'Djamena, Chad, to Paris on September 19, 1989, was demolished in midair by a bomb over the Tenere Desert in Niger. The attack killed the 170 passengers and crew. After conducting a forensic investigation, France tried six Libyan intelligence officers in absentia in 1999, finding them guilty and sentencing them to life imprisonment as well as levying restitution of $33 million against Libya. Qaddafi agreed to pay the $33 million assessment, and eventually, another $170 million, but he declined to accept responsibility or to extradite or incarcerate the defendants.

How did the international community handle evidence of Libyan complicity in the Lockerbie bombing?

In November 1991, the United States and Britain charged Abdelbaset al-Megrahi, the former head of security at the

132 LIBYA AND THE WEST

Libyan Arab Airlines office in Malta, and Al-Amin Khalifa Fhimah, a Libyan security officer, on the eyewitness testimony of a shopkeeper in Malta who had sold the pair personal effects found to have been used in the attack. The two Western powers demanded that the two suspects be extradited for trial in the United States or Scotland, and they sought United Nations approval of universal sanctions against Libya unless it complied.

Qaddafi denied the charges, deriding the evidence presented as "less than a laughable piece of fingernail." To stave off sanctions, he proposed that the two men would be tried by another Arab state or Malta—an offer that the Western powers declined—and he renounced his ties to certain international terrorist groups. But he refused the Western demands for extradition.[41]

Under British and US leadership, the UN Security Council adopted three resolutions to compel Libya on this issue. Resolution 731 of January 1992 demanded that Libya comply with the Western demands. Two months later, Resolution 748 imposed sweeping, universal economic sanctions including such important matters as arms sales, civilian travel, and spare parts for oil production equipment. Resolution 883 of November 1993 made matters worse for Qaddafi by freezing Libyan assets abroad.

Qaddafi's diplomatic interests waned under these sanctions. In contrast to the US-led sanctions of the previous decade, the UN action signaled Libya's isolation and outlaw image across the international community. A provision enshrined in the sanctions resolution made it possible for the United Nations to tighten the restrictions at any time, and, in the Iran and Libya Sanctions Act of 1996, the United States imposed sanctions on European firms conducting business in Libya worth more than $40 million per year.

To what extent did Western powers worry about Libyan development of nuclear weapons?

From his early years in power, Qaddafi took an interest in nuclear science and weaponry. King Idris's regime had approved the Nuclear Non-Proliferation Treaty in 1968, and, in 1975, Qaddafi ratified it and affirmed the International Atomic Energy Agency (IAEA) Safeguards because the Soviets conditioned their offer to build the nuclear research facility at Tajoura on such actions. The Tajoura reactor became functional in August 1981, after the Soviets provided enriched uranium and Qaddafi recruited scientists from Egypt and Pakistan to operate the facility. Libya pursued other nuclear power deals with firms in the United States, France, and India, but the governments of those countries, suspicious of Libya's intentions, denied the needed export licenses. Consistent with his erratic nature, Qaddafi oscillated in his public speaking between antinuclear idealism and rugged determination to get an "Arab bomb."[42]

During the 1980s, Qaddafi displayed growing determination to become a nuclear weapons power, both to earn international prestige and to balance Israeli and US military might. In 1980, he accepted a Soviet offer to build a large reactor at Sirte for electricity generation. The 1981 Israeli air raid on the nuclear reactor at Osirak, Iraq, alarmed Qaddafi because his recently completed Tajoura reactor was within range of Israeli air power. Israel's unauthorized use of Libyan airspace on a bombing run against Palestinian Liberation Organization (PLO) strongholds in Tunisia in 1985 further offended Qaddafi and revealed Libya's security vulnerabilities. The US airstrikes on Tripoli and Benghazi the very next year starkly exposed Qaddafi's weaknesses. "If we had possessed a deterrent— missiles that could reach New York," Qaddafi declared publicly in 1990, in reference to 1986 airstrikes, "we would have hit it at the same moment. Consequently, we should build this force so that they and others will no longer think about an attack."[43]

In this quest, however, Qaddafi faced numerous obstacles. His government and society lacked the scientific expertise needed to build a bomb and the industrial infrastructure to fabricate components. Many foreign powers remained unwilling

134 LIBYA AND THE WEST

to sell him vital commodities. In the late 1980s, Libya's partnership with the Soviets to build the large reactor at Sirte fell apart amid Soviet Premier Mikhail Gorbachev's *perestroika* reforms, doubts in Moscow about Libya's ability to pay the $4 billion cost, and Libyan worries, in the aftermath of the Chernobyl disaster of 1986, about the safety of Soviet technology.[44]

In the 1990s, Qaddafi pursued the essential components of a nuclear weapons program—including raw materials, military hardware, and scientific expertise—through backchannels in Russia, China, Pakistan, North Korea, Niger, and Iran. Once UN sanctions were suspended in 1999, Libya explored restoration of certain supply lines in Western Europe (to no avail). Libya outwardly downgraded the Tajoura Nuclear Research Center but escalated covert operations to acquire nuclear enrichment capacity via the A. Q. Khan underground supply network based in Pakistan. It was estimated that Qaddafi spent between $100 million and $500 million on equipment, blueprints, and training and that he secured uranium hexafluoride, a key component in nuclear weapons production, likely from North Korea.[45]

Given Libya's dearth of scientific expertise, industrial infrastructure, and access to uranium, Western officials remained assured that it did not pose an imminent threat of becoming a nuclear weapons power. Libya was gaining capabilities, however, and thus Western governments remained vigilant and resolved to preventing it from succeeding.[46]

How did Qaddafi's foreign conflicts shape his people's perceptions of him in the 1990s?

The Qaddafi regime faced mounting challenges at home in the 1990s because of the costly consequences of its foreign adventures. Although Qaddafi was outwardly defiant toward the UN sanctions, they caused his country significant economic hardship. In the absence of spare parts, technical upgrades, open markets, and Western engineers, the productivity of

Libyan-run oilfields declined by 8 percent per year, and Libya had to suspend explorations of new oil deposits to replace aging oilfields that were running dry. The ban on air travel limited business enterprise and tourism and forced shipment of essential commodities by slower and costlier land and sea routes. Some oil exports continued; the Italian firm AGIP remained active in developing a natural gas pipeline from Libya to Italy, under a $5.5 billion contract signed in 1993 and thus argued to be exempt from sanctions. Overall, however, the Libyan economy grew by a paltry 0.8 percent per year under sanctions, and per capita gross domestic product (GDP) fell from $7,285 in 1992 to $5,244 in 1998.[47]

Struggling with growing deprivations, the Libyan people grew less supportive of their leader. Public support of the regime noticeably cooled in reaction to the corruption, economic malaise, political suppression, and declining standard of living. Even when called by Qaddafi to protest the US military action against their country, the masses did not take to the streets to demonstrate their support of the regime, a telling signal that Qaddafi's public persona was fading. Rather, the people were shocked and despondent over their government's dereliction in defending the country and came to regret the international pariah status that Qaddafi had earned. In addition to causing economic hardships, the UN sanctions singled out Libya for worldwide reproach. Qaddafi tried to rally his people by tempering the revolutionary fervor of his regime, rescinding restrictions on individual freedoms, and easing economic regulations. But he struggled to balance between moderating the growing public backlash and allowing reforms that might reveal the obsolescence of his revolutionary ideals.[48]

The discontent with Qaddafi soon permeated the Libyan armed forces. Although the army had increased from 7,000 to 85,000 soldiers in 1969–1985 and was armed with vast quantities of weapons purchased with oil revenues, the force was neither professionalized nor entrusted to maintain internal security. Maladministration meant that soldiers often

136 LIBYA AND THE WEST

went unpaid. Military setbacks in Chad, the series of defeats to the US Navy, and an inability to defend the country against US airstrikes signaled widespread incompetence and sapped morale. The collapse of the Soviet Union, a traditional supplier of weaponry, and the imposition of UN sanctions ended the import of arms for most of the 1990s.[49]

Did Qaddafi face threats of internal rebellion?

By the late 1980s, rebelliousness simmered among the Libyan people. Falling oil revenues led to a curtailment of social services, food distribution, and the patronage that had won the loyalty, or at least the tolerance, of the people. The debilitating military involvement in Chad and the country's vulnerability to US military attacks demoralized the armed forces and eroded popular confidence in the regime.

Islamic political activism posed a growing threat to the Qaddafi regime. Across the Middle East, Islamic identity and militance rose after the Iranian Revolution of 1979 and as the *mujahedeen* resisted the Soviet occupation of Afghanistan in the 1980s. The Algerian army's cancellation of that country's 1992 elections—a step taken to prevent an Islamist takeover of the government—energized Libyan Islamists. Enjoying sanctuary in Sudan, Osama bin Laden, head of the al-Qaida network, perpetrated violence on behalf of what he considered Islamic interests. Within Libya, the Muslim Brotherhood, which had been overpowered by Qaddafi in the early years of his rule, began to rebuild chapters in some mosques. Such markers of Islamist identity as beards on men and hijabs on women grew more common within Libya. After Qaddafi crushed Islamist rebellions in 1987 and 1989, he encouraged his people to "decapitate" Islamists "as if you had found a wolf, fox, or a scorpion. This is a poison. This is a devil. This is a heretic."[50]

The most acute Islamist threat to Qaddafi came from the Libyan Islamic Fighting Group (LIFG), based in Cyrenaica and composed of Libyans who had ventured to Afghanistan to fight with the *mujahedeen* and who aspired to replace Qaddafi with an Islamist government. In February 1996, Islamists planted a bomb on a road where Qaddafi's limousine was expected to travel, but the bomb detonated when the wrong car passed over it, killing members of Qaddafi's entourage but not the leader. (Evidence that emerged later indicated the possibility that British government intelligence officers had conspired with the Islamists in planning this attack.)[51] On May 31, 1998, Qaddafi survived another assassination attempt when Islamist militants fired on his motorcade as it traveled through eastern Libya. Formation of such other groups as Ansar Allah and the Libyan Patriots Movement in 1996–1997 signaled growth in the popularity of Islamism.[52]

Sensing a serious threat to his power, Qaddafi strenuously suppressed Islamism in all its manifestations. He publicly ridiculed Islamists as lazy and thoughtless. Beginning in 1995, his security services arrested and imprisoned hundreds of suspected Islamists, thoroughly suppressing a conspiracy among LIFG leaders. Following an uprising by Islamists at the notorious Abu Slim prison, government forces shot dead more than 1,200 political prisoners. Under a 1997 collective punishment law, the regime levied penalties (such as curtailment of public utilities) on the families or tribes of Islamists as a means of deterrence on political activity. Identified as a locus of anti-Qaddafi Islamist sentiment, Benghazi was subject to crippling financial sanctions. When Army units sent to patrol Cyrenaica reportedly cavorted with rebels, Qaddafi dispatched his Security Brigades as well as warplanes piloted by Cubans and Serbs to attack rebel strongholds.[53]

Qaddafi also faced rebelliousness within his professional armed services. In 1993, Army officers belonging to the Warfalla tribe plotted to assassinate Qaddafi in their tribal stronghold, Bani Walid. The Warfalla had been one of the three tribes most loyal to Qaddafi and had dominated the army's officer corps. Upset by exclusions from the air force and by other tribal rivalries, the Warfalla officers rebelled against the bankruptcy of the revolution and Qaddafi's growing reliance on the Security Brigades, which were dominated by relatives of Qaddafi, to defend the state. Qaddafi's personal security force detected and crushed the Warfalla conspiracy, arresting its perpetrators and eventually executing the ringleaders. Qaddafi thereafter generated competition within and among the major tribes over outward demonstrations of loyalty to the regime, arresting the larger threat of rebellion based on tribalism, and he further downgraded the importance of the army.[54]

5

THE RAPPROCHEMENT BETWEEN QADDAFI AND THE WEST, EARLY 2000S

How was the controversy over the Lockerbie bombing resolved?

Following the UN Security Council's sanctions against Libya in April 1992, a complex legal stand-off ensued for six years between the United States and Britain, on the one hand, and Libya, on the other. Initially, Libya refused to comply with the demands of the Western powers to extradite the two named defendants for trial in Scotland, contending—correctly—that under the Montreal Convention of 1971, it was not obligated to extradite the two suspects but rather could try them within its own legal system. The Western powers rejected that view on the suspicion that Qaddafi would order Libyan courts to exonerate the accused.

Meanwhile, the international sanctions gradually inflicted considerable harm on Libya's economy. By 2003, annual oil production fell to 1.5 million barrels per day, the lowest rate since the 1960s. Because the Libyan government derived 75 percent of its revenue from oil, it was forced to freeze wages and hiring. Through the 1990s, unemployment reached levels of 25 to 30 percent and inflation 50 percent. Young adults murmured in discontent, and Islamist groups like the Muslim Brotherhood grew more popular. Qaddafi estimated that, between 1992 and 2001, UN sanctions cost his regime $26.5 billion.[1]

140 LIBYA AND THE WEST

Given the toll of sanctions, the government in Tripoli searched for a compromise. It offered to extradite the two defendants to Malta, where their alleged criminal deeds occurred, but Britain and the United States refused that proposal. Hoping to avoid the appearance of a total capitulation, Libya offered, in 1994, to extradite the accused for a trial in a Scottish court provided the court sat in a neutral state such as the Netherlands. Britain and the United States also refused that proposal, and the deadlock persisted.

By 1998, however, the sanctions regime began to crumble, convincing the Western powers to reconsider Qaddafi's 1994 offer. The Arab League and the Organization of African States indicated diminishing enthusiasm for sanctions and pressed the Western powers to compromise. Shifting from a pan-Arab to a pan-African foreign policy, Qaddafi directed foreign aid to 11 states in the Organization of African Unity, which resumed civilian flights to Tripoli in violation of the UN resolutions. China and Russia expressed interest in resuming trade with Libya. Citing "positive results" in religious freedom for Libya's 50,000 Catholics, the Vatican established diplomatic relations with Qaddafi's government in March 1997, and Pope John Paul II thereafter called for "an end without delay" of the sanctions. In addition, the International Court of Justice (ICJ) confirmed Libya's claim that it could satisfy its legal obligations under the Montreal Convention by trying the two suspects in a Libyan court.[2]

Support for the UN sanctions ebbed even within the NATO alliance. In 1996, Italian Foreign Minister Lamberto Dini used Italy's presidency of the European Union to explore whether Libya was prepared to embark upon a more stable relationship. To discuss that possibility, Libyan Foreign Minister Omar al-Muntasser visited Rome on July 18, 1997, in a clear violation of the sanctions resolutions. On July 4, 1998, Dini and Muntasser signed the Italo–Libyan Joint Communication in Rome, pledging to "develop bilateral relations based on equality, mutual respect, and cooperation in order to promote interests and welfare among the populations" as well as "peace and stability in the Mediterranean area and its economic development."[3]

Recognizing the unsustainability of universal sanctions, the United States and Britain decided, in 1998, to accept the terms Libya had offered in 1994 as a path to resolve the Pan Am 103 deadlock. After months of diplomatic negotiations arbitrated by such statesmen as South African President Nelson Mandela and Saudi Arabian King Fahd, the two Western powers and Libya settled on specific terms of a deal. Qaddafi would surrender the accused, Abdelbaset al-Megrahi and Al-Amin Khalifa Fhimah, for a trial in a Scottish court based in the Netherlands, at which time the UN sanctions would be suspended. To avoid any peril of arrest while in transit, the two defendants would be flown to the Netherlands on a non-stop flight under UN custody. The trial would focus solely on the charges pertaining to Pan Am 103. If acquitted, the defendants would be returned promptly to Libya. If convicted, they would be jailed at Barlinnie Prison in Scotland, and Britain would allow Libya to open a consular office in Glasgow to monitor their confinement even though the two countries did not have diplomatic relations. Based on these terms, Qaddafi extradited Megrahi and Fhimah to the Netherlands on April 5, 1999, and the UN Security Council immediately suspended (but did not formally revoke) the sanctions resolutions.

Did Qaddafi otherwise moderate his foreign policy?

In addition to compromising on the Lockerbie issue, Qaddafi moderated his overall foreign policy in the late 1990s. The collapse of the Soviet Union made him feel vulnerable to Western pressures. He also observed that other developing and non-aligned countries downplayed anti-imperialism and embraced economic globalization, that other African states resented his interference in their affairs, and that Libya's strident anti-Zionism fell out of step with the policies of other Arab powers. These factors, combined with the economic pain inflicted by sanctions, incentivized Qaddafi to transition away from the radical policies he had pursued in previous decades. "The world has changed radically and drastically," Qaddafi declared, shortly after announcing that he would extradite the Lockerbie suspects. "The methods and ideas should change, and being a revolutionary and a progressive man, I have to follow this movement."[4]

By the late 1990s, Qaddafi signaled that he sought more stable relations with Western powers. Having harbored the terrorist Abu Nidal for a decade, in 1997 or 1998 Qaddafi expelled him, seized his funds, and broke up his terrorist training camps. In the late 1990s, Qaddafi reversed his earlier tendencies to stir up armed rebellions in sub-Saharan Africa. He accepted the 1994 ICJ ruling on the Aouzou Strip dispute with Chad. He repaired relations with Egypt and collaborated with that state in formulating a plan to end civil warfare in Sudan. Qaddafi arbitrated settlement of a violent conflict between Uganda and the Congo and sent Libyan soldiers to Uganda to enforce it.[5]

Qaddafi also moderated his pan-Arabist legacy. In the late 1990s, he suspended his criticism of the Oslo peace process involving Israel and the Palestinians. He mended his troubled political relationship with Palestinian leader Yasser Arafat, recognizing the Palestine Liberation Organization (PLO) as the sole representative of the Palestinian people, allowing the opening of a PLO office in Tripoli, and instructing all Palestinian factions in Libya to submit to the PLO's direction. Arafat's attendance at a September 1999 summit of Arab leaders in Tripoli marking the thirtieth anniversary of the Libyan revolution symbolized a dramatic shift in Qaddafi's policy. While Qaddafi issued strongly worded verbal support of the Palestinian cause during the Second Intifada in the early 2000s, he refrained from offering any form of military aid that would have risked Israeli retaliation or US censure. Qaddafi valued his budding rapprochement with the West more than his earlier image as a radical pan-Arab leader.[6]

Qaddafi gave ground to his son Saif al-Islam Qaddafi, who emerged in the early 2000s as a dynamic personality with reformist inclinations. Through the Qaddafi International Foundation for Charitable Associations that he had established in 1997, Saif negotiated settlements of foreign claims on Libya for its past terrorist acts. In flawless English learned while a graduate student in London, Saif spoke regularly to the Western media, paying respect to democracy and the rule of law. "Libya is now ready to transform decades of mutual antagonism into an era of genuine friendship," he declared in 2003, in hope of winning the confidence of Western leaders. "The old times are finished," he told the Davos economic conference in 2005, in hope of impressing foreign investors, "and Libya is ready to move onto a new stage of modernization." In terms of foreign policy, Qaddafi allowed a group of reform-minded advisers to exert influence. Determined to end Libya's period of international isolation, Saif allied with such like-minded officials as Foreign Minister Abdel Rahman Shalgam, Chief of External Security Musa Kusa, Ambassador to Rome Abdul Ati al-Obeidi, and Ambassador to London Mohamed Abdul Qasim Zwai to counsel Qaddafi to transform his foreign policy by cooperating with Western powers.[7]

What verdict did the Scottish court reach in the Lockerbie trial?

The Lockerbie trial was held over 85 days between May 3, 2000, and January 31, 2001. Prosecutors presented circumstantial evidence that linked the bomb materials to the Libyan military, that connected the suitcase that contained the bomb and contents of the suitcase to the two defendants, and that placed the two defendants in Malta on the day the bomb was supposedly checked into the luggage system there. The court found Megrahi guilty of mass murder but did not convict Fhimah. Acknowledging that the evidence was circumstantial, the three judges concluded that "there is nothing in the evidence which leaves us with any reasonable doubt as to the guilt" of

144 LIBYA AND THE WEST

Megrahi. Fhimah was promptly released, and Megrahi was sentenced to 27 years in prison. Qaddafi criticized this outcome and refused to accept official responsibility for the crime, and Libyan Ambassador to the European Union Hamed al-Hudhairy called the verdict "a political decision." Libyan citizens protested the guilty verdict in front of the British embassy and the UN office in Tripoli.[8]

Was Megrahi actually guilty?

After the trial, significant doubts were aired about the guilty verdict. Various legal experts found inconsistencies in the witnesses' testimony and noted that potentially exculpatory evidence was never investigated. An Austrian who served as one of five UN observers at the trial called it "a rather spectacular case of a miscarriage of justice." In 2007, one of the key eyewitnesses confessed that he had lied about the origins of the bomb's timer. These discrepancies left many experts and journalists convinced that the trial scapegoated Megrahi for the political motive of pressuring the Qaddafi regime. Nelson Mandela, other prominent leaders, and even the families of some of the victims lobbied for Megrahi's release from prison. Megrahi lost an appeal to the Scottish Court in 2002, however, and the US and British governments consistently argued that he was guilty.[9]

In 2005, Megrahi was transferred to a more modern prison in Inverclyde, Scotland. Three years later, he was diagnosed with terminal cancer. Over protests by US President Barack Obama and many victims' families, Scotland granted Megrahi a humanitarian release from prison in August 2009, on the condition that he would not appeal his guilty verdict. Megrahi flew home to a hero's welcome in Libya. He died in 2012.[10]

After Qaddafi's death in 2011, former officials of his regime linked Qaddafi—although inconclusively—to the bombings of Pan Am Flight 103 and UTA Flight 772. Mustafa Abdel Jalil, Qaddafi's Minister of Justice who defected from the regime to lead an anti-Qaddafi rebel group, claimed to have "information that is one hundred percent sure that Gaddafi [Qaddafi] is behind the tragedy at Lockerbie," although he never produced proof of his claim. Admitting that Libya was entirely responsible for the UTA bomb, former Foreign Minister Shalgam said that "the Lockerbie operation was far more complex. While the Libyan services were implicated, I do not think it was purely a Libyan operation."[11]

What effect did the Lockerbie trial have on Libya's relations with Western powers?

The compromises that resulted in the Lockerbie trial opened an era of normalization in the relationships between Western powers and Libya. His energy for revolutionary change within Libya depleted, Qaddafi essentially decided to escape the UN sanctions and stabilize his country within the world order. Western leaders saw opportunities to reshape the Libyan state and to renew their access to its oil. This convergence of interests generated momentum toward more stable relations between Libya and the West.

European powers immediately took steps to renew interactions with Libya. Italy was especially eager to restore its oil trade. On April 6, 1999, one day after the United Nations suspended sanctions, Foreign Minister Dini visited Tripoli, applauding Libya for extraditing the two Lockerbie suspects and declaring that he hoped for "a full reintegration of Libya into the International community." At the conclusion of the meeting, Qaddafi declared that "Libya will become Italy's bridge to Africa, . . . and Italy will become Libya's door to Europe." Before Dini returned for a second visit in August, the Italian oil company Ente Nazionale Idrocarburi (ENI) and the Libyan National Oil Company formed the Western Libya Gas Project to explore for natural gas and market it in Europe. In December, Prime Minister Massimo D'Alema became the first Western head of government to visit Tripoli since 1991.

146 LIBYA AND THE WEST

D'Alema and Qaddafi issued a joint statement condemning terrorism, and the Italian leader called on the United States to improve relations with Libya. In December 2000, Italy and Libya signed another agreement to collaborate in law enforcement, counterterrorism, and immigration control.[12]

Other European powers more conditionally tried to improve relations with Libya. France moved to resolve the dispute over the 1989 bombing of UTA Flight 772. In March 1999, a French court tried in absentia, convicted, and sentenced to life imprisonment six Libyans—including Qaddafi's brother-in-law Abdullah al-Senussi—for their involvement in the attack. Qaddafi refused to admit responsibility for the bombing or to surrender the defendants, but, in July, he agreed to pay $34 million in compensation to the families of the victims as well as the airline and its insurer. The same month, Qaddafi accepted responsibility for the killing of the British police officer who was shot dead from within the Libyan People's Bureau in London in 1984, and he agreed to pay compensation to her family. Britain promptly restored diplomatic relations with Libya. In September 1999, the European Union announced that it would resume economic trade with Libya, excluding weapons.

By contrast to its European allies, the United States remained relatively cautious about normalizing relations with Libya. Despite feeling pressure from the international community to end sanctions after Qaddafi's Lockerbie concession, President Bill Clinton made clear that the lifting of sanctions and the restoration of formal diplomatic relations remained contingent on Libya's willingness to renounce terrorism and weapons of mass destruction, promote regional stability, and accept financial responsibility for the Lockerbie bombing. Accordingly, his administration affirmed the continuation of the US sanctions on Libya that predated the 1992 UN sanctions.

In practice, the United States took a few steps toward improved relations with Libya but also clarified limits. Clinton approved a meeting between US and Libyan diplomats at the

United Nations in June 1999, on the condition that Qaddafi would refrain from lobbying for the end of sanctions. At that gathering—the first official meeting between the two countries in 18 years—Qaddafi expressed concern with Islamic radicalism, offered to cooperate with the US efforts to defeat Osama bin Laden's al-Qaida network, and pledged to break ties with radical Palestinian groups and endorse the Arab–Israeli peace process. US officials acknowledged these steps but also reiterated their broader expectations. While the Clinton administration allowed some agricultural sales to Libya and authorized US oil companies to resume exploratory work in Libya, it blocked a sale of European aircraft to Libya because they contained US-made parts that were subject to the embargo. In March 2000, US foreign service officers traveled to Libya to discuss resumption of civilian air travel, but the administration renewed the ban on such travel later in the year.[13]

What was the impact of 9/11 on the US–Libyan relationship?

President George W. Bush occupied the White House in January 2001, intent on continuing sanctions on Libya until Qaddafi met the conditions articulated by President Clinton. In August 2001, Bush signed into law a bill that extended the Iran and Libya Sanctions Act of 1996 for an additional five years.

The September 11, 2001, terrorist attacks on New York and Washington, however, broke the ice on US–Libyan relations. Qaddafi expressed sympathy for the United States, extended condolences to the American people, and organized blood drives to support the victims symbolically. He publicly justified the US invasion of Afghanistan as an act of self-defense. Having come to fear Islamic militarism as a threat to his own regime, Qaddafi was pleased to see US military power applied against it. He shared with Western powers Libyan intelligence on Islamic terrorists operating in the Middle East and Europe.

148 LIBYA AND THE WEST

How did the 9/11 breakthrough contribute to the settlement of the Lockerbie issue?

Determined to escape the burden of international sanctions, Qaddafi made further concessions on the Lockerbie issues in the aftermath of 9/11. Specifically, he accepted US demands that he must accept responsibility for the bombing and pay compensation to the families of the victims. Terms were negotiated in secret talks between US Assistant Secretary of State William Burns and Musa Kusa, the Libyan intelligence officer and Qaddafi confidante. In a deal reached in August 2003, Libya agreed to pay $2.7 billion in compensation to the families of the 270 Lockerbie victims, at the rate of $10 million per victim and on a schedule of 40 percent when UN sanctions were lifted, 40 percent when US sanctions were lifted, and 20 percent when the US State Department removed Libya from its list of state sponsors of terrorism. Libya recorded its responsibility for the Lockerbie bomb in an August 16 letter from Libyan UN Representative Ahmed Own to the Security Council president. Libya "has facilitated the bringing to justice of the two suspects charged with the bombing of Pan Am 103," Own wrote, "and accepts responsibility for the actions of its officials."[14]

How did France respond to the Lockerbie settlement?

France was unhappy about the discrepancy between the value of compensation that Libya paid for the UTA bombing and for the Pan Am Lockerbie bombing. The $34 million that France had accepted in 1999 as UTA compensation equated to an average of $200,000 for each of the 170 passengers killed in the attack, whereas the Pan Am Lockerbie settlement averaged $10 million per victim. To make the imbalance worse, French officials pointed out, most of the $34 million was directed to the airline and its insurance company, while the families of the victims received only $3,000 to $30,000 each. The French government demanded that Libya rectify the inequity before France would agree to any action normalizing relations with Libya. France even indicated that it would veto any UN Security Council resolution to lift sanctions on Libya—which was a precondition of Libya's payout to the Lockerbie families. That threat angered the families of the Lockerbie victims, who decried it as a form of blackmail.

After months of diplomacy, Qaddafi and French president Jacques Chirac reached a settlement on September 1, 2003. Libya agreed to pay an additional $170 million in compensation for the UTA attack, directly to the families of those killed, at the rate of $1 million per victim. The funds were provided by the Qaddafi Foundation—technically a private charity associated with Saif Qaddafi—in an agreement formally signed in January 2004 by the foundation and a private entity representing the families of the victims. Neither Libya nor France was a party to the agreement.

Although the government of Libya refused to admit any official responsibility for the UTA bombing, the agreement fostered a new era in French–Libyan relations. Shortly after the formal settlement was signed, French Foreign Minister Dominique de Villepin met with Libyan Foreign Minister Shalgam, declaring that "all of our relations will benefit from a new dynamism from today, this new stage that's opening."[15]

On what terms did the United Nations lift its sanctions against Libya?

On September 12, 2003, the UN Security Council passed Resolution 1506, formally ending sanctions on Libya, by a vote of 13–0, with the United States and France abstaining. The resolution found that Libya had complied with the conditions stipulated in the original sanctions resolutions "concerning acceptance of responsibility for the actions of Libyan officials, payment of appropriate compensation, renunciation of terrorism,

150 LIBYA AND THE WEST

and a commitment to cooperating with any further requests for information in connection with the investigation."[16]

The United States abstained to reinforce its own additional expectations that Libya would address such other issues as production of WMD, meddling in Africa, human rights abuses, and authoritarianism. The Bush administration made clear that it would maintain unilateral sanctions as a lever in such matters. France abstained to signal its abiding displeasure with the UTA attack and its inability to achieve financial equity with the Lockerbie settlement. The two Western powers did not veto the measure, however, because they feared that such a step would undermine their economic interests when international commerce in Libya eventually resumed.[17]

When did Libya decide to renounce its weapons of mass destruction programs?

On December 19, 2003, Qaddafi announced his commitment to dismantle all WMD programs. Although that action surprised many Western officials, it marked a culmination of several years of diplomatic negotiations and Qaddafi's ongoing reassessment of his country's international disposition.

As Libya became more cooperative with the West on such issues as the Lockerbie trial and the compensation terms, it also expressed interest in renouncing its quest for WMD in exchange for concessions. At the secret negotiations in May 1999 on the Lockerbie issue, the Libyan envoy Kusa indicated a willingness to discuss WMD, and, by October, he added that Qaddafi would consider signing the Chemical Weapons Convention and submitting to international inspections. US and British officials affirmed that they would expect a renunciation of WMD before complete normalization of relations, but they also downplayed the issue because the Lockerbie and terrorism issues seemed more urgent and because Libya was not believed to be reaching WMD capacity at a rapid pace.[18]

As US and Libyan officials found common cause resisting Islamic extremists after 9/11, the two powers closed the gap between them on the WMD issue. President Bush was sufficiently encouraged to omit Libya from what he defined in January 2002 as the "Axis of Evil," those nations capable of using terrorism and WMD to upend the international order. (Bush limited the Axis to North Korea, Iran, and Iraq.) Libya signed the International Code of Conduct against Ballistic Missile Proliferation in November 2002, and raised the possibility that it would sign the Comprehensive Test Ban Treaty and the Chemical Weapons Convention.

In late 2002, British officials facilitated conversations on WMD with the United States and Libya (represented by Saif Qaddafi). On a visit to Tripoli in August, Foreign Minister Michael O'Brien secured Qaddafi's assurance that he was ready to make a deal. The next month, Prime Minister Tony Blair secured President Bush's agreement that the renunciation of WMD would lead to normal relations and conveyed those terms to Qaddafi.[19]

Yet Western experts continued to monitor with concern evidence of Libya's ongoing WMD efforts. Libya developed its ability to enrich uranium, secured uranium hexafluoride, acquired a blueprint for a nuclear weapon from the A. Q. Khan network, reportedly received Nodong ballistic missiles and technical advisers from North Korea, and showed interest in biological weapons capacities. Suspicious about Qaddafi's ultimate intentions, President Bush named Libya as one of four states targeted in a new US initiative of December 2002 to stanch the proliferation of WMD via multiple means, including possible preemptive military action against any state found to be on the cusp of acquiring WMD capacity.[20]

The diplomacy on Libya's WMD reached a breakthrough once the August 2003 Lockerbie settlement and the September 2003 revocation of UN sanctions improved Libya's relationships with the Western powers. In October, Libya allowed inspections by US and British officials of its

152 LIBYA AND THE WEST

WMD-related military, industrial, and scientific facilities. In the same month, US and Italian authorities detained the German ship *BBC China* in the port of Taranto, Italy, and seized a load of centrifuge components being shipped to Libya (in containers labeled as used machine parts) from the A. Q. Khan network. In several days of intense negotiations among US, British, and Libyan officials—which included the first-ever phone call between Blair and Qaddafi—the United States offered to lift its unilateral sanctions if Qaddafi would renounce WMD. Accepting those terms, Qaddafi requested and received a pledge by the United States and Britain that if he surrendered the deterrent effect implicit in WMD capacity, they would refrain from seeking to remove him from power.[21]

Libya thus made its surprise public announcement on December 19, 2003. Foreign Minister Shalgam revealed that the Qaddafi government "has decided of its free will to get rid of these materials, equipment and programs, and to become totally free of internationally banned weapons." The Bush administration announced that Libya had pledged specifically to eliminate all its nuclear, chemical, and biological weapons programs; eliminate ballistic missiles with a range of more than 300 kilometers or a payload capacity greater than 500 kilograms; sign all relevant arms control treaties; and allow international inspections of all WMD sites to verify compliance.[22]

Why did Libya decide to renounce its weapons of mass destruction programs?

Qaddafi decided on the momentous step of WMD renunciation on the calculation that his pursuit of WMD had become an impediment rather than an asset to his security. His WMD programs had consumed resources and earned international isolation, both of which undermined the economic and social interests of his people. He consequently faced a growing threat of Islamic militancy within his own country, while progress in the Arab–Israeli peace process diminished the likelihood of a hostile encounter with Israel. The United States seemed determined to maintain sanctions as long as he pursued WMD. On balance, the lifting of the US sanctions would prove more valuable to Qaddafi than an immature WMD program actively resisted by the Western powers.[23]

Did the US and British invasion of Iraq in March 2003 influence Qaddafi's decision to renounce WMD?

There is some controversy over the extent to which the invasion of Iraq compelled Qaddafi to surrender his WMD programs by raising his fears that the weapons programs made him vulnerable to a similar military attack. "To an extent that cannot be precisely measured," the *New York Times* editorialized, "the fate of [Iraqi president] Saddam Hussein, who was ousted from power by the American military with British backing after endless prevaricating about Iraqi weapons programs, must have been an important consideration in Libya's decision." Recounting the diplomacy leading to Qaddafi's December 19, 2003, renunciation, President Bush strongly implied such causation in his January 2004 State of the Union address. "For diplomacy to be effective, words must be credible," he intoned. "And no one can now doubt the word of America."[24]

There are reasons to be skeptical of this interpretation. Libya first considered dismantling its WMD programs in the late 1990s, when Libyan diplomats broached the topic with British officials. Qaddafi's inclination to disarm gained considerable momentum before the invasion of Iraq and for reasons pertaining to Libyan security per se. Critics of the US invasion of Iraq suggest that Bush exaggerated its effect on Libya because he was embarrassed that the absence of WMD in Iraq had undermined his justification for the invasion. As Martin Indyk, who had represented the Clinton administration in the early conversation with Libya, concluded succinctly, "Libyan disarmament did not require a war in Iraq."[25]

154 LIBYA AND THE WEST

How did Libya and Western powers follow up on the WMD deal?

Under the supervision of Western officials, Libya fulfilled its pledge to shut down its WMD programs. In December 2003, Libya turned over to International Atomic Energy Agency inspectors the nuclear weapon design plans it had secured from the A. Q. Khan network. Those plans were among 55 tons of materials including uranium hexafluoride, centrifuges, and documents that were airlifted to the United States in January 2004. In that same month, Libya acceded to the Chemical Weapons Convention and ratified the Comprehensive Test Ban Treaty. In March, it declared to the Organization for the Prohibition of Chemical Weapons (OPCW) that it had 23 tons of mustard gas produced at Rabta in the 1980s, and the OPCW supervised the destruction of 3,200 empty gas shell casings. By April, an additional 1,000 tons of centrifuges, missiles, and missile launchers were removed from Libya, and Russia hauled away 13 kilograms of enriched uranium it had supplied for the Tajura reactor.[26]

To reward Libya for these actions, the Western powers took steps to integrate Libya into the international order. In February 2004, the United States opened an Interests Section in the Belgian Embassy in Tripoli, and, in July, Libya opened an Interests Section at the United Arab Emirates Embassy in Washington. In March, Assistant Secretary of State Burns attended a meeting in Tripoli, becoming the highest-ranking US official to visit the country in 30 years. As Libya fulfilled its WMD pledges in stages, the Bush administration eased travel restrictions in February, removed some trade restrictions in April, and unfroze $1.3 billion in Libyan assets and restored all civilian air traffic in September.

In March 2004, Prime Minister Blair met Qaddafi in his signature tent near Tripoli and shook his hand in front of news cameras as a symbol that Qaddafi was reformed. The first British leader to visit Libya since Winston Churchill inspected British troops there in 1943, Blair declared that he was "reaching out the hand of partnership" to demonstrate that "it is possible for countries in the Arab world to work with the United States and the U.K. to defeat the common enemy of extremist fanatical terrorism driven by Al Qaeda."[27]

European Commission President Roman Prodi invited Qaddafi to Brussels to discuss Libyan membership in the Euro-Mediterranean Partnership, which aimed to promote free trade in North Africa, and in the World Trade Organization. Although Qaddafi publicly censured Europe's legacy of colonialism and warned that unfriendly policies might force Libya to resume violence, he also declared that "Libya, which led the liberation struggle in the Third World, has decided to lead the peace movement all over the world. . . . The time has now come to reap the fruits of this armed struggle, namely peace, stability, development."[28]

The Western powers also authorized oil firms to resume operations in Libya. The Anglo-Dutch firm Royal Dutch Shell signed a $200 million gas exploration deal with Libya, announced during Blair's March 2004 visit to Tripoli. In August, for first time in decades, Libya opened a competitive bidding process for new oil exploration concessions. Some 120 companies made bids, and, in 2005, 15 of them (11 of which were US) were selected to move forward to contracts. The 15 firms pledged to pay a total of $133 million at the outset of their work and to spend a minimum of $300 million on prospecting, with Libya poised to collect 60 to 90 percent of their eventual earnings. Given the uncertainty that the invasion of Iraq had cast over that country's oilfields, Western companies were enthused about resuming their operation in Libya.

How did French–Libyan relations evolve after sanctions were lifted?

Under the influence of Nicolas Sarkozy, France moved quickly to restore relations with Libya. As France's Minister of the Interior, Sarkozy visited Qaddafi in Tripoli on October 6, 2005,

156 LIBYA AND THE WEST

in the aftermath of the UTA settlement, in hope of achieving cooperation on counterterrorism and immigration controls. Soon after becoming president of France on May 16, 2007, Sarkozy negotiated several lucrative deals, worth several billion dollars, to sell Libya military fighter jets, anti-tank weapons, helicopters, communications gear, radar systems, and civilian aircraft. In December 2007, Sarkozy welcomed Qaddafi during an official visit in Paris, the Libyan leader's first ever to a Western country, and Qaddafi stayed for several days to sightsee.

The meeting in Paris was not without trouble. Qaddafi contested Sarkozy's proposal to build a so-called Mediterranean Union because it would rival the Arab League and the African Union. During Qaddafi's sightseeing tour of Paris, human rights activists greeted his entourage with furious protests, which put political pressure on Sarkozy to speak firmly to Qaddafi about his abysmal human rights record. Rather than submit, Qaddafi reciprocated by making an unscheduled visit to the UNESCO headquarters in Paris, where he levied charges that the European powers maltreated African immigrants, and publicly disputing Sarkozy's claims that he had spoken firmly to Qaddafi on human rights.[29]

What was the nature of Italy's relationship with Libya?

Italy emerged as a champion of reintegrating Libya into international relationships. As early as 2000, Italy and Libya signed an agreement to cooperate in countering terrorism, drug trafficking, organized crime, and illegal immigration. The following year, Prime Minister Silvio Berlusconi approved a Treaty of Friendship, Cooperation, and Good Neighbor Policy with Libya and began a series of visits to the North African country to promote trade ties. By 2004, Qaddafi agreed to consider compensating the 6,000 Libyan Jews who had been expelled from the country in 1967 and readmitting some of the 20,000 Libyan-born Italians who had been expelled in 1970.

As US and British ties with Libya improved, ironically, Italy's relationship with Libya experienced turbulence. In 2002, Qaddafi demanded that Italy pay reparations to Libya for losses incurred during the colonial era. In 2004, a spike in unauthorized immigration from Africa led Italy to charge that Libya was not policing its borders as it had agreed to do. Italian firms operating in Libya noted a chilling of the business atmosphere, and Libya failed to name an ambassador to Rome from October 2004 to July 2006, which Italy viewed as a sign of political discontent. The relationship hit bottom in February 2006, when Italian Reforms Minister Roberto Calderoli publicly supported the Danish artist who had published cartoons unfavorably depicting the Prophet Mohammed. Although Berlusconi asked Calderoli to resign, a mob of demonstrators set fire to the Italian consulate in Benghazi.

The relationship improved again by 2008. Berlusconi and Qaddafi signed a new Treaty of Friendship, Partnership, and Cooperation, in which Italy pledged $5 billion over 20 years as compensation for its colonial past while Libya opened itself to Italian investment and pledged to stem immigration. The Italian firm ENI pledged to invest $28 billion in Libya, extend oil and gas contracts to 2020, and develop new oilfields. In March 2010, Berlusconi visited Tripoli and kissed Qaddafi's hand in a symbolic gesture of friendship.[30]

Why did the United States restore diplomatic relations with Libya?

Despite the dramatic changes in Libya's foreign policy, the United States delayed the restoration of diplomatic relations with Libya through 2005 because the government in Tripoli remained authoritarian and in violation of human rights protocols. In addition, intelligence officials detected evidence that Qaddafi might have been involved in a planned terrorist attack in Saudi Arabia.

158 LIBYA AND THE WEST

By early 2006, however, President Bush was persuaded by the overall trajectory of Libyan behavior to extend diplomatic recognition. On May 15, Secretary of State Condoleezza Rice announced that the United States would restore relations with Libya and remove Libya from the State Department's list of state sponsors of terrorism. "We are taking these actions," she declared, "in recognition of Libya's continued commitment to its renunciation of terrorism and the excellent cooperation Libya has provided to the United States and other members of the international community in response to common global threats faced by the civilized world since September 11, 2001." Within a few weeks, the US Embassy in Tripoli reopened for the first time since 1980, and the Libyan Embassy in Washington reopened for the first time since 1981.[31]

While their relations improved thereafter, the United States and Libya did not resolve all differences. The two powers signed agreements on trade, security, and counterterrorism in the years that followed the reopening of embassies. Yet the State Department consistently labeled Libya an "authoritarian" state with a "poor" human rights record. When Secretary of State Hillary Clinton received Qaddafi's son and envoy Moatassim Qaddafi in Washington, in April 2009, she pressed, without success, for the release of Fathi al-Jahmi, a Libyan dissident jailed since 2002.[32]

What was Qaddafi's international reputation after diplomatic relations were normalized?

To a degree, Qaddafi's reputation among Western powers was rehabilitated. In January 2009, he published a column in the *New York Times* proposing a settlement of the Israeli–Palestinian conflict via the creation of a single, unified state that he referred to as "Isratine." Eight months later, Qaddafi was invited to address the UN General Assembly for the first time in his 40 years in power. Speaking immediately after US President Barack Obama, Qaddafi paid tribute to Obama as the first "son of Africa" to be elected US president and expressed the hope that Obama would remain president indefinitely.[33]

Like his larger reputation, however, Qaddafi's visit to New York did not lack controversy. Libyan dissidents staged mass protests in the streets outside the UN building during his visit. Qaddafi overnighted in the Libyan diplomatic mission after several prominent hotels refused to host him. His usual practice of erecting a tent wherever he traveled as a symbol of his Bedouin roots was stymied because several public and private venues denied him permission to use their land. Critics found Qaddafi's UN address provocative, defiant, and rambling; he spoke for 90 minutes although allotted only 15. He called for prosecution of those who committed "mass murder" in Iraq and defended the Taliban's right to establish an Islamic emirate. He ripped up a copy of the UN Charter and proposed renaming the Security Council the "terror council" because its five permanent members held veto powers. As a rebuke to Qaddafi, British Prime Minister Gordon Brown declared during his own address, "I stand here to reaffirm the United Nations charter, not to tear it up."[34]

As revealed in Qaddafi's General Assembly appearance, Western officials remained concerned by Qaddafi's behavior on international issues even as relations were normalized. When Swiss police arrested Qaddafi's son Hannibal in July 2008, after he allegedly beat his domestic staff in a Geneva hotel room, for example, Qaddafi retaliated by withdrawing $7 billion from Swiss banks, imposing an embargo on Swiss imports and on oil exports to Switzerland, and jailing two Swiss nationals for visa irregularities. When the convicted Lockerbie bomber was granted early release from a Scottish prison on humanitarian grounds in 2009, Qaddafi arranged a hero's welcome for him in Tripoli, which Western officials considered a contradiction of the contrition Libya had previously expressed. Western oil firms reported that their operations in Libya became increasingly difficult in the face of growing corruption, graft, and arcane regulations. In addition, negotiations between Western

160 LIBYA AND THE WEST

firms and Libya on grand schemes to develop critical infrastructure, tourism establishments, industrial facilities, and transportation never materialized amid the firms' doubts about Libya's business environment.

Finally, Western leaders continued to puzzle over Qaddafi's eccentric behaviors, such as his infatuation with Secretary of State Rice. "I support my darling black African woman," Qaddafi declared in a 2007 interview. "I admire and am very proud of the way she leans back and gives orders to the Arab leaders . . . . Leezza, Leezza, Leezza, . . . I love her very much." Despite Qaddafi's "slightly eerie fascination with me personally," Rice recorded, she traveled to Libya in September 2008, in the hope that her visit would mark "a major milestone on the country's path to international acceptability." But Qaddafi acted erratically during their meeting and presented her with a recording featuring a new song called "Black Flower in the White House," which he had commissioned in her honor. "I came away from the visit," Rice later wrote, "realizing how much Qaddafi lives inside his own head, in a kind of alternate reality."[35]

What type of domestic leader did Qaddafi become in the early 2000s?

After the end of UN sanctions in April 1999, the Libyan people anticipated that Qaddafi would use the thirtieth anniversary of his revolution to announce an era of domestic reform that would parallel his new foreign policy. They were disappointed, however, when Qaddafi focused his September 1 anniversary address on such banalities as an automobile that he had designed to avoid accidents. Indeed, Qaddafi generally doubled down on his revolutionary fervor, announcing there would be no political reforms, dissolving the General People's Committee (his cabinet), and declaring that he expected young men to read the *Green Book* and reinvigorate the revolution. As domestic criticism and Islamic rebellion mounted, Qaddafi made a few additional gestures, like abolishing people's courts in 2004 and blaming the deprivations of the 1990s on bureaucrats, although little changed in the political rights or quality of life of the people.

Qaddafi attempted to revitalize Libya's economy in the early 2000s. He solicited foreign investments and signed on to International Monetary Fund regulations that enhanced business prospects. In 2003, he reconstituted his cabinet, naming oil economist Shukri Ghanem as its general secretary (equivalent to prime minister). Ghanem moved to eliminate corruption, downsize Libya's public sector workforce of 800,000 (13 percent of the total population), and privatize hundreds of state-run businesses and eliminate their subsidies. But his efforts were staunchly resisted by government workers who viewed their jobs as entitlements even when little or no work was performed and who saw few opportunities in the private sector. The elites who managed state-subsidized firms also objected strenuously to Ghanem's proposals. Growth in private enterprise was limited generally to hotels and restaurants that catered to Western business executives. Qaddafi fired Ghanem in 2006.

Perhaps as a gambit to build his popularity among the people of Libya, Qaddafi's son Saif al-Islam launched a series of domestic reforms in 2004. Saif led campaigns to recognize victims of human rights abuses, reconnect with Libyan dissidents abroad, and release jailed Islamic militants if they promised to remain apolitical. He offered some $120 million in financial compensation to the families of the 1,200 political prisoners massacred at the Abu Salim prison in 1996. He founded the Al-Ghad media company, which freely published news and dissent. In 2004–2008, Saif headed a committee purportedly charged to write a new constitution, although the effort foundered because the committee could not resolve his erratic and inconsistent proposals on terms.

Saif achieved sufficient stature to generate speculation that his aging father was grooming him for succession to the helm of Libya. Moammar Qaddafi never indicated any intention of transitioning power to anyone, however, and might have allowed his son to crusade as a means of venting popular discontent and raising hopes of a brighter future. Saif's brother Moatassim, who did not share Saif's reformist inclinations, also appeared to be building alliances with conservative elites as part of a possible bid for succession. Critics noted that while Saif shared his father's grandiosity, flamboyance, and distractedness, he also accumulated vast wealth and indulged in an ostentatious lifestyle that stood in stark contrast to his father's Bedouin-rooted, Islamic puritanism.[36]

Despite the reforms promoted by Saif, antiregime resistance festered in some quarters. Given their revulsion at the Western invasions of Afghanistan and Iraq, Islamists became even more disgruntled with Qaddafi after he mended his relations with the Western powers. Many of the families of the victims of the Abu Salim massacre refused to accept the offers of financial compensation, insisting instead that the perpetrators be brought to justice. Meanwhile, the Imazighen of western Libya felt troubled by edicts from Qaddafi requiring the use of Arabic language in their homes and the giving of Arab names to their children. "You can call yourselves whatever you want inside your homes—Berbers [Imazighen], Children of Satan, whatever," Qaddafi callously declared during a visit to an Amazigh community in 2008, "but you are only Libyans when you leave your homes."[37]

6

THE LIBYAN REVOLUTION OF 2011

What were the long-term origins of the Libyan revolution of 2011?

Living conditions that had developed over decades set the stage for an anti-Qaddafi revolt in 2011. To be sure, some measures of quality of life improved in Libya during Muammar al-Qaddafi's decades in power. Life expectancy increased from 51 years to 74 years between 1969 and 2011, while literacy rates reached 88 percent of the population and per capita income grew to $12,000 per year. Qaddafi's stature, however, dimmed in the shadow of his persistent administrative incompetence, corruption, wastefulness, and profligacy. The Libyan people tired of his mercurial leadership style as they suffered persistent economic stagnation, food shortages, and high unemployment. "Corruption was one of the most corrosive elements of Gaddafi's [Qaddafi's] Libya," Lin Noueihed and Alex Warren noted. Having distributed patronage to win the loyalty of select tribal leaders, family members, and potential rivals, Qaddafi had neglected to build strong state institutions, such as a national military or a professional civil service, and private entities, such as labor unions or political parties. "For all Qaddafi's pretensions of ideological revolution and professed commitment to ruling on behalf of a people who loved him," Jason Pack observed, "his regime had become an old-fashioned

164 **LIBYA AND THE WEST**

family dictatorship." Denied any legitimate forms of political discourse or dissent, the Libyan people gravitated into tribal and familial networks and gradually came to view violent rebellion as their best, if not only, option to remedy their intolerable circumstances.[1]

Qaddafi's failure to develop a sense of national identity meant that historic schisms among the people of Libya persisted. Having always bristled at their loss of authority from the Senussi era and at the discrimination the state levied against them, Cyrenaicans periodically had attempted rebellions, and they remained poised for opportunities to try again. The Imazighen and other non-Arab tribes of western and southern Libya resented the regime's pan-Arabism pursuits. The rise of Islamic militancy in the 1990s exacerbated the mounting disloyalty of the people, especially in Cyrenaica, where clerics affiliated with the Muslim Brotherhood urged the faithful to join protest movements against the Qaddafi regime.[2]

An important generational shift also made the country more prone to rebellion. Composing one-third of Libya's population in the early 2000s, young adults (ages 15–29) faced daunting levels of unemployment and food shortages. They saw few opportunities for personal advancement within Libya. Exposed via cellphones, social media, and other new technologies to ideas, values, material objects, and inspirations from other countries, they were able to visualize alternatives to the corrupt, isolated, and decrepit regime under which they had been born. More highly educated and better informed than their elders, young adults were able to imagine active resistance to rather than passive acceptance of the conditions they faced.[3]

What were the immediate triggers of the Libyan uprising?

The immediate triggers of the Libyan revolt were uprisings in Tunisia and Egypt that marked the start of the Arab Spring, a wave of unrest that swept across the Arab world. Over decades, conditions had developed in many Arab states that rendered them vulnerable to revolt. Authoritarian regimes repressed political aspirations and prevented peaceful means of redress. Class inequality, economic sluggishness, and rising food prices generated mass discontent and anxiety. A surging population of young adults enjoyed few opportunities for personal or professional fulfillment. The growing availability of cellphones and social media created new opportunities for dissenters to organize collective action.

The Arab Spring revolts erupted suddenly in late 2010. As Joel S. Migdal observed, "the upheaval in the Middle East . . . surprised everyone, including Washington policy makers."[4]

In Tunisia, to Libya's west, a spontaneous uprising in late December led to the resignation of President Zine El Abidine Ben Ali on January 14, 2011, after 23 years in office. Then, a mass uprising in late January in Egypt, to Libya's east, forced President Hosni Mubarak to resign on February 11, 2011, after nearly 30 years in power. These revolts and the stirring of unrest in other Arab states inspired the people of Libya and galvanized them to action.

In January 2011, Libyans in Benghazi organized street demonstrations about the failures of the Qaddafi regime. Protests targeted such matters as late paychecks, inadequate housing, and food shortages; some citizens took occupation of unfinished apartment complexes that for years had been under construction, mired in administrative incompetence. Inspired by the events in Tunisia and Egypt, a group named the National Conference for the Libyan Opposition planned the so-called Days of Rage, a series of rallies in Benghazi to protest political repression and economic misery. They set a starting date of February 17, 2011—the fifth anniversary of the attack on the Italian consulate in Benghazi by a mob protesting anti-Islamic cartoons.

A popular revolt erupted even before the planned start of the Days of Rage. On February 15, regime authorities tried to

166 LIBYA AND THE WEST

prevent the scheduled rallies by arresting Fathi Terbil, one of their organizers and an attorney who had been representing the families of the political prisoners massacred by security forces at Abu Salim Prison in 1996—but that arrest backfired. Hundreds of citizens, including families of the massacre victims as well as members of the legal profession, took to the streets to protest Terbil's arrest. The government released Terbil in hope of containing the unrest, but the streets of Benghazi filled with thousands of demonstrators. Police officers sent to contain the turmoil used lethal force, killing 11 protestors on February 17. Such police action provoked even more widespread protests, leading to more intense suppression and a cycle of escalating turmoil.

The revolt in Benghazi quickly intensified and spread to other cities. Although originally targeted against the tangible failures of the Qaddafi regime, the protestors soon embraced regime change as their objective, symbolized by the appearance of pre-1969 Libyan flags at the demonstrations. On February 19, unrest erupted in Misrata, where demonstrators threw rocks and homemade explosives at police, who responded with deadly force. One day later, even Tripoli—long considered Qaddafi's political foundation—was in the throes of unruliness. On that city's famed Green Square, gunfire from armored vehicles killed scores of demonstrators and police arrested hundreds of others.

Did US policies trigger the Arab Spring uprisings?

During the decade preceding the Arab Spring revolts, two US presidential administrations expressed calls for democratic reform in the Arab world. In a 2003 speech that was a part of his "freedom agenda" initiative, President George W. Bush rejected the notion that democracy and Arab culture were incompatible, declaring that "I believe every person has the ability and the right to be free." He continued, "As long as the Middle East remains a place where freedom does not flourish, it will remain a place of stagnation, resentment, and violence ready for export." Two years later, Secretary of State Condoleezza Rice added, "liberty is threatened by undemocratic governments. Some believe this is a permanent fact of history. But there are others who know better. These impatient patriots can be found in Baghdad and Beirut, in Riyadh and in Ramallah, in Amman and in Tehran and right here in Cairo."[5]

Shortly after taking office in 2009, President Barack Obama amplified this theme in an address in Cairo designed to chart a path for improved relations between the United States and the Muslim world. "I do have an unyielding belief that all people yearn for certain things," he declared, "the ability to speak your mind and have a say in how you are governed; confidence in the rule of law and the equal administration of justice; government that is transparent and doesn't steal from the people; the freedom to live as you choose. These are not just American ideas; they are human rights. And that is why we will support them everywhere." Rhetorically addressing leaders in Muslim states, Obama added, "You must maintain your power through consent, not coercion; you must respect the rights of minorities, and participate with a spirit of tolerance and compromise; you must place the interests of your people and the legitimate workings of the political process above your party."[6]

The spontaneous eruption of the Arab Spring within 18 months of Obama's address created the appearance of causality, the notion that the peoples who took to the streets of the Arab states were inspired to some degree by such US declarations. While there might be a degree of truth in that conclusion, however, there are reasons to doubt it. In much of the Muslim world, President Bush's characterization of his invasions of Afghanistan and Iraq as promotions of democracy had tarnished his credibility on that topic. In addition, the antecedents to the rebellions, notably in Libya, predated the US oratories and were substantial enough to lead to rebellion even in the absence of such US rhetoric.[7]

168 LIBYA AND THE WEST

How did Qaddafi react to the protests?

Initially, Qaddafi misread the danger to himself inherent in the uprisings in Tunisia and Egypt. He reasoned that Ben Ali and Mubarak had been targeted because of their association with the West and that his own revolution had met the essential needs of the Libyan people. Before long, however, Qaddafi sensed the potency of the broader Arab Spring, and he endorsed both Ben Ali's and Mubarak's holds on power even though they had embraced values and policies in conflict with his own.

Qaddafi tried multiple tactics to head off the mounting unrest in the streets of Libya. In the early days, he aimed to persuade people that he would lead them through a period of reform, staging elaborate meetings with common people to hear their grievances and pledge immediate fixes. He promised to double the salaries of state employees. He organized pro-government counterdemonstrations in Tripoli and elsewhere, hoping that displays of mass loyalty would deter protesters. These measures proved ineffective; Qaddafi had left unfulfilled so many grandiose promises over the years that many people placed no confidence in his pledges to reform.

As the protests grew, Qaddafi increasingly relied on strongarm techniques. He ordered his security forces to use deadly force and mass arrests. He pressured organizers to cancel rallies, warned journalists not to cover the protests, and ordered the arrest of anyone who spoke to the media. Qaddafi used patronage and pressure to reinforce the loyalty of such crucial security forces as the militias commanded by his sons and of such leading tribes as the Qaddafa, Warfalla, and Magarha. In the hope of containing the unrest to Benghazi, he severed that city's phone lines, disrupted its cellphone networks, and erected roadblocks on the highway to Tripoli. Qaddafi mobilized the Islamic Pan-African Brigade composed of mercenaries from Chad, Sudan, and Niger; recruited additional mercenaries from among Libya's community of migrant laborers; and dispatched the Tawergha, an ethnic community in El Goush that was descended from sub-Saharan African slaves, to help suppress the violence in Misrata. (Having hollowed out Libya's professional army over many years, Qaddafi did not have to fear that that institution would become an instrument of regime change like those in Tunisia and Egypt had.)

The Qaddafi regime's ruthless determination to crush the revolt was made clear by a televised address given by Saif al-Islam Qaddafi, the dictator's son who earlier had developed a reputation as a reformer. Initially, Saif had welcomed the revolt in Tunisia as a catalyst for rapid, progressive reform in Libya. When street demonstrations erupted in Tripoli on February 20, by contrast, he abandoned all pretensions of reform and endorsed his father's regime. Blaming the revolt on "an Islamic group with a military agenda," Saif predicted that it could cause civil war, economic collapse, and foreign occupation; called on the people to support Qaddafi and crush the revolt; and vowed that "we will fight until the last man, the last woman, the last bullet." Delivered in a condescending tone, his address seemed especially galling to those many Libyans who had anticipated that Saif would announce a wave of major reforms or even a transition of power from his father to himself.[8]

As he sensed the gravity of the protests, Muammar Qaddafi adopted an uncompromising demeanor. In a televised address on February 22, he called the rebels "drug addicts, jihadis, and rats" and vowed that his security forces would "clean Libya inch by inch, house by house, home by home, alleyway by alleyway, person by person, until the country is cleansed of dirt and scum." Despite its firm tone, this speech soon inspired widespread derision of Qaddafi among his opponents. Protestors adopted the phrase "alleyway by alleyway" (*zenga zenga* in Arabic) as a cynical expression of contempt for the regime. The Internet soon broadcasted so-called *Zenga Zenga*

170 LIBYA AND THE WEST

videos that mocked Qaddafi by depicting belly dancers and playing pop music interspersed into his speech.[9]

What was the result of Qaddafi's decision to suppress the demonstrations with force?

The clashes between the street demonstrators and government security forces morphed into a nationwide armed revolt and a political revolution. Given the intensity of the rebellion in Cyrenaica and that province's long-standing mistrust of his regime, Qaddafi made a strategic decision to withdraw his forces from that region and prioritize saving Tripoli, where loyalty to the regime was widespread and where street protests were suppressed relatively quickly. Openly disparaging the rebels in the East as crazed Islamic militants, Qaddafi proclaimed that he would launch a massive offensive to retake Benghazi and punish the insurgents.

The opposition soon organized into paramilitaries capable of engaging Qaddafi's security forces. Drawing from the universal military training that Qaddafi had provided under his ideology of building a people's army to defend the state, the rebels formed structured fighting units. Moreover, they raided armories where Qaddafi had stockpiled massive quantities of weapons purchased from overseas suppliers, purportedly to be used in the liberation of Palestine. The rebellion was bolstered by the defection of several military officers and their troops. Most famously, Major General Abdul Fatah Younis, a confidante of Qaddafi who was ordered to attack rebel forces in Benghazi on February 22, instead joined the insurgency. The hardline speeches by Qaddafi and his son Saif convinced the rebels that they were in a fight to the finish. The only outcome acceptable to them would be a revolution that ousted Qaddafi and his family and demolished the *Jamahiriya*. "We have liberated the east areas," the lawyer and activist Fathi Terbil declared on February 21. "Now we need to go to Tripoli and liberate Tripoli."[10]

The conquest of Tripoli, however, proved to be daunting. As rebels took control of much of the country, well-armed paramilitaries loyal to Qaddafi massed in the capital city. On February 25, Qaddafi delivered a public address on Green Square, vowing to arm loyal citizens who would kill the rebels and declaring that "people who don't love me don't deserve to live." Recognizing the vast superiority of Qaddafi's arsenal of weapons, rebel leaders in Benghazi openly discussed the prospect of asking for foreign airstrikes to offset the imbalance of power between state and rebel forces.[11]

In early March, intense battles between government forces and rebel militias raged along coastal land between Tripoli and Benghazi. Qaddafi's forces launched a major offensive on March 6 that gradually advanced from Tripoli toward the rebel stronghold in Benghazi. While an intense battle for Misrata remained unresolved, the regime besieged the city. Using air, artillery, and naval power, government forces gradually overran Ran Lanuf, Ajdabiya, and Zuwetina, gaining a corridor for an assault on Benghazi itself. By March 18, military units loyal to Qaddafi were at the gates of Benghazi, poised to overrun the birthplace of the uprising.

Why did the Libyan opposition form the National Transition Council?

As popular determination to oust Qaddafi increased, opponents of the regime constructed a governmental entity to organize the rebellion, administer those regions of the country liberated from Qaddafi's control, and, they hoped, serve as an interim government after Qaddafi's ouster. Founded on February 27, in Benghazi, the National Transitional Council (NTC) was composed of rebel leaders, prominent exiles, and defectors from the Qaddafi regime. Although they represented a broad cross-section of competing ideologies, members were united by their staunch opposition to Qaddafi.

172 LIBYA AND THE WEST

Mustafa Mohammed Abdul Jalil, Qaddafi's Minister of Justice from 2007 until he defected to the rebels in late February 2011, was a key organizer of the NTC and its first chairman. The identities of the other members, originally 33 in number, were kept secret to protect them and their families from reprisals by the regime. As cities and towns were liberated from Qaddafi's control, the NTC invited them to send delegates to the council. On March 5, the council declared itself the sole representative of all Libyan people.

Jalil launched initiatives to secure international recognition, seize government assets, produce and market oil, and provide governmental service and structure in the liberated cities. But his most urgent challenge was coordinating military operations against the Qaddafi regime, which remained extremely dangerous to the NTC and to the multitudes of people who supported the popular uprising.

How did Western governments view the uprising in Libya?

Caught off guard by the Arab Spring uprisings, leaders of Western states faced acute dilemmas between backing existing regimes or endorsing the pro-democracy movements. While many of the existing regimes protected the Western powers' diplomatic, security, and financial interests, the pro-democracy movements were consistent with their ideological values. Western governments faced difficult decisions between sticking with an old regime or taking a chance on a new movement, well before it became clear which side would prevail. Supporting a side that was destined to lose would cause serious consequences.

In the case of Libya, revulsion among Western governments at the level of violence Qaddafi inflicted on his people quickly eroded the rapprochement that had developed between Libya and the West during the preceding decade, exposing a foundation of lingering resentments about historic grievances as well as tensions over recent policy disagreements. There were deterrents, on the other hand, to decisive action in favor of the anti-Qaddafi movement, such as the realization that, if Qaddafi prevailed, he would reward commercially those states that supported him—like China and Russia—over any state that broke with him.

Among the Western powers, France was the first to turn against the Qaddafi regime. Long suspicious that Qaddafi was a spoiler in France's quest to promote a European–African trade partnership, President Nicolas Sarkozy had ill feelings for the Libyan dictator at the outset of the Arab Spring. A hardline policy toward Qaddafi, moreover, seemed likely to advance Sarkozy's prospects for reelection in the April 2012 French presidential polling. Domestic challengers had criticized Sarkozy for associating with dictators after members of his government spent holidays with friends in the Tunisian and Egyptian regimes and after Foreign Minister Michele Alliot-Marie offered President Ben Ali of Tunisia the assistance of French police in maintaining order. Sarkozy calculated that endorsing the Libyan rebels would burnish his reputation as a human rights advocate and thereby boost his sagging domestic popularity.[12]

Two days after Qaddafi's February 22 speech denouncing the rebels, Sarkozy became the first European leader to call for Qaddafi's resignation, declaring during a visit to Turkey that "Mr. Qaddafi must leave." On the next day, Sarkozy expressed disgust at the violence Qaddafi's regime perpetrated against unarmed protestors, proclaiming that "the international community cannot remain a spectator to all the massive violations of human rights." Given "what is happening in Libya," he added on February 27, "the French have a duty to react."[13]

The United States echoed Sarkozy's concern with human rights. The Obama administration conveyed to the Qaddafi regime "strong objections about the use of lethal force" against peaceful protestors, State Department spokesman Philip J. Crowley indicated on February 20. "The suffering and bloodshed is [sic] outrageous, and it is unacceptable," President

174 LIBYA AND THE WEST

Obama publicly declared on February 23. "These actions violate international norms and every standard of common decency. This violence must stop."[14]

Obama initially refrained from calling on Qaddafi to resign out of concern that the Libyan leader might take US citizens in Tripoli as hostages. US plans to evacuate some 600 Americans, including diplomats' dependents and oil company staff, were suspended when the Libyan government denied permission to land the aircraft sent to extricate them. State Department officials made alternative arrangements for an evacuation by sea, but as long as the group remained in harm's way, Obama moderated his words. Once the evacuation was accomplished on February 26, the president called for Qaddafi's removal. "When a leader's only means of staying in power is to use mass violence against his own people," he intoned, "he has lost the legitimacy to rule and needs to do what is right for his country by leaving now."[15]

British leaders soon echoed the French and US pronouncements. "For the future of Libya and its people," Prime Minister David Cameron stated in the House of Commons on February 28, "Colonel Qadhafi's [Qaddafi's] regime must end and he must leave." To pressure the Libyan leader, Cameron vowed to hold him accountable for human rights abuses and promised to seek a UN Security Council resolution imposing financial sanctions and possibly even authorizing military action against his regime. "It is clear that this is an illegitimate regime that has lost the consent of its people," Cameron added. "My message to Colonel Qadhafi is simple: Go now."[16]

At the outset, Italy expressed reluctance about breaking with Qaddafi because its relationship with him advanced several national interests. Since 2004, Italy had been Libya's top trading partner and top arms supplier. The Italian energy company Ente Nazionale Idrocarburi (ENI) had invested tens of billions of dollars in Libya, and other Italian firms had contracts to develop a coastal highway, railways, and fiber optics there. In turn, Libya owned 7.6 percent of UniCredit, the

The Libyan Revolution 175

Italian government's central bank; 2 percent of Finmeccanica, the defense contractor; and nearly 2 percent of Fiat, the automaker. Italy relied on Libya for 25 percent of the oil and 10 percent of the natural gas it consumed. In addition, Italian leaders viewed the Qaddafi regime as a sturdy container against the potential migration of tens of thousands of prospective African migrants who, they feared, would aggravate Italy's economic and unemployment woes. During the early days of turmoil in Libya, Prime Minister Silvio Berlusconi indicated he would not "disturb" Qaddafi.[17]

To what extent did human rights concerns motivate the Western powers to act against Qaddafi?

Motivated by evidence that Qaddafi was taking extreme measures against his people, French, British, and US leaders matched their firm words with diplomatic action during the last week of February. Human rights groups reported the deaths of hundreds of unarmed demonstrators at the hands of regime security forces using ground and air power, and two Libyan Air Force officers defected with their military jets to Malta, claiming to have defied orders to strafe protestors in Benghazi. After announcing his own defection from the Qaddafi regime because it prepared to massacre thousands of its citizens, Libya's Ambassador to the United Nations Abdurrahman Mohamed Shalgam asked the international body to intervene.

Considering the evidence of impending genocide, France, Britain, and the United States agreed to seek UN Security Council sanctions on Qaddafi's regime. They were motivated in part by the "Responsibility to Protect" ("RtoP" or "R2P") doctrine enshrined by the United Nations in 2005, in response to episodes of genocide in the Balkans and Rwanda. "RtoP" doctrine clarified that states were responsible to take collective action against any government committing genocide of its own people. On February 24, President Obama, President Sarkozy,

176 LIBYA AND THE WEST

Prime Minister Cameron, and Prime Minister Berlusconi conferred by telephone, and, the following day, the United States, Britain, France, and Germany proposed a UN Security Council resolution to limit Qaddafi's destructive capacity.[18]

What action did the UN Security Council take against Qaddafi's regime?

On February 26, the UN Security Council unanimously adopted Resolution 1970 to contain Qaddafi's capacity for genocide. The resolution imposed an arms embargo on Libya, required member states to freeze Libyan financial assets deposited in their countries, imposed a travel ban on Qaddafi and members of his family, and directed the International Criminal Court (ICC) to investigate whether the Qaddafi regime had committed war crimes. The resolution called upon the Libyan government to cease its violent practices, "to fulfill the legitimate demands of the population," and to ensure the safety of all foreign nationals in the country. The endorsement of this resolution by the Arab League and by Ambassador Shalgam persuaded such countries as Russia, China, and India to vote for it. There were limits to the UN action. Out of concern that such terms would become the basis for Western military intervention, Russian blocked a proposal by Libyan defectors to include enforcement of a No-Fly Zone (NFZ) in Libyan airspace as well as a British proposal to authorize "all measures necessary" to stop the violence.[19]

Western leaders promptly implemented the terms of Resolution 1970. The Obama administration imposed sanctions and froze some $30 billion in Libyan assets in US banks. Pledging to hold Qaddafi and his aides accountable for any war crimes violations, US Secretary of State Hillary Clinton declared, "It is time for Gaddafi to go. Now, without further violence or delay." Prime Minister Cameron cancelled export licenses for the dozens of arms deals which Libya negotiated with British firms during the rapprochement. Germany froze

Libyan accounts at 14 financial institutions, its Finance Ministry declaring that "the brutal oppression of Libyans' right to freedom can no longer be financed with money that has been placed in German banks." France transported medical personnel and supplies to the rebels in Benghazi as a symbol of its support for the ouster of Qaddafi. Despite diplomatic appeals by Qaddafi envoys in Belgium, Greece, Portugal, and Malta, the European Union adopted stringent measures as directed by the UN Security Council. Overcoming its earlier reluctance to break with Qaddafi, Italy suspended its 2008 treaty with Libya that had facilitated economic ties and prohibited Italy from allowing use of its military bases for military action against Libya.[20]

How did Western policy toward Qaddafi evolve in March 2011?

In early March 2011, Western powers debated taking additional action to stymie Qaddafi's military offensive against the rebel stronghold in Benghazi. France took the lead in advocating for the isolation of the Qaddafi regime and the elevation of the NTC as the legitimate government of Libya. France's approach sparked an intense debate among the Western powers. Britain soon echoed France's policy, the United States and Italy gradually embraced it, but Germany and Turkey expressed deep disagreement. After about a week of intense conversation, most Western powers agreed on a proposal to secure UN Security Council authorization to use military force against Qaddafi's regime.

France seized the lead in advocating for regime change when President Sarkozy welcomed NTC leaders Mahmoud Jibril and Ali Al-Esawi to a meeting in Paris on March 10, becoming the first head of state to receive them. The French president proceeded to declare that the NTC had become the sole legitimate representative of the Libyan people and that France and the NTC would soon exchange ambassadors. By taking this step, France broke international precedent by recognizing

178 LIBYA AND THE WEST

a government rather than a state. In response, Qaddafi severed diplomatic relations with France.[21]

Over succeeding days, Western leaders debated the possibility of military actions against Qaddafi. At the European Union summit meeting in Brussels on March 11, Sarkozy and Cameron proposed enforcement of an NFZ in Libyan airspace to stop what appeared to be impending genocide by the regime. "Qaddafi is still on the rampage, waging war on his own people," Cameron said. "We simply do not know how bad this could get, or what horrors already lie hidden in the Libyan desert." Several delegates, however, were upset at Sarkozy for his unilateral recognition of the NTC, and German Chancellor Angela Merkel said she was "fundamentally skeptical" of any military intervention. The EU meeting reached a consensus that Qaddafi should resign but that military action should be avoided in the absence of Arab state approval, a UN mandate, and precise legal parameters.[22]

The topic of Libya also divided the foreign ministers of the Group of Eight (G-8) meeting in Paris on March 15. The British and French ministers advocated for an NFZ, citing the Arab League's March 12 endorsement of this idea as a necessary measure to prevent Qaddafi from slaughtering his people with airpower. Secretary of State Clinton remained noncommittal on an NFZ, even after meeting NTC chair Jibril and hearing his request for an NFZ and arms supply. German Foreign Minister Guido Westerwelle cautioned that "we do not want to get sucked into a war in North Africa and we would not like to step on a slippery slope where we all are, at the end, in a war." Dutch Prime Minister Mark Rutte called France's recognition of the NTC "a crazy move." Deadlocked, the G-8 foreign ministers agreed to refer the topic to the UN Security Council. Because of this diplomacy, Qaddafi declared in a media interview, Libya would shift oil production "to Russian, Chinese, and Indian firms," adding that "the West is to be forgotten."[23]

Overcoming its initial hesitation, the United States eventually signed on to the British and French initiative. At first,

President Obama professed that the revolution most likely would succeed if it were accomplished by the Libyan people alone. He acknowledged the concern expressed by Secretary of Defense Robert M. Gates that enforcing an NFZ in Libya might not prevent Qaddafi from inflicting carnage on his people, that it would serve no US security interest, that it would distract from US operations in Afghanistan and Iraq, and that it might escalate into a broader intervention. "As much as I shared the impulse to save innocent people from tyrants," Obama recalled in his memoirs, "I was profoundly wary of ordering any kind of military action against Libya. . . . War is never tidy and always results in unintended consequences, even when launched against seemingly powerless countries on behalf of a righteous cause."[24]

Obama relented, however, to the advice of his Ambassador to the United Nations Susan Rice and National Security Council advisor Samantha Power that the world community must act under the "RtoP" doctrine to protect the Libyan people from looming genocide. Secretary of State Clinton came to agree with Rice and Power after the Arab League endorsed an NFZ and after Clinton visited advocates of democracy in Egypt and Tunisia and imagined the horrors awaiting their counterparts in Libya. Qaddafi's imminent attack on Benghazi threatened to kill tens of thousands of Libyans, Obama realized, and "I was perhaps the one person in the world who could keep that from happening."[25]

After consulting his National Security Council on March 15, Obama resolved to support Western intervention in Libya but to impose strict limits on the US role. Motivated by the concerns about genocide, he directed that the United States support a broad intervention against Qaddafi's forces. Such an intervention would demand early and significant US action to destroy Qaddafi's air defense system. Obama directed the Pentagon to prepare for that mission but also made clear that Britain and France must take the lead in sustaining all subsequent operations needed to prevent Qaddafi's troops from

180 LIBYA AND THE WEST

attacking civilians. "America would go along," James Mann noted, "so long as it didn't have to carry the military burden on its own." Obama's decision soon became known as a policy of "leading from behind."[26]

What action did the UN Security Council take in March 2011?

Pointing to the potential impact of Qaddafi's imminent assault on Benghazi, France, Britain, and the United States petitioned the UN Security Council to debate a resolution authorizing military intervention in Libya. The Western states warned that inaction would result in the conquest of Benghazi, with massive loss of life. "This is urgent," French Foreign Minister Alain Juppé declared publicly. "We have often seen in our contemporary history that the weakness of democracies leaves the field open to dictatorships. It is not too late to defy this rule." Secretary of State Clinton added, "We are all well aware that the clock is ticking."[27]

Joined by Lebanon, the three Western powers co-sponsored Resolution 1973 when the Security Council convened on March 16–17. The resolution reiterated the terms of Resolution 1970 and added two very important provisions to safeguard the people of Libya against mass killings by their government. First, it imposed an NFZ in all Libyan airspace and authorized member states "to take all necessary measures to enforce compliance with the ban on flights." Second, it authorized member states "to take all necessary measures . . . to protect civilians and civilian populated areas under threat of attack in the Libyan Arab *Jamahiriya*, including Benghazi, while excluding a foreign occupation force of any form on any part of Libyan territory." In both cases, member states were authorized to act "nationally or through regional organizations or arrangements," provided they coordinated actions with the UN Secretary-General and the Arab League.[28]

Western states took the lead in arguing for adoption of this resolution. Presenting the case to the Security Council,

Foreign Minister Juppé argued that "the will of the people has been crushed by the murderous repression led by Colonel al-Qadhafi's [Qaddafi's] regime." British representative Mark Lyall Grant observed that the regime "has begun air strikes in anticipation of what we expect to be a brutal attack using air, land, and sea forces." US Ambassador Rice defined the purpose behind the resolution as "clear—to protect innocent civilians."[29]

Several states initially resisted the proposed resolution. Germany remained skeptical, Foreign Minister Guido Westerwelle declaring that his country "is not prepared to be dragged into a civil war." Representatives of Russia and China expressed concern with the consequences of foreign military intervention in Libya, but they conceded that Qaddafi's maltreatment of his people was repugnant. Lebanon's co-sponsorship of the resolution, as well as the Arab League's earlier endorsement of its provisions, also mitigated their resistance to intervention.[30]

After a relatively short debate, the Security Council adopted Resolution 1973 on March 17 by a vote of 10–0, with five nations (Russia, China, Germany, India, and Brazil) abstaining. "Resolution 1973 affirms, clearly and unequivocally," UN Secretary-General Ban Ki-Moon observed, "the international community's determination to fulfill its responsibility to protect civilians from violence perpetrated upon them by their own government." Passage of Resolution 1973 within five weeks of the start of the violence was a notable accomplishment for the United Nations. "By the standards of international diplomacy," Richard Northern and Jason Pack observed, "this was a remarkably swift, concerted, and coordinated action."[31]

What military action did Western powers take under the Security Council resolutions?

Western powers used Resolution 1973 as an ultimatum to Qaddafi to cease his violent suppression of his people or face

182 LIBYA AND THE WEST

the wrath of the international community. One day after the resolution was adopted, President Obama publicly demanded that Qaddafi must cease fire; withdraw forces from Benghazi, Misrata, and other besieged cities; and allow humanitarian relief to reach his people. "Let me be clear, these terms are not negotiable," Obama declared. "If Qaddafi does not comply with the resolution, the international community will impose consequences, and the resolution will be enforced through military action." To put teeth into the ultimatum, representatives of Western states (France, Britain, the United States, Canada, Germany, Norway, Denmark, Belgium, Spain, Poland, and Italy), Arab states (Qatar, Morocco, and the United Arab Emirates [UAE]), the Arab League, the European Union, and the United Nations huddled in Paris to plan coordinated military operations to neutralize Libyan airpower and protect civilians from attack by regime forces.[32]

Any hope that such an ultimatum would deter Qaddafi from further military action quickly faded. In a radio address on March 17, Qaddafi starkly warned the people of Benghazi that his troops would invade the city and that "we will come house by house, room by room. . . . We will find you in your closets. We will have no mercy and no pity." In response to Resolution 1973, Qaddafi wrote in public letters to Obama and Sarkozy, "Libya is not yours. Libya is for all Libyans. This is injustice, it is clear aggression, and it is uncalculated risk for its consequences on the Mediterranean and Europe." On March 19, Qaddafi's military forces barraged Benghazi with artillery, infiltrated it with snipers, and invaded it with tanks, provoking an intense battle near the city center.[33]

Citing the authority granted by Resolution 1973, Western states responded by launching aerial attacks on Qaddafi's war-making capacities. Within hours of Qaddafi's assault on Benghazi, French warplanes bombed Libyan armored vehicles in and near the city. US Navy ships positioned in the Mediterranean launched more than 100 cruise missiles against communications, radar, and missile sites at Tripoli,

Misrata, and Sirte. British warplanes also immediately entered the fray, and Qatar and the UAE joined by March 26. Qaddafi denounced the external action as "colonial crusader aggression that may ignite another large-scale crusader war."[34]

How did the Western powers justify their military assaults?

The Western powers justified their action as enforcement of Resolution 1973 and the broader "RtoP" doctrine. US officials calculated that although hard evidence of actual genocide was limited, the combination of Qaddafi's current threats and his legacy of past atrocities provided reason to fear the worst and to preempt it. "I want the American people to know that the use of force is not our first choice, and it's not a choice that I make lightly," President Obama stated. "But we can't stand idly by when a tyrant tells his people that there will be no mercy."[35]

Critics of Obama's decision to intervene suggest that the president exaggerated the likelihood of genocide in Libya. He overlooked or downplayed that many of the forecasts of a looming bloodbath in Benghazi originated among Libyan expatriates in Geneva who had political motives to disparage Qaddafi and limited first-hand information. US intelligence should have noted that when Qaddafi's forces overran such other cities as Misrata, Zawiya, and Ajdabiya, they targeted only armed rebels, not masses of civilians, the critics suggest. A careful analysis of Qaddafi's February 22 speech should have noted that its terrifying threats were directed to rebel combatants only and that non-combatants were promised mercy.[36]

European powers viewed the situation in Libya as Obama did. "We simply cannot have a situation where a failed pariah state festers on Europe's southern border," Prime Minister Cameron declared to the House of Commons, by way of justifying the Cabinet's decision to participate in the airstrikes. "This would potentially threaten our security, push

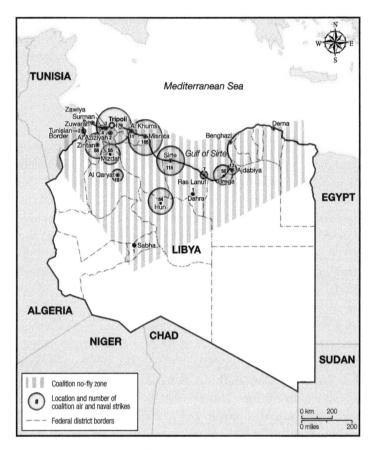

Map 5 Coalition No Fly Zones and Strike Locations during the 2011 Intervention

people across the Mediterranean, and create a more dangerous and uncertain world for Britain and for our allies as well as for the people of Libya." A French Foreign Ministry spokesman observed, "Libya shows that there is a political and diplomatic dynamic of European construction and an active European voice in world affairs." Italian Foreign Minister Franco Frattini stressed that military operations would be limited to protecting civilians and "shouldn't be a war on Libya." While refusing to participate in the fighting, Germany made such mild concessions as sending an additional 300 soldiers to Afghanistan to relieve Allied soldiers needed for redeployment to Libya. Chancellor Merkel specified that while Germany did not approve the tactics used against Qaddafi, she supported the objective of preventing maltreatment of civilians.[37]

To be sure, unarticulated factors also motivated the military action. Western leaders naturally cheered for the democratic movements birthed during the Arab Spring. The Qaddafi regime, by contrast, was blemished by its incompetence and corruption, its legacy of bad behavior that was not fully mitigated by the recent rapprochement, and now its brutal violence against its people. France still nursed suspicions of Qaddafi meddling in Chad and elsewhere in Francophone Africa. The European powers favored a restoration of stability both to prevent a surge of illegal migration from Libya to southern Europe and to ensure the steady production of Libyan oil, which supplied 10 percent of the European Union's needs and 25 percent of Italy's. (The United States, which imported less than 1 percent of its oil from Libya and which was not easily accessible to migrants from Africa, did not share these concerns.) In the domestic political context, President Sarkozy remained committed to human rights as an election strategy, the Conservative Party leaders of Britain hoped to distinguish their approach from the former Labour government's engagement with Qaddafi, and Chancellor Merkel's reluctance to join the battle was shaped by the dynamics of German parliamentary elections scheduled for March 27.[38]

What was the impact of the Western intervention on the civil war in Libya?

The impact of Western airstrikes on the Libyan civil war was dramatic but initially inconclusive. Qaddafi's March 19 invasion of Benghazi quickly fizzled after Anglo–French airpower demolished dozens of armored vehicles, potentially sparing that city a cruel fate. By nightfall on March 20, rebel forces

186 LIBYA AND THE WEST

recaptured Benghazi and advanced some 40 miles along the highway to Ajdabiya. Allied airstrikes then degraded Qaddafi's ground units near Ajdabiya, Misrata, and Zintan and demolished a government airbase near Misrata, with goal of sparing those cities from invasions by regime soldiers. As Qaddafi suppressed a nascent rebellion and consolidated his authority in Tripoli, Allied airpower wrecked his sprawling compound on the perimeter of the city. "We hit a lot of targets," Admiral Mike Mullen, the chairman of the US Joint Chiefs of Staff told reporters on March 20, "focused on his command and control, focused on his air defense, and actually attacked some of his forces on the ground in the vicinity of Benghazi." Qaddafi would never recover from his defeat in Benghazi, leading US diplomat Ethan Chorin to conclude that his "fixation on making a bloody example of Benghazi was probably his single largest strategic error."[39]

While the Western airstrikes stymied Qaddafi's offensive operations, they did not enable a rapid rebel victory. Within Misrata and other coastal towns, fighting raged between loyalists and rebels, while the Allies withheld airstrikes to avoid inflicting casualties on civilians. During the last 10 days of March, rebel units captured Ajdabiya and two oil refineries near Brega and Ras Lanuf and reached the outskirts of Sirte, a Qaddafi stronghold, before Qaddafi's forces sent them into headlong retreat all the way back to Ajdabiya. Such dynamic warfare divided Libya into regime- and rebel-controlled zones with fluid borders. While Western airpower clearly averted a Qaddafi triumph, shortages of experience, skill, and weapons prevented a rebel victory.[40]

Did the Allies try to overthrow or kill Qaddafi with their airstrikes?

Whether the Allies deliberately sought Qaddafi's downfall or death became a matter of speculation and controversy from the initial stages of intervention. Discussion centered on the discrepancy between the calls by Western leaders for Qaddafi's departure from leadership and the authorization by Resolution 1973 for military action limited to the purpose of protecting civilian lives. As Allied airpower pummeled Qaddafi's assets, foreign nations as well as Western citizens and journalists openly speculated that regime change was an unacknowledged objective of the air operations. Such observers found credibility in the complaint from Libyan government spokesman Musa Ibrahim that foreign attacks on regime troops retreating from battle fronts indicated a determination to weaken the Qaddafi regime to the strategic advantage of the rebels. "Clearly NATO is taking sides in this civil conflict," Ibrahim charged. "It is illegal. It is not allowed by the Security Council resolution. And it is immoral, of course."[41]

Western heads of state addressed these criticisms by delicately arguing that they indeed sought Qaddafi's departure but were not using military means to accomplish that end. "It is U.S. policy that Qaddafi needs to go," Obama declared on March 21, "and we've got a wide range of tools in addition to our military effort to support that policy." Echoing this rationale, Secretary of State Clinton declared, on March 29, that Libya "belongs not to a dictator, but to its people." In an editorial published on April 14, Obama, Cameron, and Sarkozy jointly declared that their aim "is not to remove Qaddafi by force. But it is impossible to imagine a future for Libya with Qaddafi in power."[42]

While denying that they were trying to kill Qaddafi, Allied military commanders made statements that fueled public speculation to the contrary. The commanders argued that their operations were consistent with the stipulations of Resolution 1973 and that Qaddafi's fate was a political matter separate from their military mission. After denying that Qaddafi was a target when his compound near Tripoli was bombed, however, US Navy Vice Admiral William E. Gortney observed, "If he happens to be in a place, if he's inspecting a surface-to-air missile site, and we don't have any idea if he's there or not, then,"

188 LIBYA AND THE WEST

before his voice trailed off. "We are not targeting Gaddafi directly," British General David Richards added in May, "but if it happened that he was in a command and control centre that was hit by NATO and he was killed, then that is within the rules."[43]

The longer hostilities persisted, the more that Western military actions revealed determination to overthrow Qaddafi. The Western powers broadened target lists to include critical infrastructure and Libyan Army assets, and they deployed helicopter gunships to coordinate assaults with fixed-wing aircraft, signaling growing resolve to prevail. NATO officers affirmed the principle that only Qaddafi, and not the rebels, could pose a threat to civilians as defined by the Security Council resolution. In April, an airstrike on a residence believed to be used by Qaddafi killed his son, Saif al-Arab. Western states and Qatar supplied arms via sea and air routes to Misratan rebels, who broke Qaddafi's siege of their city in May. British, French, and US officers were deployed covertly to rebel areas to oversee the weapons distribution; to vet, train, and counsel rebel commanders; and to identify targets for airstrikes.[44]

Why did NATO become involved in air operations against Libya?

As it became clear that hostilities would endure for some time, France, Britain, and the United States transitioned their military operations to a unified NATO command. Despite President Obama's initial reservations about intervention, the United States initially took on the central role in the air operations given that success depended heavily on US warplanes and missiles, aircraft carriers, intelligence assets, command and control capabilities, communication technologies, and such tactical skills as in-flight refueling, reconnaissance, and search and rescue. The head of the US Africa Command, Army General Carter F. Ham, assumed the lead role in coordinating military operations. As early as March 18, however, the president called on Britain, France, and the Arab League "to take a leadership role in the enforcement of this resolution, just as they were instrumental in pursuing it." From the start of operations, Secretary of State Clinton added, "President Obama has stated that the role of the U.S. military would be limited in time and scope."[45]

During the last week of March, an inter-Allied discussion ensued on the possibility of NATO assuming responsibility for the air war. Wanting to play a lead role, France opposed the idea, predicting Arab opposition to NATO command. Britain favored NATO leadership, by contrast, while Italy and Norway warned that they would refrain from supporting the operations in the absence of NATO command. Turkey expressed opposition to NATO leadership but agreed to go along if ground troops were not deployed. Germany remained uncommitted. When NATO met in Brussels on March 21 to discuss this topic, tempers flared, and the French and German ambassadors walked out of the room.[46]

Cooler heads soon prevailed. The North Atlantic Council, the decision-making body within the alliance, reached a consensus in favor of NATO accepting the responsibility for air operations in Libya. By month's end, NATO launched Operation Unified Protector, a coordinated plan to ground Libyan air forces, protect civilians from harm by the regime, and enforce arms embargoes. "NATO will implement all aspects of the U.N. resolution," Secretary General Anders Fogh Rasmussen clarified on March 27. "Nothing more, nothing less." General Ham transferred his responsibilities to Canadian Lt. General Charles Bouchard, who was named by NATO to the leadership role. By May 1, 14 NATO powers (as well as Qatar, the United Arab Emirates, and Sweden) were involved in the air operations in Libya. By October 2011, the Western air campaign against Qaddafi would involve some 25,000 sorties and 7,000 airstrikes. France and Britain conducted 40 percent of all missions and destroyed 34 percent of all targets. To stanch the flow of weapons to Qaddafi's regime, NATO naval units conducted 3,100 marine actions and 400 boardings.[47]

190 LIBYA AND THE WEST

Were efforts made to end the fighting via diplomacy?

As NATO airstrikes weakened his military, Qaddafi explored political pathways to saving his regime. Within Libya, he appealed to tribal leaders on patriotic grounds to defend the government. He asked conservative Islamic scholars—whom he had long feared and denigrated—to declare that the rebellion was inconsistent with Islam. He floated offers to transition power to his son Saif Al-Islam, who would practice more democracy. He proposed that if the NTC accepted a ceasefire, he would hold free elections within six months and thereafter resign.

These initiatives fell flat. The rebellious factions remained determined to overthrow Qaddafi and refused his overtures. NTC leaders calculated that accepting a ceasefire would incur the risk that Qaddafi would regain the strength to crush them. In fact, the NTC assured the rebel forces in Misrata—who worried that a compromise partitioning the country would leave them to a cruel fate within Qaddafi-controlled western Libya— that it would fight for the liberation of the entire country. When he realized that the NTC would not negotiate, Qaddafi denounced it as the "tail of the colonisers" and called on the people to "explode against those bisexuals who are fighting under the cross and under the American, French, and British flags."[48]

International efforts to find a diplomatic solution to the civil war similarly foundered. Russia, China, and Arab League Secretary General Amr Moussa criticized the Western powers for exceeding the mandate intended by the Security Council and pressured them to deescalate. Various African states called for a mediated settlement that would allow Qaddafi to remain in power, and South African President Jacob Zuma visited Qaddafi in Tripoli in hope of negotiating a compromise. Qaddafi himself repeatedly offered to negotiate with the West, and Turkey offered to mediate such talks. In response to the many Western calls for his resignation, Qaddafi declared that "the rulers of the states of the alliance who decided to wage a second crusade between Muslims and Christians should step down."[49]

The United States, Britain, and France, however, viewed these diplomatic options with deep skepticism. While cognizant of the risk that Qaddafi's downfall might open Libya to Islamic extremism, they recognized that the Libyan rebels lacked faith in Qaddafi and would not accept any scenario in which he retained any degree of power. As the NTC gained stature and planned a transition to democracy, Western states viewed it as the foundation of a new, post-Qaddafi government. Following France's lead, Italy recognized the NTC as the government of Libya on April 4, followed in turn by Germany (June 13), Canada (June 14), the United States (July 15), and Britain (July 27). Once recognized, the NTC gained access to the considerable financial assets of the Libyan government that the Western powers previously had frozen.[50]

How did the rebels ultimately prevail?

Through mid-summer 2011, the outcome of the civil war hung in the balance. While the rebels held Benghazi, Qaddafi remained in firm control of Tripoli and battles raged over other territories. NATO powers and several Arab states supported the rebel militias with airstrikes, arms supply, and military advice. Rebel militias in Misrata and Zintan gained strength and edged toward Tripoli. As public and parliamentary support for intervention eroded in several Western states, President Sarkozy of France pressed NTC leaders to coordinate an operation to liberate Tripoli and win the war.[51]

Rebel militias and their Western backers prepared for such a final offensive in August. Over several weeks of fighting, militias from Zintan expelled regime troops from western Libya and opened crucial supply lines from Tunisia. Their capture of Zawiya, only 30 miles west of Tripoli, and Gahryan,

192 LIBYA AND THE WEST

43 miles south, on August 13–20 indicated the weaknesses of Qaddafi's defensive lines and left his capital city encircled by rebel forces. Rebel sleeper cells, organized within Tripoli to rise up once an invasion began, stockpiled weapons. The commander of one of Qaddafi's powerful security brigades agreed to betray the dictator once an invasion started. NATO airpower further degraded Qaddafi's defensive capabilities, and British, French, and Qatari troops provided weapons, fuel, and intelligence to the rebels.[52]

Rebel forces launched Operation Mermaid Dawn to conquer Tripoli on the night of August 20–21, and it quickly succeeded. Militias attacked the city from the west and east, under NATO air cover, and armed residents seized control of various neighborhoods. Several regime commanders declared their loyalty to the rebels. Rather than resist to the death, many units of Qaddafi's army collapsed, their soldiers discarding uniforms and weapons as they fled their duty stations. Rebel militias gained control of most of the city within 48 hours and overran Bab al-Aziziyah, Qaddafi's massive military complex northeast of the city, on August 23. Throngs of people poured into the streets to celebrate, destroy such vestiges of Qaddafi's power as billboards and statues, and ransack the offices and villas belonging to Qaddafi, his family, and other regime elites. "The momentum against the Qaddafi regime has reached a tipping point," Obama observed publicly. "Tripoli is slipping from the grasp of a tyrant. . . . The people of Libya are showing that the universal pursuit of dignity and freedom is far stronger than the iron fist of a dictator."[53]

What happened to Qaddafi?

As Tripoli fell to rebel militias, Qaddafi and the remnants of his regime fled to his ancestral lands near Bani Walid and Sirte. The NTC and the rebel militias searched intensively for Qaddafi and his family, and, on September 21, NATO agreed to extend its mission for 90 days to stabilize the new government and join the hunt for Qaddafi. From mid-September through mid-October, rebel militias launched a series of attacks on Sirte that met staunch resistance but slowly degraded the fighting strength of Qaddafi's forces. Qaddafi desperately tried to rally his troops, in one radio address calling the rebels "germs and rats" and declaring that "this magnificent regime cannot be toppled."[54]

On October 20, NATO surveillance teams detected a convoy of vehicles suspected (correctly, it turned out) of carrying the Qaddafi entourage on a road outside of Sirte. After a US drone and a French warplane struck the convoy, Qaddafi fled his vehicle and took refuge in a drainage pipe beneath the roadway. Overpowering his bodyguards, a rebel militia dragged Qaddafi into the sunlight for a final reckoning. He remained delusional to the end, reportedly asking his captors, in what proved to be his final words, "What's wrong with you? What's happening?"[55]

Qaddafi's captors beat him, tortured him, and shot him to death. Motivated by rage and revenge over the depravities of his regime and the brutality of his counter-insurrectionary methods, they ignored directives from the NTC to take Qaddafi alive so that he could be tried in a court of law—an omen of future trouble for the country. "The cruelest irony of all in this very public death," Alison Pargeter noted, "was that after years of the Colonel calling on the masses to 'rise up' in the service of his revolution, . . . they did so in order to destroy him and all that he had created."[56]

Qaddafi's captors took his body to Misrata and displayed it in a refrigerated meat locker. Over several days, hundreds of Libyans filed past the body, as if seeing it brought them closure on the 42-year Qaddafi era. Qaddafi "had grown into a larger-than-life demon-like figure—terrifying even to his followers," the scholar Lisa Anderson observed. "It was inevitable that someone would need to vanquish the monster and that everyone would be called to witness it." The NTC eventually gained custody of Qaddafi's body and arranged a burial in an unmarked desert grave without Islamic rituals.[57]

194 LIBYA AND THE WEST

Qaddafi's family dynasty collapsed with him. His son Moatassim as well as his Minister of Defense Abu Bakr Younis, who were traveling in Qaddafi's fateful motorcade, were also executed on the spot by the rebel militia. (In death, Moatassim joined his brothers Saif al-Arab and Khamis, who were killed in battles during the rebellion.) Qaddafi's wife, daughter, and two other sons fled into Algeria, where they were given asylum on condition of silence, and his son Saadi fled into Niger, which offered asylum on similar conditions. Saif al-Islam, the son who was once considered to be reform-minded, fled toward Niger but was captured by rebel gunmen from Zintan. Rather than summarily execute him, they flew him to Zintan and held him for several years as a hostage.[58]

How did Qaddafi's legacy shape the political situation in Libya?

Occurring almost exactly one century after the October 3, 1911, Italian invasion of Cyrenaica and Tripoli, Lisa Anderson notes, Qaddafi's death on October 20, 2011, marked the end of "a hundred years of almost unrelieved cruelty, incompetence, and corruption in government" in Libya by Italy, Britain, King Idris, and Qaddafi. Whatever advantages accrued to the Libyan people from his downfall, however, the legacy of Qaddafi's 42 years in power made it difficult to stabilize and govern the country. As Akram al-Turk observed, "the fall of the Qadhafi regime . . . was the easy part."[59]

In the aftermath of his downfall, Qaddafi's legacy made the task of state-building extremely difficult. Qaddafi had dismantled the administrative state, downgraded the army, and ended the political process. He had abolished or suppressed such institutions as political parties, labor unions, government ministries, nongovernmental organizations, and independent media. He had neglected the infrastructure, eviscerated the middle class, suspended civic life, and promoted a culture of shirking hard work but expecting a paycheck from the state.

Those Libyans who wanted to establish a stable, national government for the post-Qaddafi era faced monumental foundational challenges. "Gaddafi had ruled the country in his addled way for more than 40 years, and had deeply affected the life of every single Libyan throughout that time," BBC editor John Simpson commented in 2015. "You don't just kill a dictator like that, destroy his portraits, and put him behind you."[60]

The political situation in Libya was chaotic after the downfall of Qaddafi. Having been unified by a shared resolve to oust the dictator, the anti-Qaddafi rebellion fragmented along regional, tribal, familial, ideological, and religious lines. Dozens of militias, formed organically in the fight against the regime, claimed checkerboard authority over various towns and tribal areas. Heavily armed, they occasionally battled each other for such spoils as control of airports and trade routes. When fighters from Misrata who had helped liberate Tripoli lingered in occupation of that city, they wore out their welcome among its residents. Intense and complicated quarrels erupted over property as citizens and returning expatriates competed for ownership of assets that Qaddafi had nationalized.[61]

The NTC struggled to stabilize this situation. In August, it promulgated a constitution declaring that Libya would become a democracy governed by the will of the people, and, in September, it gained recognition from the United Nations as the de facto government of Libya.

As a self-appointed body of elites, however, the NTC lacked credibility among the people of Libya. Many rebels, especially Islamists, harbored deep suspicions about Chairman Jibril, given his past ties to the Qaddafi regime. Militias defied the NTC's claim of national authority over military and security matters and resisted its efforts to transition them into a national army. On July 28, 2011 (even before Qaddafi was overthrown), a rebel militia assassinated General Abdel Fattah Younes, a former government minister whom the NTC had designated as the commander of rebel forces, on suspicion that he was a secret agent of Qaddafi. The limited authority of the NTC was also revealed by the ineffectiveness of its directives to capture rather than kill Qaddafi.

The NTC also faced massive tactical challenges. The Council was able to recover Libyan financial assets overseas that the United Nations had frozen under Qaddafi and to revive oil production to 1.5 million barrels per day (83 percent of prewar levels) by May 2012. But the rebellion had taken the lives of some 30,000–50,000 Libyans and had seriously damaged the country's physical infrastructure. The NTC continually struggled to manage the budget, eradicate corruption, impose law and order, and provide such basic services as a potable water supply and waste removal.[62]

Could the Western intervention in Libya be deemed a long-term success?

At the time of Qaddafi's downfall, Western leaders voiced nuanced views on the success of their actions to overthrow the regime. On the one hand, they realized that Libya would encounter monumental challenges in transitioning to democratic government. "We're under no illusions," Obama remarked. "Libya will travel a long and winding road to full democracy." On the other hand, Obama and other leaders positively assessed the impact of the Western aerial intervention in facilitating the downfall of a brutal dictator. "Without putting a single U.S. service member on the ground," Obama boasted, "we achieved our objectives." Prime Minister Cameron declared, "I'm proud of the role that Britain has played" helping the Libyan people overthrow the dictator. Germany was "relieved and very happy," Chancellor Merkel noted. Invoking a popular Latin phrase to describe the historic watershed in Libyan history, Prime Minister Berlusconi observed, "now the war is over. *Sic transit gloria mundi* [Thus passes the glory of the world]."[63]

Assessments of the Western intervention became more critical in succeeding years as Libya failed to make a smooth transition to a democracy and instead devolved into a failed state afflicted with violence and instability. Obama eventually expressed considerable regret with the Western intervention even though it prevented massive state-sanctioned violence against Libyan citizens. "Even as we helped the Libyan people bring an end to the reign of a tyrant," he remarked to the UN General Assembly in September 2015, "our coalition could have and should have done more to fill a vacuum left behind." In 2016, Obama admitted that the intervention "didn't work" given that "Libya is still a mess." When asked by a television journalist to identify his "worst mistake" as president, Obama replied metaphorically, "probably, failing to plan for the day after" the downfall of Qaddafi.[64]

Secretary of Defense Robert M. Gates, who opposed Obama's decision to intervene, later publicly faulted the president for committing two strategic errors: expanding the mission to include regime change and failing to plan for the post-Qaddafi era. Obama could have used airpower to ground the Libyan air force and protect Benghazi, Gates argued, setting the stage for a political accommodation. By ousting Qaddafi and doing nothing to fill the political void, however, Obama set the stage for a debilitating civil war, the spread of the Islamic State, and strategic gains by Russia.[65]

While Obama expressed his misgivings, the foreign affairs committee of the British House of Commons released a scathing report on the Cameron government's policy in Libya. Cameron's strategy "was founded on erroneous assumptions and an incomplete understanding of the evidence," the committee concluded, and it unwisely embraced "an opportunist policy of regime change . . . not underpinned by a strategy to support and shape post-Gaddafi Libya." The results—which were foreseeable and thus avoidable—included "political and economic collapse, inter-militia and intertribal warfare, humanitarian and migrant crises, widespread human rights violations, the spread of Gaddafi regime weapons across the region and the growth of ISIL [Islamic State of Iraq and the Levant] in North Africa."[66]

Because it triggered Libya's descent to a failed state, the Western intervention in Libya garnered extensive public analysis. On the one hand, critics of the intervention argued that Western officials misread the evidence about the likelihood of imminent genocide. They could have decided to work with Qaddafi to stymie militant extremists and eventually to transition authority to his son Saif al-Islam or some other enlightened successor. The intervention, moreover, caused collateral damage in Libya and across the Middle East. By creating a vacuum of power in Libya, it facilitated eventual intervention by the Arab powers, Russia, and Turkey. By creating political instability conducive to the transit of fighters and weapons, it allowed terrorism to flourish and intensified the civil war in Syria. By expanding the mission from protecting civilians to regime change, the Western powers undermined their credibility and trustworthiness in the UN Security Council, the Arab League, and other international bodies. By turning against a small state leader who had relinquished his nuclear aspirations in exchange for their support, the Western powers undermined their broader nonproliferation objectives by discouraging other states from following Qaddafi's example.[67]

On the other hand, many observers continued to justify the intervention. They noted the popularity of the intervention among millions of Libyan people and the unusual international consensus on the necessity of intervention under "RtoP" doctrine. They reasoned that the chaos that afflicted Libya in the years following Qaddafi's ouster would have been even more violent, lethal, and destabilizing had the dictator remained in some degree of power; in Syria, often cited as a comparative example, prolonged state suppression of the Arab Spring uprisings resulted in hundreds of thousands of deaths. To these observers, the inability of the Libyan people to transition easily and promptly to a stable democracy and the failure of outside powers effectively to facilitate such an outcome did not negate the justification for the original intervention. "Even when interventions fail to end civil wars or resolve factional differences immediately," the scholars Jon Western and Joshua S. Goldstein concluded, "they can still protect civilians."[68]

7

CIVIL WAR, FOREIGN MEDDLING, AND POLITICAL DEADLOCK

LIBYA SINCE 2011

What steps were taken to establish a stable government after the downfall of Qaddafi?

The National Transitional Council (NTC) planned to build a democracy for the post-Qaddafi era. Even before the conquest of Tripoli, it clarified a plan to transition to an elected government in 18 months after Qaddafi's removal. The NTC prescribed that voters would elect 200 delegates to a new General National Congress (GNC), 120 as individual candidates and 80 as political party representatives. The GNC would replace the NTC, appoint a government to administer the country, and form a committee to write a constitution. Once ratified by popular referendum, the constitution would govern another round of elections to determine a permanent government. On October 23, 2011, three days after Qaddafi's death, the plan was set in motion with a target completion date of May 2013. Days later, Mahmoud Jibril resigned as NTC chairman, and the council named Abdel Rahim al-Keeb to succeed him as prime minister. An electrical engineer who had lived in exile since 1976 and was a dual US–Libyan citizen, Keeb had a clean slate and technocrat credentials but struggled to earn credibility among the people.[1]

This transition plan faced severe handicaps. Libya had no democratic tradition, no political parties, no system for registering voters or conducting elections, and no consensus on whether the state should practice religious or secular law or whether women should exercise equal rights. Militias remained reluctant to yield their power even to an elected government. Residents of Benghazi, fearing that the more populous Tripolitania would determine the new constitution and dominate an elected national government, openly talked about secession into a self-governing autonomous region. The NTC doggedly pressed on, passing an election law, founding an elections commission, and scheduling the first national elections for July 7, 2012. Only days before the polling, the council addressed the emerging separatism in Benghazi by transferring the authority to write a constitution from the GNC to a small committee to be determined by a separate election.[2]

Although there were outbreaks of violence and other irregularities, the July 2012 election was widely considered remarkably stable given the chaos that had dominated the country since Qaddafi's downfall. Some 1.7 million voters, 62 percent of those deemed eligible, cast ballots for the 200 delegates to the GNC. The National Forces Alliance, headed by the former NTC chairman Jibril, won the most seats, with 39. The Justice and Construction Party, formed by the Muslim Brotherhood to espouse Islamic ideology, by contrast, secured only 10 percent of the vote and 17 seats. On August 8, the NTC transferred power to the GNC, which elected Mohammed Yousef al Magariaf as GNC president and interim head of state.[3]

The GNC faced challenges from the outset. Given the absence of a legislative culture in the Qaddafi era, delegates grappled over the processes to set up a government, make decisions, and pass laws. Although elected, the parliament struggled to claim the mantle of authority and win public trust. The absence of a clear majority forced delegates to form coalitions, which proved unstable. Tensions between the secularist majority and the Islamist minority, the scholar Mary Fitzgerald noted, "triggered deep unease" and "became impossible to bridge." On September 11, the GNC elected Mustapha Abushagur as prime minister, but then rejected his slate of Cabinet nominees and, on October 7, passed a vote of no confidence in him. Ali Zeidan was named his successor a week later.[4]

How did the Western powers view the new government of Libya?

Western officials initially viewed the political situation in Libya with ambivalence. On the one hand, the GNC had limited authority and credibility. The militias were well-armed, independent-minded, and increasingly assertive. There was potential for Islamic extremists to exploit the instability. All Libyan factions seemed resistant to Western influence, and such Arab states as the United Arab Emirates (UAE) and Qatar were meddling in Libyan politics for their own purposes. "Nobody knows now what the political fabric of this country is going to look like after 42 years in which there was no political fabric," US Ambassador Gene Cretz remarked upon his return to Tripoli on September 21, 2011, after an absence of nine months. "So I think there is a genuine cause to be concerned that things could go wrong."[5]

On the other hand, Western officials found reasons to hope that Libya would emerge as a stable democracy. Libya's oil industry had the capacity to generate considerable wealth. Libyans were relatively homogeneous in their language and sectarian traditions, and, despite their historic disunity and fragmentation, they were more culturally cohesive than the peoples of such unstable countries as Iraq and Syria. Libya's desert landscape was not conducive to a guerilla insurgency. Even as the outcome of the rebellion hung in the balance, US, French, British, and Italian experts on Libya devised elaborate plans to build a democracy, stimulate the economy, stabilize the military situation, and prevent Islamic extremism.

Not long after the downfall of Qaddafi, however, Western powers tended to withdraw from Libya. Mired in Afghanistan and Iraq, US President Barack Obama indicated that he expected the European states to handle Libya. For their part, the Europeans looked to the United Nations to take charge. "We acted to protect you," NATO Secretary General Anders Fogh Rasmussen declared in Tripoli, while announcing the formal end of NATO's mission on October 31, 2011. "Together we succeeded. Libya is finally free." The United Nations, however, lacked the resources and power to achieve stability among Libya's rivalrous factions and militias. In 2012, the UN Support Mission in Libya (UNSMIL) tried to transition the three dominant militias in Tripoli into a unified military and police force, but the initiative was understaffed and underfunded, and the militias were not eager to follow UNSMIL's lead in any case.[6]

What were the origins of the deadly attack on the US consulate in Benghazi on September 11, 2012?

Given the reluctance of President Obama to use military power in Libya, the State Department took responsibility to shape Libya's future through diplomacy. Appointed in April 2012, Ambassador Christopher Stevens relished the opportunity to engage openly with the Libyan people and their leaders, in hope of steering them toward democratic stability. Conversant in Arabic and people-oriented, Stevens met with members of all Libyan factions and encouraged them to move forward together.[7]

Meanwhile, episodes of violence portended the emergence of Islamic extremism in Benghazi. There was a series of assassinations of former officials of the Qaddafi regime. In April and June, small explosive devices were used against the US Consulate, and someone rolled a grenade under the UN envoy's armored vehicle. After its officials were targeted in bomb and gun attacks, Britain closed its mission in Benghazi in early June. The US Consulate remained open (as did those of

204 LIBYA AND THE WEST

France, Italy, Turkey, Malta, and the European Union), although recommended enhancements of the US Consulate's security apparatus—its personnel, fortifications, and weaponry—remained uncompleted by late summer because of resource scarcity and bureaucratic inefficiency. Despite warnings that the security situation in Benghazi was deteriorating and that the US Consulate would be hard to defend against a coordinated attack, the State Department recruited and relied upon untested local militias to protect it.[8]

Despite knowing the risks, Ambassador Stevens and his information officer arrived in Benghazi in early September intent on recruiting local militia leaders as partners in a quest for stability. Senate investigators later determined that Stevens had declined an offer from the Pentagon's Africa Command to send additional security personnel to the city. Several militia leaders with whom Stevens met expressed appreciation for US assistance in deposing Qaddafi and expressed interest in attracting US business franchises to the city, but they also warned that the US diplomats should leave the city because conditions had become unsafe. These warnings, which proved to be prescient, were disregarded.

Turmoil erupted on September 11, the eleventh anniversary of the 2001 terrorist assaults on New York and Washington. In Muslim countries, public discourse fixated on an anti-Islamic video that a US citizen had produced and posted on the Internet. Backlash against the video, laced with anti-Americanism, quickly spread via social media throughout the Muslim world, and Egyptian television flooded Benghazi with content about the film, stoking outrage. In this context, about 120–150 militants launched an armed attack on the US Consulate at about 9:40 PM. The marauders occupied parts of the compound and started a fire that killed Stevens and his information officer. Fighting between US security personnel and militants continued sporadically through the night at both the consulate and a nearby Central Intelligence Agency (CIA) facility, claiming the lives of two US security officers.[9]

Why did the Benghazi attack become a prominent issue in US domestic politics?

Within the United States, a debate over the causes of the raid escalated into an embittered political dispute. Partisanship was elevated by the coincidence that the raid occurred less than two months before the US presidential election and only two weeks before the first of three debates between Obama and his Republican challenger, Mitt Romney. Heated public discourse ensued before time allowed intelligence officers and other investigators to determine exactly what had happened in Benghazi.

Obama administration officials initially explained the raid as a spontaneous escalation of a street demonstration against the anti-Islamic film. Prominent Republicans, by contrast, argued that the attack was premeditated, probably by al-Qaida, and that the administration had committed a major intelligence and security failure in not preventing or defeating it. Encouraged by confirmation that no street demonstration had preceded the raid—which disproved the administration's initial claims—the Republicans accused the administration of deliberately covering up al-Qaida's lethality to preserve the accolades Obama had earned by ordering the killing of al-Qaida's leader, Osama bin Laden, in May 2011.

In the context of growing partisan conflict within the United States, the Benghazi raid became a fixture of political debate in Washington for several years. Republicans in Congress launched a series of investigations into the attack that stretched more than two years and consumed millions of dollars in public funds. As former Secretary of State Hillary Clinton emerged as a leading candidate for the Democratic Party's nomination for president in 2016, Republicans focused on her role in the debacle. The House of Representatives Benghazi Committee, chaired by a Republican, released an 800-page report in June 2016 that sharply faulted the State Department, the CIA, and the Pentagon for security lapses and intelligence failures. The

206 LIBYA AND THE WEST

Clinton campaign characterized the report as a collection of "discredited . . . conspiracy theories." Presumptive Republican presidential nominee Donald J. Trump, by contrast, charged on June 22 that Ambassador Stevens "was left helpless to die as Hillary Clinton soundly slept in her bed."[10]

Official and media investigations into the Benghazi raid eventually determined that there were elements of truth in the views of both sides. Although there were no street demonstrations immediately before the attack, the anti-Islamic film had generated anger among Benghazi residents. The attack on the consulate was organized and conducted by several Islamist militias that had ties to al-Qaida, but there is no evidence that the attack was a grand scheme premeditated by al-Qaida. Rather, local, Islamist militias opportunistically exploited the anger surrounding the film to pursue their own interests of bloodying the US government and gaining political capital in the Libyan internal conflict.[11]

In a report approved on a bipartisan basis, the US Senate Select Committee on Intelligence (SSCI) concluded in 2014 that the Benghazi raid was preventable. The SSCI found that, given the growing intensity of security threats in Benghazi, the State Department should either have fortified or evacuated the consulate. Tragically, Ambassador Stevens himself overestimated the reliability of local militias to protect him from harm and missed opportunities to protect himself and his colleagues. The SSCI also found that more robust security protocols by the State Department or better coordination and communication among the State Department, the CIA, and the Pentagon could have averted the deadly outcome of the incident.[12]

How well did the elected government of Libya stabilize and administer the country?

The Libyan government elected in July 2012 never achieved the stature needed to govern the country. It proved incapable of exerting national authority over the various militias, providing basic civil and social services, stabilizing the consumer economy, or fostering such reforms as job training and development. While the government enjoyed access to overseas financial assets that were unfrozen by foreign states after Qaddafi's downfall, it struggled to translate that largesse into effective action or popular credibility. The corruption and infighting endemic in the Qaddafi era persisted into the new age. "The country's new leaders know nothing else but the old ways," a UN official commented privately, "which in turn fuels the impression that the old ways are back."[13]

The government was handicapped by the emergence of broad, cross-cutting schisms among the Libyan people. The historic rivalry between eastern and western Libya persisted, and, by 2013, some eastern tribes pursued separatism, declaring the autonomy of Cyrenaica. In addition, there was mistrust between members of different tribes and towns, between the secular and the religious, between those who had and those who had not served the Qaddafi regime, and between those who returned from exile and those who had never left the country. Such conflicts aggravated the usual tensions generated by competition for power and wealth, and, with the country awash in weapons, the conflicts often triggered violence. Human rights monitors documented a rising tide of abuses, detentions, torture, and revenge killings by multiple parties.[14]

In 2012–2013, the elected government enacted two policies that severely weakened its own foundations. First, in the hope of securing their loyalty and integration, Prime Minister Keeb decided to pay the militias that remained in occupation of most of the country and defiant of national authority. That decision, however, caused a result that was opposite of the intention. Because the payments were not dependent on concessions, militias continued to operate independently even after accepting the funding. In the absence of other job opportunities, in fact, multitudes of *new* members joined militias as their new riches became evident. Within a year of

Qaddafi's downfall, the number of registered militias swelled to 500 and their fighters increased in number from 60,000 to 200,000. The largesse stimulated rising expectations among the militias, many of which threatened or used violence to extort increasingly larger payments from administration officials.[15]

Second, the GNC passed the Political Isolation Law, which banned any former official of the Qaddafi regime from public office for 10 years. Enacted on May 5, 2013, the ban included not only high-ranking Qaddafi loyalists but also apolitical technocrats and military officers. No exceptions were made for those who had defected early and risked their lives in the revolt. Passed under pressure from militia leaders who sought to flex their muscle and eliminate political rivals, the law denied the government the expertise and experience of former officials, thereby weakening public trust in the government and fomenting tension between those who supported the ban and those who opposed it.[16]

How did the Western powers try to stabilize Libya after the Benghazi raid?

Seeing that Libya was destabilizing, Western leaders tried to shore up its government. President Obama welcomed Prime Minister Zeidan to the White House in March 2013 and listened sympathetically to a request for funds to create a new security force that would offset the militias. British Prime Minister David Cameron invited Zeidan to the June 2013 Group of Eight (G-8) meeting in Northern Ireland, where Britain, the United States, Italy, and Turkey agreed on a plan to train 20,000 soldiers to serve the Libyan government in the so-called General Purpose Force. "I'm proud of the role Britain played in getting rid of Colonel Gaddafi [Qaddafi] in Libya," Cameron said, in announcing the training program. "But we need to help that country secure its future" by training troops "to help Prime Minister Z[e]idan disarm and integrate the militias and take the fight to the extremists."[17]

This training program failed miserably. The Pentagon showed little enthusiasm for it, doubtful of its efficacy, fearful that it would drain human resources from more important priorities in Afghanistan and Iraq, and frustrated by the inability of Libyan officials to execute agreements and make expected financial payments. Serious concerns emerged about the vetting of the recruits, which made the trainers seem vulnerable to insider attacks. The attrition rate among recruits neared 75 percent, and those who finished programs seemed to melt into the population rather than join the national army. Several training programs were beset by gross misconduct by the recruits, including widespread drunkenness among trainees in Turkey. The United States cancelled a program in Libya after trainees facilitated massive theft of US property from the training base. The British government cancelled a program at a base in Bassingbourn, England, after trainees committed a wave of sexual assaults against British citizens in nearby Cambridge in October 2014.[18]

Why did the elected government of Libya decline in 2014?

In 2013–2014, it became clear that the elected government lacked the stature to govern the country or contain emergent armed conflicts among the militias. In October 2013, the government's impotence was demonstrated when militias kidnapped Prime Minster Zeidan and briefly held him for ransom before releasing him to an intermediary. The GNC remained in session after its original mandate expired on February 7, 2014, provoking a crescendo of criticism and opposition from multiple detractors. In this context of government dysfunction, the equilibrium among the militias that had pacified the country since Qaddafi's downfall gave way to flares of violence between armed groups that soon escalated into sustained fighting in Misrata, Benghazi, and elsewhere.

In a consequential move on February 14, Major General Khalifa Haftar announced the suspension of the GNC, declared

210 LIBYA AND THE WEST

himself the commander of the army, and pledged to organize elections of a new government reflective of the popular will. Long concerned with Islamist militants, Haftar claimed that his action was justified by the GNC's close ties to Islamists as well as the expiration of its original mandate. It was widely suspected that Haftar modeled himself on Egyptian General Abdel Fattah al-Sisi, who, in July 2013, had overthrown the elected government in Cairo because it was dominated by the Muslim Brotherhood. Haftar echoed al-Sisi when he stated, in a video sent to journalists, that "the national command of the Libyan army is declaring a movement for a new road map."[19]

A power struggle ensued between the GNC and General Haftar. "Libya is stable," Prime Minister Zeidan declared in reply to Haftar's announcements. "The GNC is doing its work and so is the government. The army is in its headquarters and Khalifa Haftar has no authority. No military units have moved to touch any institutions." In March, however, Zeidan fled to Germany to avoid an investigation into alleged corruption in his government. His successor, Abdullah Thinni, soon became the target of multiple threats of violence.[20]

Haftar escalated the power struggle by launching a military campaign that he called Operation Dignity on May 16. Commanding a coalition of eastern tribal militias and army and air force units that he christened the Libyan National Army (LNA), the general attacked Islamist militias in Benghazi like Ansar al-Sharia as well as pro-GNC forces. When the GNC declared Haftar's move unlawful, Zintani militias that favored Haftar moved into Tripoli and shelled the GNC's meeting hall.

The GNC tried to appease the growing rebellion by promptly scheduling national elections for a new parliament to be called the House of Representatives, but that move did little to stabilize the country. Held on June 25, the elections were marred by low voter turnout: whereas 2.8 million people had registered and 1.7 million (62 percent) had voted in the 2012 election, only 1.5 million registered and 630,000 (42 percent) voted in 2014. The low turn-out reflected both widespread doubts about the legitimacy of Haftar's moves as well as personal security concerns, especially among women, in the face of escalating violence. After faring poorly in the polling, Muslim Brotherhood and other Islamist groups came to fear that the new parliament would pass unfriendly laws, and thus gradually resorted to violent resistance. Overall, the incoming House of Representatives had limited credibility and a modest popular mandate.[21]

What triggered the start of full-scale civil war?

Galvanized by Haftar's aggressiveness and by the election results, Islamist, Misratan, and Amazigh militias launched a counteroffensive against Operation Dignity on July 13. Called Libya Dawn, the initiative initially focused on taking military control of the Tripoli Airport, which Haftar had used to supply his allies in the capital city. Dawn forces captured the airport in late July and controlled most of the capital by the end of August. The leaders of Dawn proclaimed themselves the heirs of the anti-Qaddafi, democratic revolt of 2011 and cast their adversaries as usurpers with ties to the old regime. They portrayed Haftar as a protégé of al-Sisi and vowed to defeat his effort to derail their democratic movement.

For several weeks, Dignity and Dawn forces settled into two hostile camps that focused on eradicating pockets of resistance within the territory they controlled: Dignity attacked Islamists in Benghazi, while Dawn went after Zintanis in Tripoli. Hostilities soon spread across the entire country, however, including an intense and prolonged fight for Benghazi. While Dawn probably counted more fighters, Dignity had airpower and better weapons. The violence catalyzed the alignment of nearly all Libyan militias into two coalitions broadly identified as non-Islamist and Islamist, although other axes of disagreement like tribal and geographic loyalties blurred the lines. It became increasingly difficult for moderates to occupy a neutral ground. The fighting disrupted the oil industry, with production falling from 1.6 million to 400,000 barrels per day from 2012 to 2014, stressing the country's financial infrastructure. The violence took a toll on the Libyan people, who faced food and fuel shortages, blockaded roads and closed ports, waves of crime, and the breakdown of civic life and social services.[22]

The violence between Dignity and Dawn spawned a deep division in the political structure of the country. The new House of Representatives was inaugurated on August 4 in Tripoli. Citing security concerns after Misratan militias seized the Tripoli airport from the Zintanis, however, its non-Islamist, two-thirds majority voted weeks later to relocate to Tobruk, some 800 miles to the east and under the control of Dignity. Denouncing this move as unlawful, the Islamist one-third minority of the House of Representatives remained in Tripoli, where they reconvened the GNC and formed the so-called Government of National Salvation (GNS) under Prime Minister Khalifa al-Ghwell. By January 2015, Libya had two rival governments and two central banks. The division was so complete that some of Libya's overseas embassies represented Dawn and others, Dignity. Plans for the parliament elected in 2014 to write a new constitution stalled.[23]

Why did Muslim-majority states become involved in the Libyan civil war?

Several Arab states became involved in the Libyan civil war in support of different factions. The UAE and Qatar both had intervened militarily to back the revolt against Qaddafi and were welcomed by the Western powers seeking Arab League partners in their mission to stymie the old regime. Once Qaddafi was removed, however, the UAE and Qatar remained involved in support of competing militias. Eager to protect its home front against Islamic extremism, the UAE supported General Haftar and Dignity, surreptitiously bombing Dawn and Islamist units near Tripoli, in Benghazi, and in Derna in 2014–2018. Egypt also backed Dignity for the same antiextremism purpose. Qatar, by contrast, backed Dawn's Islamist militias because it favored a more inclusive Libyan government. Eventually, Turkey and Sudan offered tactical assistance to Dawn. Both foreign coalitions sent weapons to their proteges, in violation of UN arms embargoes and No Fly Zone restrictions in effect since 2011.[24]

How did the Western powers assess the Libyan civil war?

Western powers deeply regretted that Libya's revolution against Qaddafi gave way to a debilitating civil war, but they were adamantly opposed to intervening to end it. In the aftermath of the murder of Ambassador Stevens, President Obama redoubled his conviction that he would not again become involved militarily in Libya. While State Department officials viewed the rise of General Haftar with concern that civil war might result, the Pentagon and the CIA saw value in the general's counterterrorism actions. When opposition militias seized the Marsa al-Hariga and Zueitina oilfields and diverted the royalties to eastern Islamists in 2013, the United States flatly denied a request from Prime Minister Zeidan for airstrikes on the attacking forces.[25]

As the civil war intensified in late 2014, Western states withdrew their diplomats from Libya. The United Nations, France, the United States, and Britain shuttered their embassies and missions in Tripoli in July and August, as gun battles raged nearby. As she closed the US embassy and evacuated its staff to Tunisia, US Ambassador Deborah Jones commented privately that "it's not worth losing even a finger over this bullshit." The last Western power to withdraw, Italy closed its embassy in February 2015, one month after Turkish Air, the last foreign carrier serving Libya, suspended flights to the country.[26]

Western powers generally backed UN diplomacy to curtail the fighting. In late 2014, UN Special Envoy Bernardino Leon developed a plan to create a national unity government at

214 LIBYA AND THE WEST

Ghadames, a town near the Algerian border. In January 2015, Leon proposed that such measures as escrowing oil revenues, refreezing Libyan overseas assets, and embargoing arms might compel the militias to accept a ceasefire monitored by UN peacekeepers. Leon admitted, however, that he was engaged in "wishful thinking," and his diplomacy made no headway.[27]

What kind of threat did the Islamic State in Iraq and Syria pose in Libya?

As civil war between Dawn and Dignity raged, Libya was further destabilized by the emergence of militias loyal to the Islamic State in Iraq and Syria (ISIS), a conservative, militant Islamic movement that was battling for control of Syria and Iraq. In April 2014, the Islamic Youth Shura Council (*Majlis Shura Shabab al-Islam* in Arabic or MSSI)—filled with local Islamists who had returned from battling against the Assad regime in Syria—claimed that it was Derna's security force and that it would impose Sharia law in the city. In October, MSSI declared that its domain in Derna was part of the caliphate controlled by ISIS. By early 2015, ISIS appointed a Tunisian as the Emir of Tripoli and a Yemeni as the Emir of Derna—signaling its intentions to expand across the country.[28]

Exploiting Dignity's and Dawn's preoccupations with each other, ISIS spread its influence across Libya in 2015. It distributed charity and propaganda to win hearts and minds and used social media to recruit fighters from across the Middle East and Africa. It engaged in terrorist attacks, such as the early 2015 car bombing of a luxury hotel in Tripoli and the beheadings of 21 Egyptian Coptic Christians. It engaged in sporadic gun battles with rival militias in both the Dawn and Dignity coalitions, fighting even rival Islamist militias like Ansar al-Sharia. By mid-2015, ISIS controlled Sirte and outlying territory stretching some 200 miles along the coastline, and its influence reached Benghazi and Tripoli. It was believed to have some 5,000 fighters deployed. In areas under its control, ISIS rigorously enforced sharia law, suppressing women, destroying tobacco products, requiring observance of prayer rituals, and extremely punishing anti-Islamic offenses.[29]

How did the Western powers respond to the rise of ISIS in Libya?

The Western powers viewed the rise of ISIS in Libya with alarm. They were concerned that ISIS would not only destabilize Libya but also use it as a base to launch terrorist attacks in Europe and to expand into other African states. European leaders feared that ISIS fighters would infiltrate the growing stream of African migrants crossing the Mediterranean from Libya to Italy. A series of eight deadly terrorist attacks across France in 2015 and early 2016—attributed to ISIS—made the threat seem real and acute. ISIS posed an "imminent" threat to Italy, Defense Minister Roberta Pinotti asserted in early 2015. "Italy has defense needs and cannot have a caliphate ruling across the shores from us." At the conclusion of a meeting in November, French President Francois Hollande and Italian Prime Minister Matteo Renzi publicly warned that ISIS in Libya must be dealt with urgently.[30]

At first, however, Western leaders expressed reluctance about militarily battling ISIS in Libya. Even when Prime Minister al-Thinni urged Western action against ISIS to ensure the security of Europe as well as Libya, British and US leaders reasoned that Libya's divided government and fractured militias made it difficult to intervene effectively. Obama feared that Western intervention might undermine the new, fragile Government of National Accord established in 2015. Instead, US and British officials encouraged and equipped both Dignity and Dawn to counter ISIS, hopeful that, in the process, the two coalitions would develop practices of cooperation on a common purpose. "Our strong preference, as has always been the case, is to train Libyans to fight," Obama stated in February 2016. "There's a whole bunch of constituencies who are hardened fighters and

216 LIBYA AND THE WEST

don't ascribe to ISIS or their perverted ideology. But they have to be organized and can't be fighting each other."[31]

To this end, the Western powers dispatched special operations forces to Benghazi and Misrata in 2016, to coordinate anti-ISIS operations by Dignity and Dawn, respectively. US and British special forces (aided by Jordanian troops serving as interpreters) reportedly concentrated on mobilizing anti-ISIS militias and gathering intelligence on ISIS targets in and near Sirte. In August 2016, Obama authorized a broad US air campaign to support Misratan militias that attacked the ISIS stronghold in Sirte. In a campaign aided by nearly 500 sorties by US war planes, the Misratans liberated Sirte from ISIS control in December.[32]

French paramilitary troops organized by the General Directorate for External Security (DGSE) mobilized militias to strike at the framework of ISIS. Some of them even fought alongside Haftar's troops, a point that the government in Paris reluctantly acknowledged only after three of its soldiers were killed when Islamic militants shot down their helicopter near Benghazi in July 2016. Fearing a public backlash over any civilian casualties, Italy did not participate in the air attacks and denied use of its airbases to conventional US combat aircraft. It allowed the United States, however, to use a base in Sicily to launch armed drones that were sent aloft in defense of Allied special forces in Libya.[33]

In addition to supporting ground operations by anti-ISIS Libyan militias, the United States, Britain, and France conducted surgical airstrikes to destroy ISIS's infrastructure and kill its leaders. In November 2015, a targeted US airstrike in Derna, facilitated by French ground forces, killed Abu Nabil, an Iraqi who commanded ISIS in Libya. Abu Nabil's death "will degrade ISIL's ability to meet the group's objectives in Libya," a Pentagon spokesman asserted (using an alternative acronym for ISIS), "including recruiting new ISIL members, establishing bases in Libya, and planning external attacks on the United States." Two months later, British and

French ground operatives coordinated another US airstrike, this one on an ISIS training base and armory at Sabratha, west of Tripoli. That assault killed dozens of ISIS fighters including Noureddine Chouchane, a Tunisian-born commander believed to have perpetrated attacks in his native country in 2015. On January 19, 2017, the day before his term ended, Obama authorized one final, massive airstrike on two ISIS training camps near Sirte, killing 80 militants.[34]

Degraded by Haftar's army and Western airpower, ISIS in Libya devolved in 2017 to an estimated 500 militants organized in cells hidden in the deserts of southern Libya. They remained a continuing concern to their adversaries, however, as they sporadically launched terrorist attacks in Libya and Europe (including a suicide bombing that killed 22 people at a concert in Manchester, England, in May 2017). With the support of Prime Minister Fayez al-Sarraj, US President Donald J. Trump ordered a drone strike in September 2017 that killed 17 ISIS fighters at a camp south of Sirte.[35]

Thereafter, ISIS in Libya organized episodic terrorist attacks against government buildings, military bases, and oil facilities, and the United States conducted periodic airstrikes to interdict them. The tumult surrounding General Haftar's April 2019 attack on the GNA in Tripoli (see below) enabled ISIS to regroup and renew its campaign of violence, given that Haftar's forces were distracted from their usual vigilance against ISIS and that the United States withdrew its counter-terrorism special operations forces from Tripoli for security reasons. ISIS opportunistically conducted nine terrorist attacks between April and November 2019, mostly in southern Libya but also in Derna. In September, the United States retaliated by conducting drone strikes on ISIS targets in southern Libya.[36]

Why did the United Nations fail to resolve the civil war?

UN officials searched for a diplomatic settlement of the civil war between Dignity and Dawn forces. On December 17, 2015, they brokered the Libyan Political Agreement (LPA), signed in Skhirat, Morocco, by representatives of the GNC and the House of Representatives whose war weariness was intensified by the growth of ISIS. The LPA established the Government of National Accord (GNA), which included a Presidency Council (PC), an advisory High State Council (HSC), and the existing House of Representatives as a legislative branch. The GNA was given a mandate of two years, at the end of which it would hold national elections. Led by Prime Minister Sarraj, members of the Presidential Council and the cabinet of the GNA arrived in Tripoli on March 30, 2016. The UN Security Council unanimously recognized the GNA as the national government of Libya.[37]

The GNA, however, faced substantial obstacles from the start. After organizing in Tunisia, in January 2016, Sarraj's cabinet had to travel to Tripoli by sea after unfriendly militias denied it use of the airport, and most cabinet officers were confined to a naval base in Tripoli for security reasons. Lacking enforcement mechanisms like a national army or police force, the GNA struggled to run the country because several militias and factions defied its decisions and directives on such core matters as financial policy and oil production. By 2017, policy disagreements inspired two of the nine members of the Presidency Council to boycott meetings and issue statements contradicting government policies.

General Haftar, moreover, continued to accrue political influence, to the detriment of the GNA. Although the chairman of the House of Representatives initially had endorsed the new government, Haftar expressed his lack of confidence in it. The House of Representatives blocked several cabinet appointments, and, in 2016, it withdrew its earlier endorsement of the GNA. As Haftar fought to suppress ISIS—in partnership with France and other foreign states—he gained political influence and international stature on par with the GNA. By 2018, Haftar's forces controlled two-thirds of Libya's territory containing 70 percent of its people and all its oil production capacity.

Arab state diplomacy to reconcile the GNA and Haftar's regime came to naught. Egypt invited Sarraj and Haftar to work out a reconciliation plan at a meeting in Cairo in February 2017, but Haftar declined to meet. Three months later, Sarraj and Haftar met in Abu Dhabi under UAE auspices but failed to reach any accord.[38]

In part because of Western pressures, the GNA and Haftar were able to develop a tenuous tactical partnership on national financial matters. When his forces captured the ports of Ras Lanuf and Es Sider in June 2018, Haftar gained control of Libya's oil export infrastructure. He declared that he would redirect oil export revenues to the oil company and bank associated with his regime in eastern Libya rather than to the National Oil Corporation (NOC) and Central Bank of the GNA. The international community refused, however, to make transactions with the eastern firms, insisting that all foreign sales must be conducted by the NOC. Haftar relented, and an uneasy partnership developed in which the GNA paid the salaries of public employees and soldiers who answered to Haftar, while Haftar allowed the oil to flow to foreign markets under the domain of the GNA. But political quarrels between the two factions led to a series of disruptions in oil production in the early 2020s, resulting in an output of 1.2 million barrels per day in 2024 (down from the peak of 3.8 million in 1970).[39]

How did the civil war shape patterns of human migration in Libya?

The instability in Libya intensified the long-standing concern among European powers (especially Italy) that migrants would use the north African country as a corridor for unauthorized transit to Europe. Whereas Qaddafi had prevented the mass exodus of disaffected persons, the vacuum of state authority that followed his downfall provided optimal conditions for unauthorized migration. The insecurity of Libya's land borders enabled thousands of migrants—mostly from sub-Saharan

Africa—to enter the country. Militias, organized crime, and other opportunistic entities put together a shadowy, lucrative human trafficking network that shepherded migrants to the north coast and conveyed them across the Mediterranean aboard rickety watercraft. By 2015–2016, an estimated 10,000 migrants per month exited Libya for Europe, with nearly 500 per month perishing enroute. In the first half of 2017, Italy reported the arrival of 93,000 migrants, a 17 percent increase from the first half of 2016, and, by early 2018, some 400,000 Africans had reached Italy.[40]

Italy worked hard to stem that human tide. The responsibility to care for the thousands of newly arrived migrants—and to rescue those whose voyages became imperiled—consumed budgetary resources. The migration stimulated nativism among the Italian electorate, threatening an electoral upheaval against the government of Prime Minister Paolo Gentiloni. In 2017, therefore, Gentiloni negotiated the Libya–Italy Memorandum of Understanding on Migration (LIMUM) with the GNA in Tripoli. Under the deal, the GNA pledged to stem the outflow of migrants in exchange for some $100 million in Italian and EU funding for such ends as equipping the Libyan coast guard and building detention centers in Libya. Italy also reportedly paid several Libyan militias to cease and suppress trafficking. LIMUM achieved its stated purpose; the arrival in Italy of 11,000 Africans in January–April 2018 represented a 75 percent decline in the rate of migration compared to the same period in 2017.[41]

This decline, however, came too late to avert an electoral upheaval in Italy. The influx of African migrants over several years had generated anti-immigration and nationalist movements that were embraced by such populist parties as the Five Star Movement (FSM) and the League. In the national elections of March 4, 2018, FSM won 33 percent of the vote, the largest single party plurality. On June 1, it coalesced with the League to form a government under Prime Minister Giuseppe Conte.[42]

After the onset of the COVID-19 pandemic in 2020, Italy forcibly blocked the arrival of migrant vessels, impounded rescue ships of humanitarian-minded nongovernment organizations that had traditionally picked up migrants at sea and delivered them to Italian ports, and extended LIMUM to 2023. The rate of unauthorized immigration to Libya fell dramatically: in 2017–2023, 108,000 migrants (including 24,680 in 2022 alone) were forcibly returned to Libya, where they faced captivity in harsh detention centers. When Italian courts ruled it unlawful for the government to return migrants picked up at sea to a war zone like Libya, Prime Minister Giorgia Meloni of the conservative Brothers of Italy party negotiated an extension of the LIMUM to 2026, paying Libyan militias to detain migrants seeking to reach watercraft on the Mediterranean.[43]

How did European powers attempt to resolve the political deadlock in Libya?

In 2018, France and Italy launched competing political initiatives to broker a settlement between the GNA and General Haftar. Rivals for oil and gas contracts in Libya, the two European powers vied for the reputation of being the leading European power on Libyan matters.

Moving first, French President Macron hosted the May 2018 Paris Peace Forum, a multinational conference attended by Libyan leaders and African heads of state (but not Italy, which was not invited). During the conference, Prime Minister Sarraj, General Haftar, House of Representatives President Aguila Saleh, and Chairman of the State Council Khaled al-Mishri agreed in principle to hold elections on December 10, 2018. Two months later, Sarraj and Haftar returned to Paris, where Macron presided over their signing of an agreement providing for a ceasefire, recognition of Haftar's command of the LNA, and elections by the end of 2018. British Foreign Minister Boris Johnson visited Haftar near Benghazi, Sarraj in Tripoli, and militia leaders in Misrata to encourage them to honor the Paris agreement. The Paris agreement, however, did little to curb violence or build stability in Libya.[44]

Italy matched the French initiative by hosting a conference in Sicily on November 12–13, 2018, attended by 36 nations. Having recently been formed in a populist backlash against the migration of Africans from Libya, the government of Prime Minister Conte hoped to stabilize Libya and thereby mitigate the exodus of Africans from its coast, as well as reclaim its legacy as the European leader on Libyan affairs. Viewing the French plan for elections in December 2018 as unviable, Italy aimed for an agreement among the Libyan factions to hold a national unity conference in January 2019 and elections soon thereafter. General Haftar belatedly reneged on his pledge to attend the conference, citing his objection to the presence there of Turkish delegates and Libyan Islamists, and he showed up only for a private sidebar meeting with Sarraj, Egyptian President al-Sisi, and Russian foreign minister Dmitry Medvedev. There, Haftar and Sarraj reaffirmed their commitment to holding democratic elections, and Haftar pledged that he would not attempt to overthrow Sarraj in the meantime.[45]

Did US policy in Libya change under President Donald J. Trump?

Under President Trump, US policy in Libya reflected reluctance to become involved in Libya. By issuing an executive order in January 2017 banning entry into the United States of all travelers from Libya and six other Muslim-majority states, the new president insulted those Libyans who had looked favorably on the United States and who battled ISIS within their borders. At a March 2017 press conference with Italian Prime Minister Paolo Gentoloni, Trump declined Gentoloni's request to become more involved in stemming unauthorized migration from Libya. "I do not see a role in Libya," Trump stated. "I think the United States has, right now, enough roles. We're in a role everywhere." He added that the United States would play a "primary role" in "ridding the world of ISIS . . . whether it's in Iraq or Libya or anywhere else." In July 2017, however, political adviser Stephen K. Bannon stymied an initiative by National Security Adviser H. R. McMaster and Secretary of Defense James Mattis to increase the number of US special operatives in Libya as a safeguard against the revival of ISIS. Bannon argued that Libya was not a high enough security priority to justify the risks of escalation inherent in the requested troop increase. Perhaps not coincidentally, Bannon resigned from Trump's staff in August, about a month before the president, for the first time, authorized an airstrike on an ISIS facility in Libya.[46]

US policy also reflected ambivalence between support for General Haftar and support for the GNA. On the one hand, Trump did not disrupt the State Department's policy of backing the GNA. He received Prime Minister Sarraj at the White House in December 2017, but declined Sarraj's request to become more involved in stabilizing Libya. "President Trump underscored the United States' continued support for the Government of National Accord," the White House press office stated discreetly after the meeting, "and the United Nations-facilitated efforts to achieve political reconciliation in Libya." Trump signaled limited interest in the GNA by leaving vacant key government posts (including Ambassador to Libya), limiting the number of special operatives on duty in Libya, and remaining reticent about and uninvolved in diplomacy pertaining to Libya.[47]

On the other hand, Trump took a liking to Haftar. The general appealed to Trump by extolling his own counterterrorism credentials and providing US intelligence and special forces officers access to Benghazi. President al-Sisi of Egypt lobbied Trump to back Haftar as the best guarantor of stability in Libya. Trump and such officials as Mike Pompeo, who served as Director of Central Intelligence in 2017–2018 and Secretary of State in 2018–2021, found favor in Haftar's anti-Islamist missions.[48]

224 LIBYA AND THE WEST

Why did the Libyan civil war resume in 2019?

Large-scale civil war erupted anew on April 4, 2019, when General Haftar launched a major military attack on Tripoli. This move violated the agreements Haftar had made during the various peace and reconciliation initiatives led by the international community since 2015. Haftar launched his attack, in fact, one day after UN Secretary-General António Guterres arrived in Tripoli to plan the envisioned national reconciliation conference. The offensive signaled Haftar's determination to displace the GNA, avoid elections, and consolidate his power over the entire country. Eschewing diplomacy and democracy, he gambled on his ability to capture control of the capital through force of arms.

On the first day of the attack, Haftar's troops occupied Gharyan, 60 miles south of Tripoli; Surman, 50 miles west; and Azizia, 25 miles southwest. The general apparently calculated that his advance would catalyze supporting actions by friendly Tripoli-area militias, leading to his conquest of the city. Rather than a rapid victory, however, Haftar's bold action provoked determined resistance by the GNA and Islamic militias. Prime Minister Sarraj openly defied Haftar and called on all militias to resist attacks "from terrorist groups, criminals, outlaws, and all who threaten the security of every Libyan city." As Misratan brigades moved to defend Tripoli against Haftar, its leaders declared that "we are ready for this tyrant with every strength we have. We are ready as always to stop this advance."[49]

How did the Western powers react to Haftar's offensive on Tripoli?

Western powers regretted the onset of the hostilities. The United States, Britain, France, Italy, and the UAE "urge all parties to immediately de-escalate tensions," the five powers declared jointly. "Our governments oppose any military action in Libya and will hold accountable any Libyan faction that precipitates further civil conflict." While generally considering Haftar at fault, the Western states also were bothered that the coalition that rallied to defend Tripoli included militias that had been linked to terrorism and trafficking of migrants. The European Union issued a statement expressing concern "at the involvement of terrorist and criminal elements." After Sarraj charged that French support of Haftar had encouraged his lawless militarism, Macron distanced himself from the general and voiced support of the GNA.[50]

In contrast to the five-power statement opposing hostilities, the Trump administration soon conveyed mixed views of Haftar's action. Given his own anti-Islamist principles, National Security Adviser John Bolton apparently saw value in Haftar's attack on Islamist militias in Tripoli. When Haftar phoned him days before the offensive began, Bolton reportedly said nothing to discourage the attack and instead indicated that if Haftar were going to attack, then he should do so rapidly. Once the attack started, by contrast, Secretary of State Mike Pompeo publicly declared that "we oppose the military offensive by Khalifa Haftar's forces and urge the immediate halt to these military operations against the Libyan capital." The State Department encouraged the British to draft a UN Security Council resolution condemning the offensive and demanding a ceasefire.[51]

President Trump soon reversed Pompeo's declared opposition to Haftar's attack. In an April 9 meeting in the White House, Egyptian President al-Sisi lobbied Trump to endorse Haftar's offensive because it targeted Islamists. On April 15, the US president phoned General Haftar; while the transcript of that conversation remains classified, the White House released a statement four days later reporting that "the President recognized Field Marshal Hifter's [Haftar's] significant role in fighting terrorism and securing Libya's oil resources, and the two discussed a shared vision for Libya's transition to a stable, democratic political system." Haftar apparently discerned strong support from the US president,

226 LIBYA AND THE WEST

evident in his forces' intensified shelling of Tripoli the day after the phone call. Within days, moreover, the US delegation at the United Nations withdrew its earlier support for a Security Council resolution condemning Haftar's attack, effectively blocking its passage.[52]

A report by the United Nations, leaked to the *New York Times* and the *Washington Post*, indicated that Haftar enjoyed the support of Erik Prince, the former head of the Blackwater security firm. The United Nations found that, at a meeting in Cairo on April 14, Haftar recruited Prince to organize an $80 million operation in which mercenaries would deliver weapons to Haftar's forces and assassinate GNA military commanders and other prominent adversaries of Haftar. In June, the *New York Times* reported, 20 mercenaries from Britain, South Africa, Australia, and the United States reached Libya, but Haftar criticized them for bringing weapons of lower-than-expected quality, forcing the mercenaries to abandon the operation and flee to Malta by sea. Prince firmly denied the UN report, calling it "a hatchet job."[53]

How did non-Western powers react to Haftar's offensive?

Several non-Western powers became involved in the battle for Tripoli between Haftar's militias and the GNA. The UAE continued its long-term support of the general, supplying him weapons that were mostly of Russian and Chinese origin. In June 2019, GNA forces overran a Haftar stronghold near Tripoli and found US-made Javelin anti-tank missiles that apparently had been sold by France to the UAE and then supplied to Haftar.[54]

Russia had been grooming Haftar since January 2017, when it sent its only aircraft carrier to Libya and welcomed the general aboard for an electronic meeting with the Ministry of Defense in Moscow. The government of Vladimir Putin became active in supporting the Haftar offensive on Tripoli because it promised to undermine Islamist militants and restore order through authoritarianism. Russia supplied Haftar's forces with military jets, artillery, missiles, and other weapons. The Wagner Group, a supposedly private entity with close ties to the Kremlin and headed by oligarch Yevgeniy Prigozhin, supplied 1,200 mercenaries to engage in hostilities, particularly sniper duty, on Haftar's behalf. Russia printed massive quantities of counterfeit Libyan currency for Haftar to pay his militias and manipulated social media and television news in Libya to generate popular support for the general's cause.[55]

The GNA, in turn, received considerable assistance from Turkey. President Recep Tayyip Erdogan resolved to rescue the Islamist militias in Tripoli from conquest by Haftar as well as to out-maneuver his rivals in the UAE (and Egypt). Beginning in late 2019, Turkey sent military advisers, supplied heavy weapons and electronic warfare systems, and recruited Syrian mercenaries, all in defense of the GNA. Erdogan indicated that his objective was to neutralize UAE and Russian actions and thereby force Haftar to suspend his offensive and enter peace talks with the GNA.[56]

What was the outcome of the battle for Tripoli?

The fight between Haftar and the GNA lasted for 14 months, killing or displacing thousands of people and laying waste to vast sectors of Tripoli. UN diplomacy to curtail the fighting proved futile. On June 10, 2019, the UN Security Council renewed the arms embargo against Libya, and, on January 19, 2020, world leaders conferencing in Berlin signed a 55-point pledge to uphold the embargo and promote a ceasefire in Libya. But these actions did little to stem the flow of weapons from the UAE, Russia, and Turkey and thereby had no immediate effect on the war. On January 30, UN special envoy Ghassan Salame complained to the Security Council that "unscrupulous actors . . . cynically nod and wink toward efforts to promote peace and piously affirm their support for the U.N.," only to "double down on a military solution, raising the

228 LIBYA AND THE WEST

frightening specter of a full-scale conflict and further misery for the Libyan people." His peacemaking in shambles, Salame resigned his post in March.[57]

In early 2020, the GNA gained the upper hand in the battle for Tripoli. The tide turned because Turkish-supplied drones proved effective at destroying the Russian-built, UAE-supplied, truck-mounted anti-aircraft missiles that had defended Haftar's ground troops, leaving them vulnerable to counterattack. By May, GNA militias liberated several towns from Haftar's control. Sensing a shift in momentum, Russia withdrew its mercenaries from Tripoli, leaving Haftar further exposed there, while sending 14 war jets to eastern Libya as a sign of support for Haftar on his home terrain. His offensive depleted, Haftar withdrew his forces from the Tripoli area beginning on June 5.[58]

Was the United Nations able to broker a postwar settlement?

Once Haftar withdrew his forces from the Tripoli theater, UN officials pursued a peace settlement. In a deal struck in October 2020, the GNA and Haftar's Libyan National Army agreed to a nationwide cessation of hostilities, a recall of all combatants to home bases, and the expulsion from Libya of all foreign fighters and mercenaries—estimated to be about 20,000 combatants at 10 military bases—by January 23, 2021. The two sides agreed to reopen roads and air travel routes, unify all military forces and armed factions under national authority, and restore the oil industry and central bank under government authority. They pledged to participate in follow-up meetings, to be held in Tunis beginning in November 2020, in pursuit of a comprehensive settlement of all major political issues.[59]

The intervening foreign powers did not immediately comply with the terms of this deal. Mercenaries and foreign troops remained within the country, and Russia and Turkey continued their arms supply lines to their respective clients. Stephanie Williams, a US diplomat who served for a time as

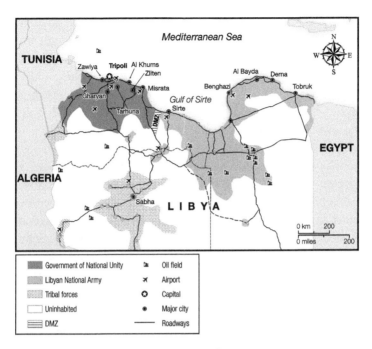

Map 6 Zones of Control in the Aftermath of the Libyan Civil War, 2022

a UN representative in the ceasefire talks, met with Libyan factions in Tunisia to encourage them to establish the independence of their country. "You may believe that these foreigners are here as your guests," she said, "but they are now occupying your house." Williams reflected the policy of the Joseph R. Biden administration of seeking to remove external powers from Libya and deny opportunity for ISIS or al-Qaida to infiltrate the country.[60]

In the follow-up negotiations facilitated by UN officials, representatives of Libya's political parties, factions, and tribes agreed in February 2021 on a new unified, transitional government. Abdul Hamid Dbeiba, a wealthy Misrata businessman and reputed deal maker, was elected interim prime minister. Dbeiba was charged to establish a cabinet, work with a parliament (balanced between eastern and western factions) to pass an electoral law, and hold elections for a permanent government on December 24, 2021. He was also expected to govern the country, revive the economy, resuscitate the oil industry, expel foreign troops and mercenaries, and tame the militias that controlled towns and neighborhoods. General Haftar, chastened and deflated by the defeat of his attack on Tripoli, endorsed the interim government.[61]

The electoral process, however, was rife with problems. None of the three leading contenders for the prime minister's position (out of a field of about 100 declared candidates) seemed likely to unify the country after an electoral victory. By refusing to resign as interim prime minister before launching his electoral campaign, as was required by the peace agreement, Dbeiba generated significant opposition among voters. General Haftar, another major contender, was deemed untrustworthy by western Libyans given his escalation of the civil war in 2018. The third candidate, the former dictator's son Saif al-Islam Qaddafi, had tried to rehabilitate his pre-2011 reputation as a reformist visionary. But the memory of his ruthlessness toward Arab Spring protestors—for which the International Criminal Court had indicted him for war crimes in 2015—made him unacceptable to another broad swath of the Libyan people. "After reviewing the technical, judicial and security reports," the president of the parliamentary election committee announced on December 22, a mere two days before the polling, "we would like to inform you that it will be impossible to hold the elections on the date set by the elections law."[62]

Thereafter, Libya remained in the throes of instability. The envisioned national elections remained postponed into mid-2024, despite discussions between the factions in Tripoli and Benghazi on how to schedule them. Episodic violence among militias caused scores of deaths. Natural disaster compounded the popular suffering: in September 2023, record rainfall induced the failure of two dams and caused a massive flood that pushed neighborhoods of Derna into the Mediterranean, killing an estimated 10,000 residents.[63]

NOTES

Introduction

1 For an overview of research conditions in Libya during the Qaddafi era, see Vandewalle, "Research Facilities."

Chapter 1

1 Tinniswood, *Pirates of Barbary*, 205–303.

2 Jefferson quoted in Wheelan, *Jefferson's War*, 44. See also Tinniswood, *Pirates of Barbary*, 274–75.

3 Wheelan, *Jefferson's War*, 102–305.

4 Leiner, *End of Barbary Terror*, 51–151.

5 Tinniswood, *Pirates of Barbary*, 286.

6 Vitelleschi quoted in Wright, *Emergence of Libya*, 221.

7 Italian government quoted in Wright, "Italian Fascism and Libyan Human Resources," 46.

8 Graziani quoted in Baldinetti, *Origins of the Libyan Nation*, 47; Badoglio quoted in Wright, "Italian Fascism," 46. See also de Grazia, *Perfect Fascist*, 144–81.

9 Metz, *Libya*, 23–31.

10 Mussolini quoted in Wright, *History of Libya*, 153; postage stamp cited in Philipps, "Fourth Shore."

11 Balbo quoted in McLaren, *Architecture and Tourism*, 18.

12 Wright, *History*, 153, 156.

13 Balbo quoted in Segrè, *Fourth Shore*, 88.

14 Moore, *Fourth Shore*, 117.

15 Mussolini quoted in McLaren, *Architecture and Tourism*, 20.

16 "Mussolini in Italy" (film), March 18, 1937.

17 Balbo quoted in Wright, "Italian Fascism," 50–55.

232 Notes

18 Mussolini quoted in Wright, "Italian Fascism," 47.

19 Wright, "Italian Fascism," 50–55.

20 Baldinetti, *Origins of the Libyan Nation*, 69–109.

21 Kelly, *Lost Oasis*, 82–114; "Secret Laval-Mussolini Agreement," 69–78.

22 Liddell Hart, *History*, 109, 137; Uldricks, *Second World War*, 228–46.

23 Kolinsky, *Britain's War in the Middle East*, 17–24, 146–53, 170–87; Carver, *Dilemmas of the Desert War*; Murray and Millett, *War to Be Won*, 92–108.

24 DeCandole, *Life and Times of King Idris*, 63–69.

25 Statement by Eden, "Libya Operations (Senussi Force)," January 8, 1942, accessed May 31, 2024, https://hansard.parliament.uk/commons/1942-01-08/debates/a6a225a9-b302-4227-b49c-6fc32 5128cf3/LibyaOperations(SenussiForce).

Chapter 2

1 Bills, *Libyan Arena*, 23.

2 Cumming and Arundell quoted in Bills, *Libyan Arena*, 21.

3 Proceedings of the Berlin Conference, August 1, 1945, accessed April 8, 2015, http://avalon.law.yale.edu/20th_century/decad e17.asp.

4 Bills, *Libyan Arena*, 10.

5 Bills, *Libyan Arena*, 159–60; Louis, *British Empire*, 265–95.

6 "Treaty of Peace with Italy," February 10, 1947, accessed May 31, 2024, https://www.loc.gov/item/lltreaties-ustbv004/.

7 Kelly, "Britain," 58.

8 Summary by McGhee, October 25, 1950, *Foreign Relations of the United States, 1950*, 5:1570. See also Kelly, "Britain," 59.

9 Wright, *Emergence of Libya*, 331; Kelly, *Cold War in the Desert*, 81–84.

10 Kelly, "Britain," 57; Wright, *Emergence of Libya*, 330.

11 Vandewalle, *History of Modern Libya*, 40. See also, UN General Assembly Resolution 289, November 21, 1949, accessed May 31, 2024, https://www.refworld.org/legal/resolution/unga/1949/en/7706.

12 Baldinetti, *Origins of the Libyan Nation*, 116–37; Gurney, *Libya*, 1–3.

13 Muschik, *Building States*, 74–76.

14 Proceedings of NCAL, December 2, 1950, quoted in Pelt, *Libyan Independence*, 445.

Notes   233

15 Constitution of the United Kingdom of Libya, October 7, 1951, in Pelt, *Libyan Independence*, 902–21.

16 Anglo-Libyan "Treaty of Friendship and Alliance," July 29, 1953, Treaty Series 003/1954: Cmd9043, accessed May 31, 2024, https://treaties.fcdo.gov.uk/data/Library2/pdf/1954-TS0 003.pdf.

17 Dulles to Wilson, December 13, 1954, *FRUS 1952–1954*, 11:598; Heefner, "Slice of Their Sovereignty," 50–77.

18 Toaldo, "Italo-Libyan Relationship," 87.

19 Gurney, *Libya*, 106.

20 Wright, *History of Libya*, 186–87.

21 Gurney, *Libya*, 17–39, 106.

22 Gurney, *Libya*, 42–62; Dietrich, *Oil Revolution*, 72–76.

23 Bini, "From Colony to Oil Producer," 49–50.

24 Bini, "From Colony to Oil Producer," 50–53.

25 John Kormann, "Recalling the Attack on the U.S. Compound in Benghazi–from June 1967," Association for Diplomatic Studies and Training Oral History Project, accessed May 31, 2024, http://adst.org/2012/11/recalling-the-attack-on-embassy-benghazi-from-june-1967/.

26 Proclamation of the Republic, September 1, 1969, "Libyan Revolution in the Words of Its Leaders," 211–12.

27 Saunders to Kissinger, September 2, 1969, *Foreign Relations of the United States, 1969–1976*, Volume E-5, Part 2, *Documents on Africa, 1969–1972*, doc. 37.

Chapter 3

1 BBC, "Bloodless Coup in Libya," accessed May 31, 2024, http://news.bbc.co.uk/onthisday/hi/dates/stories/september/1/newsid_3911000/3911587.stm.; and statement by crown prince, September 8, 1969, Ansell and al-Arif, *Libyan Revolution*, 73.

2 "Proclamation of the Republic," September 1, 1969, in "Libyan Revolution in the Words of Its Leaders," 211–12.

3 NSC Policy paper, November 10, 1969, *Foreign Relations of the United States, 1969–1976*, Vol. E–5, Part 2, *Documents on North Africa, 1969–1972*, doc. 44. See also Haley, *Qaddafi and the United States*, 20–26; minutes of Washington Special Action Group meeting, November 24, 1969, *Foreign Relations of the United States, 1969–1976*, Vol. E–5, Part 2, *Documents on North Africa, 1969–1972*, doc. 45.

234 Notes

4 Intelligence Memorandum, Washington, September 16, 1969, *FRUS, 1969–1976*, Vol. E-5, Part 2, *Documents of North Africa, 1969–1972*, doc. 39.
5 "Papers Bare Libya King's Plea in '69," *Chicago Tribune*, January 1, 2000.
6 Qaddafi statement, October 1, 1969, and RCC member statement, October 8, 1969, "Libyan Revolution in the Words of Its Leaders," 214.
7 Address by Qaddafi, September 22, 1970, Ansell and al-Arif, *Libyan Revolution*, 72–77; address by RCC member, September 18, 1969, "Libyan Revolution in the Words of Its Leaders," 204.
8 Qaddafi quoted in El-Khuwas, "Qaddafi and Islam," 62.
9 Qaddafi quoted in Hweio, "Muslim Brotherhood," 5–12; and in Obaid, *Failure of the Muslim Brotherhood*, 23.
10 Qaddafi address, October 16, 1969, "Libyan Revolution in the Words of Its Leaders," 206.
11 Qadhafi, *Green Book*, Part 1.
12 Vandewalle, *History*, 97. See also Metz, *Libya*, 47; Wright, *History*, 207.
13 Address by Qaddafi, September 16, 1969, "Libyan Revolution in the Words of Its Leaders," 207; address by Qaddafi, September 22, 1969, in Ansell and al-Arif, *Libyan Revolution*, 72–77. See also, Qadhafi, *Green Book*, part 2.
14 Vandewalle, *History*, 92.
15 Qaddafi quoted in Pargeter, *Libya*, 95.
16 Remarks by Qaddafi, November 28, 1969, "Libyan Revolution in the Words of Its Leaders," 210–11.
17 Address by Qaddafi, October 16, 1969, in Ansell and al-Arif, *Libyan Revolution*, 86–93. See also Ronen, "Britain's Return to Libya," 680.
18 Labbate, "Italy and Its Oil Dealings with Libya," 85–89.
19 Toaldo, "Italo-Libyan Relationship," 89–90; Seale and McConville, *Hilton Assignment*.
20 Maghrabi interviews, September 18, 30, 1969, "Libyan Revolution in the Words of Its Leaders," 209.
21 Mabruk quoted in Dietrich, *Oil Revolution*, 210.
22 Dietrich, *Oil Revolution*, 191–262.
23 Qaddafi quoted in Graf, "Making Use of the 'Oil Weapon,' " 195.
24 Wright, *History*, 206–7.
25 Wright, *Libya*, 201.

Notes 235

26 Qaddafi address, September 16, 1969, "Libyan Revolution in the Words of Its Leaders," 216.

27 Sadat quoted in Hilsum, *Sandstorm*, 62.

28 Ronen, "Libya's Qadhafi," 85–89.

29 Transcript of Qaddafi interview, October 14, 1969, Ansell and Al-Arif, *Libyan Revolution*, 77–86; Qaddafi address, October 16, 1969, "Libyan Revolution in the Words of Its Leaders," 216.

30 US Department of State, "U.S.-Libyan Relations since 1969," *Current Policy* No. 216. See also Haley, *Qaddafi and the United States*, 35–55.

31 Qaddafi quoted in Francis, "Libya's Empire of Terror," 9–10.

32 Qaddafi quoted in Wright, *History*, 212.

33 Nolutshungu, *Limits of Anarchy*, 145–49.

34 Nimeiri quoted in Hilsum, *Sandstorm*, 62.

35 Nolutshungu, *Limits of Anarchy*, 149–57.

36 Nolutshungu, *Limits of Anarchy*, 149–53.

37 Toaldo, "Italo-Libyan Relationship," 90.

38 US Department of State, "U.S.–Libyan Relations since 1969."

39 Qaddafi quoted in Youssef M. Ibrahim, "Qaddafi Terms the $220,000 Given to Billy Carter a Loan Tied to Business," *New York Times*, June 27, 1981.

40 Carter quoted in St. John, *Libya and the United States*, 114.

41 "Message of Leader Brother Muammar Qadhafi to Mr. Carter and Mr. Reagan," *Washington Post*, October 22, 1980.

Chapter 4

1 Vandewalle, *History*, 135–38.

2 Gurney, *Libya*, 195–215.

3 Haig quoted in Woodward, *Veil*, 116–17.

4 NSDD 322, December 14, 1988, accessed May 31, 2024, https://www.reaganlibrary.gov/public/archives/reference/scanned-nsdds/nsdd322.pdf. See also Frank Jacobs, "The World's Largest Sandbox," *New York Times*, November 7, 2011; Simons, *Libya and the West*, 63–81.

5 Simons, *Libya and the West*, 63–81; Nolutshungu, *Limits of Anarchy*, 202–28.

6 "Remarks at the Welcoming Ceremony for the Freed American Hostages," January 27, 1981, accessed September 27, 2021, https://www.reaganlibrary.gov/archives/speech/remarks-welcoming-ceremony-freed-american-hostages-0.

236 Notes

7 CIA quoted in Woodward, *Veil*, 113–14.

8 Casey quoted in Stanik, *El Dorado Canyon*, 25.

9 CIA quoted in Woodward, *Veil*, 114–15; Reagan quoted in Little, "Shores of Tripoli," 84.

10 Reagan Diary, June 1, 1981, Brinkley, *Diaries*, 22.

11 "Remarks on Board the U.S.S. Constellation off the Coast of California," August 20, 1981, accessed September 27, 2021, https://www.reaganlibrary.gov/archives/speech/remarks-board-uss-constellation-coast-california.

12 Reagan quoted in Woodward, *Veil*, 227. See also Stanik, *El Dorado Canyon*, 40–42.

13 Reagan quoted in Woodward, *Veil*, 227–28. See also NSDD 16, December 10, 1981, accessed September 27, 2021, https://www.reaganlibrary.gov/public/archives/reference/scanned-nsdds/nsdd16.pdf.

14 Brittan quoted in "Thatcher's Discussions over Murder of PC Yvonne Fletcher Revealed," *The Guardian*, January 2, 2014.

15 Qaddafi quoted in Hilsum, *Sandstorm*, 119.

16 Woodward, *Veil*, 401.

17 Casey quoted in Woodward, *Veil*, 348; interagency report, quoted in Woodward, *Veil*, 366.

18 CIA paper, "LIBYA: Qadhafi's Prospects for Survival," August 5, 1985, accessed October 1, 2021, https://www.cia.gov/readingroom/docs/CIA-RDP85T01058R000506710001-7.pdf. See also Little, "Shores of Tripoli," 87–89; Toaldo, *Origins of the US War on Terror*, 136–38.

19 Reagan Diary, December 29, 1985–January 3, 1986, Brinkley, *Diaries*, 380.

20 NSDD 138, April 3, 1984, accessed September 27, 2021, https://www.reaganlibrary.gov/public/archives/reference/scanned-nsdds/nsdd138.pdf; NSDD 179, July 20, 1985, accessed September 30, 2021, https://www.reaganlibrary.gov/public/archives/reference/scanned-nsdds/nsdd179.pdf. See also NSDD 30, April 10, 1982, accessed September 30, 2021, https://www.reaganlibrary.gov/public/archives/reference/scanned-nsdds/nsdd30.pdf.

21 NSDD 205, January 8, 1986, accessed September 30, 2021, https://www.reaganlibrary.gov/public/archives/reference/scanned-nsdds/nsdd205.pdf.

22 NSDD 205, January 8, 1986, accessed September 30, 2021, https://www.reaganlibrary.gov/public/archives/reference/scanned-nsdds/nsdd205.pdf; Wright, *History of Libya*, 213–14.

23 "The President's News Conference," January 7, 1986, accessed September 28, 2021, https://www.reaganlibrary.gov/archives/speech/presidents-news-conference-28; "The President's News Conference," April 9, 1986, accessed September 28, 2021, https://www.reaganlibrary.gov/archives/speech/presidents-news-con ference-26.

24 NSDD 205, January 8, 1986, accessed September 30, 2021, https://www.reaganlibrary.gov/public/archives/reference/scanned-nsdds/nsdd205.pdf.

25 "Libya Threatens Sea of Fire," *New York Times*, March 25, 1986. See also George P. Wilson, "Navy Prepares to Leave Gulf," *Washington Post*, March 27, 1986.

26 Reagan, "Address to the Nation on the United States Air Strike against Libya," April 14, 1986, accessed October 1, 2021, https://www.reaganlibrary.gov/archives/speech/address-nation-uni ted-states-air-strike-against-libya. See also NSDD 224, April 12, 1986, accessed September 30, 2021, https://www.reaganlibrary.gov/public/archives/reference/scanned-nsdds/NSDD224.pdf.

27 Stanik, *El Dorado Canyon*, 147–52.

28 Toaldo, *Origins of the US War on Terror*, 143–44.

29 Brian D. Johnson, "The Anger and the Expectation," *Maclean's*, April 28, 1986, accessed May 31, 2024, https://web.archive.org/web/20220425230347/https://archive.macleans.ca/article/1986/4/28/the-anger-and-the-expectation.

30 Whitehead quoted in Bernard Gwertzman, "John C. Whitehead: Parting the Fog at Foggy Bottom," *New York Times*, January 30, 1986. See also Steven J. Dryden, "Europeans to Halt Arms Sales to Nationals Backing Terrorism," *Washington Post*, January 28, 1986.

31 Tildemans quoted in E. J. Dionne, "Attack on Libya: Reproaches from Far and Wide," *New York Times*, April 16, 1986. See also Richard Bernstein, "French Say They Favored Stronger Attack on Libya," *New York Times*, April 23, 1986; E. J. Dionne, "Tension over Libya: Echoes in Rome and Tripoli," *New York Times*, April 20, 1986.

32 Qaddafi quoted in Ronen, "Libya's Conflict with Britain," 276. See also Stanik, *El Dorado Canyon*, 171–74; St. John, *Libya*, 133–34.

238 Notes

33 Joseph Lelyveld, "In Britain, Anti-Americanism Rises after Strikes on Libya," *New York Times*, April 26, 1986; William Drozdiak, "Bonn Cites Own Proof of Libyan Bomb at Disco, *Washington Post*, April 17, 1986.

34 Emmanuel de Margerie, "France's Side on the Libyan Raid," *Chicago Tribune*, May 7, 1986.

35 E. J. Dionne, "Attack on Libya: Reproaches from Far and Wide," *New York Times*, April 16, 1986. See also Rachel Donadio, "Turmoil in Libya Poses Threat to Italy's Economy," *New York Times*, March 5, 2011.

36 "Tokyo Economic Summit Conference Statement on International Terrorism," May 5, 1986, accessed October 4, 2021, https://www.reaganlibrary.gov/archives/speech/tokyo-economic-summit-conference-statement-international-terrorism; Reagan quoted in Bernard Weinraub, "U.S. Says Allies Asked for More in Libya Attack," *Washington Post*, April 22, 1986.

37 CIA quoted in Little, "Shores of Tripoli," 91; Qaddafi quoted in St. John, *Libya*, 139.

38 NSDD 234, August 16, 1986, accessed October 1, 2021, https://www.reaganlibrary.gov/public/archives/reference/scanned-nsdds/nsdd234.pdf. See also Bob Woodward, "Gadhafi Target of Secret U.S. Deception Plan," *Washington Post*, October 2, 1986.

39 Lou Cannon and David B. Ottaway, "New Attack on Libya Discussed," *Washington Post*, December 22, 1988; Michael R. Gordon, "U.S. Intelligence Aides Say Libya Is Again Making Chemical Arms," *New York Times*, March 7, 1990; R. Jeffrey Smith and Patrick E. Tyler, "Fire Strikes Chemical Plant in Libya," *Washington Post*, March 15, 1990.

40 Robert Pear, "U.S. Downs Two Libyan Fighters, Citing Their 'Hostile Intent,'" *New York Times*, January 5, 1989; Nicholas M. Horrock, "U.S. Says Tape Proves Libyan Jets Were Armed," *Chicago Tribune*, January 6, 1989.

41 Qaddafi quoted in Pargeter, *Libya*, 153.

42 Bowen, *Libya*, 18–31.

43 Bowen, *Libya*, 14–23 (Qaddafi quoted on p. 21).

44 Bowen, *Libya*, 31–36.

45 Jentleson and Whytock, "Who 'Won' Libya?," 67–74; Craig, "'Islamic Bomb.'"

46 Kemp, "Nonproliferation Emperor Has No Clothes," 53–54, 70–71.

Notes 239

47 "GDP per capita (current US$)—Libya," accessed September 17, 2021, https://data.worldbank.org/indicator/NY.GDP.PCAP.CD?locations=LY.

48 Wright, *History*, 216; Vandewalle, *History*, 142.

49 Vandewalle, *History*, 144–52.

50 Qaddafi quoted in Ronen, "Qadhafi and Militant Islamism," 5.

51 Eric Margolis, "Britain's Plot to Kill Khadaffi," *Toronto Sun*, August 20, 1998.

52 "Gaddafi's Motorcade Ambushed," *Glasgow Herald*, June 10, 1998; Ronen, "Qadhafi and Militant Islamism," 6–12.

53 Pargeter, *Libya*, 145–71; Wright, *History*, 218–21.

54 Wright, *History*, 218–21.

Chapter 5

1 Bowen, *Libya*, 45–56; Takeyh, "Rogue," 63–65.

2 "Vatican Establishes Full Ties with Libya," *New York Times*, March 11, 1997; "Pope Urges Immediate End of Libyan Sanctions," *Chicago Tribune*, November 2, 1997.

3 Colafrancesco, "Paradiplomacy," 98–99.

4 Takeyh, "Rogue," 63–67 (Qaddafi quoted on p. 66).

5 James Risen, "A Much-Shunned Terrorist Is Said to Find Haven in Iraq," *New York Times*, January 27, 1999; Vandewalle, *History*, 175–84.

6 Ronen, "Libya's Qaddafi," 93–98.

7 S. Qaddafi quoted in Bowen, *Libya*, 62–63; S. Qaddafi quoted in Pargeter, *Libya*, 190–93.

8 Donald G. McNeil Jr., "The Lockerbie Verdict: The Overview; Libyan Convicted by Scottish Court in '88 Pan Am Bombing," *New York Times*, February 1, 2001.

9 Observer quoted in "UN Monitor Decries Lockerbie Judgment," *BBC News*, March 14, 2002, accessed October 8, 2021, http://news.bbc.co.uk/2/hi/1872996.stm. See also "Vital Lockerbie Evidence 'Was Tampered With,'" *The Guardian*, September 1, 2007.

10 Robert D. McFadden, "Megrahi, Convicted in 1988 Lockerbie Bombing, Dies at 60," *New York Times*, May 20, 2012.

11 Jalil and Shalgam quoted in Hilsum, *Sandstorm*, 187–88.

12 Dini quoted in Colafrancesco, "Paradiplomacy," 100; Qaddafi quoted in Alessandra Stanley, "Italian in Libya on First Visit by a Western Leader in 8 Years," *New York Times*, December 2, 1999.

240 Notes

13 Martin Indyk, "The Iraq War Did Not Force Gadaffi's Hand," *Brookings Opinions*, March 9, 2004, accessed October 11, 2021, https://www.brookings.edu/opinions/the-iraq-war-did-not-force-gadaffis-hand/.

14 Own to Wehbe, August 16, 2003, accessed October 12, 2021, http://news.bbc.co.uk/2/hi/uk_news/scotland/3155825.stm. See also Matar and Thabit, *Lockerbie*, 233–45.

15 Keith B. Richburg, "Libya to Pay $170 Million in Bombing of Airliner in '89," *Washington Post*, January 10, 2004.

16 UN Security Council Resolution 1506, September 12, 2003, accessed October 18, 2021, http://unscr.com/en/resolutions/doc/1506.

17 UN Security Council Press Release SC/7868, September 12, 2003, accessed October 18, 2021, https://www.un.org/press/en/2003/sc7868.doc.htm.

18 Jentleson and Whytock, "Who 'Won' Libya?" 68–71; Bowen, *Libya*, 58–63.

19 Bowen, *Libya*, 58–63; Jentleson and Whytock, "Who 'Won' Libya?," 71–74.

20 Jentleson and Whytock, "Who 'Won' Libya?" 67–74.

21 Bowen, *Libya*, 63–69; Nutt and Pauly, "Caught Red-Handed," 27–32.

22 Libyan Foreign Ministry statement, December 19, 2003, published in *New York Times*, December 20, 2003. See also White House Fact Sheet, December 19, 2003, accessed October 18, 2021, https://georgewbush-whitehouse.archives.gov/news/releases/2003/12/20031219-8.html.

23 Bowen, *Libya*, 48–51.

24 "Lessons of Libya," *New York Times*, December 20, 2003; Bush, State of the Union Address, January 20, 2004, accessed October 18, 2021, https://georgewbush-whitehouse.archives.gov/news/releases/2004/01/20040120-7.html.

25 Indyk, "The Iraq War." See also Nincic, "Getting What You Want," 138–83.

26 Squassoni and Feickert, "Disarming Libya."

27 Patrick E. Tyler, "Blair Visits Qaddafi, Ending Libya's Long Estrangement," *New York Times*, March 26, 2004. See also, Glenn Frankel, "In Historic Visit, Blair Meets with Gaddafi," *Washington Post*, March 26, 2004.

28 Craig S. Smith, "Qaddafi Makes First Visit to Europe in 15 Years," *New York Times*, April 27, 2004.

Notes   241

29 Hilsum, *Sandstorm*, 188–89; Rasmi, "Beyond the War," 4–6.
30 Rachel Donadio, "Turmoil in Libya Poses Threat to Italy's Economy," *New York Times*, March 5, 2011; Paoletti, *Migration of Power*, 131–37.
31 Statement by C. Rice, May 15, 2006, State Department Archive, accessed October 18, 2021, https://2001-2009.state.gov/secret ary/rm/2006/66235.htm. See also Bush to Rice, May 12, 2006, White House Archives, accessed October 18, 2021, https://geor gewbush-whitehouse.archives.gov/news/releases/2006/05/ text/20060515-5.html; Eben Kaplan, "How Libya Got off the List," *Foreign Affairs*, October 16, 2007.
32 "Clinton Raises Case of Jailed Dissident with Libya," *Reuters*, April 21, 2009, accessed October 19, 2021, https://www.reuters. com/article/us-libya-usa/clinton-raises-case-of-jailed-dissident-with-libya-idUKTRE53K5BR20090421.
33 Muammar Qaddafi, "The One-State Solution," *New York Times*, January 21, 2009.
34 MacFarquhar, "Libyan Leader Delivers a Scolding in U.N. Debut," *New York Times*, September 23, 2009.
35 Qaddafi quoted in David Pallister, "Condoleezza Rice Meets Gadafy in Libya," *The Guardian*, September 5, 2008; Rice, *No Higher Honor*, 702–3.
36 Pargeter, *Libya*, 200–12.
37 Qaddafi quoted in Hilsum, *Sandstorm*, 36–37; See also pp. 7–12, 101–16, 131–42.

Chapter 6
1 Noueihed and Warren, *Battle*, 175; Pack, "Qaddafi's Legacy."
2 Fitzgerald, "Finding Their Place," 179–86.
3 Wright, *History*, 213–25; Joffé, "Civil Activism."
4 Migdal, *Shifting Sands*, 330.
5 "Remarks by the President at the 20th Anniversary of the National Endowment for Democracy," November 6, 2003, accessed May 31, 2024, https://millercenter.org/the-presidency/presidential-speeches/november-6-2003-remarks-freedom-iraq-and-middle-east; Condoleezza Rice, "Remarks at the American University in Cairo," June 20, 2005, accessed October 26, 2021, https://2001-2009.state.gov/secretary/rm/2005/48328.htm.
6 "Remarks by the President at Cairo University," June 4, 2009, accessed May 31, 2024, https://obamawhitehouse.archives.gov/the-press-office/remarks-president-cairo-university-6-04-09.

242 Notes

7 Packer, "Two Speeches and a Tragedy"; Gelvin, *Arab Uprisings*, 141–43.

8 S. Qaddafi quoted in Ian Black, "Libya on Brink as Protests Hit Tripoli," *The Guardian*, February 20, 2011.

9 Qaddafi quoted in Hilsum, *Sandstorm*, 39. See also Isabel Kershner, "Qaddafi YouTube Spoof by Israeli Gets Arab Fans," *New York Times*, February 27, 2011.

10 David D. Kirkpatrick and Mona El-Naggar, "Qaddafi's Grip Falters as His Forces Take on Protesters," *New York Times*, February 21, 2011.

11 Leila Fadel and Liz Sly, "Gaddafi Forces Fire on Protesters in Tripoli, *New York Times*, February 25, 2011. See also Leila Fadel and Liz Sly, "Gaddafi Foes Consider Requesting Foreign Airstrikes as Stalemate Continues," *Washington Post*, February 28, 2011.

12 Utley, "France and the Arab Upheavals," 69–73.

13 Rasmi, "Beyond the War," 1–7.

14 Eric Schmitt, "U.S. 'Gravely Concerned' over Violence in Libya," *New York Times*, February 20, 2011; Helene Cooper and Mark Landler, "Obama Condemns Libya amid Stalled Evacuation," *New York Times*, February 23, 2011.

15 Colum Lynch, "U.N. Votes to Impose Sanctions of Gaddafi," *Washington Post*, February 26, 2011.

16 "Prime Minister's Statement on Libya," February 28, 2011, accessed November 11, 2021, https://www.gov.uk/government/speeches/prime-ministers-statement-on-libya--2.

17 Henry Chu, "Britain, Italy Condemned for Libya Ties," *Los Angeles Times*, February 21, 2011. See also Rachel Donadio, "Turmoil in Libya Poses Threat to Italy's Economy," *New York Times*, March 5, 2011.

18 Kareem Fahim and David D. Kirkpatrick, "Libyan Rebels Repel Qaddafi's Forces near Tripoli," *New York Times*, February 24, 2011.

19 UN Security Council Resolution 1970, February 26, 2011, accessed November 2, 2021, https://www.undocs.org/S/RES/1970%20(2011); Colum Lynch, "U.N. Votes to Impose Sanction on Gaddafi," *Washington Post*, February 26, 2011.

20 Clinton quoted in Joby Warrick and Karen DeYoung, "U.S. Freezes Libyan Assets, Takes Steps to Aid Refugees," *Washington Post*, February 28, 2011; German Finance Ministry quoted in Elisabeth Bumiller, "NATO Steps Back from Military Intervention

in Libya," *New York Times*, March 10, 2011. See also Rachel Donadio, "Turmoil in Libya Poses Threat to Italy's Economy," *New York Times*, March 5, 2011.

21 Alan Cowell and Steven Erlanger, "France Becomes First Country to Recognize Libyan Rebels," *New York Times*, March 10, 2011.

22 Stephen Castle, "European Leaders Don't Rule Out Armed Intervention in Libyan Conflict," *New York Times*, March 11, 2011.

23 Rutte quoted in Weighill and Gaub, *Cauldron*, 48; Steven Erlanger, "G-8 Ministers Fail to Agree on Libya No-Flight Zone," *New York Times*, March 15, 2011. See also Ethan Bronner and David E. Sanger, "Arab League Endorses No-Flight Zone over Libya," *New York Times*, March 12, 2011.

24 Obama, *Promised Land*, 654–55. See also Elisabeth Bumiller, "Gates Plays Down Idea of U.S. Force in Libya," *New York Times*, March 1, 2011.

25 Obama, *Promised Land*, 658. See also David E. Sanger and Thom Shanker, "Discord Fills Washington on Possible Libya Intervention," *New York Times*, March 7, 2011.

26 Mann, *Obamians*, 300. See also Obama, *Promised Land*, 659–62; Kaplan, "Obama's Way," 47–49.

27 Juppé quoted in Edward Cody, "France Pleads for Military Intervention as Gaddafi Forces Attack Libyan Rebels," *New York Times*, March 17, 2011; Clinton quoted in Scott Wilson, Colum Lynch, and Karen DeYoung, "Obama Administration Seeks More U.N. Authority to Intervene in Libya," *Washington Post*, March 17, 2011.

28 UN Security Council Resolution 1973, March 17, 2011, accessed November 3, 2021, https://www.undocs.org/S/RES/1973%20 (2011).

29 Minutes of Security Council meeting, March 17, 2011, accessed November 3, 2021, https://www.securitycouncilreport.org/ atf/cf/%7B65BFCF9B-6D27-4E9C-8CD3-CF6E4FF96FF9%7D/ Libya%20S%20PV%206498.pdf.

30 Westerwelle quoted in Judy Dempsey, "Europe Split over Libya No-Flight Zone," *New York Times*, March 17, 2011. See also Dan Bilefsky, "Security Council Uncertain about Intervening in Libya," *New York Times*, March 16, 2011.

31 Ban quoted in Hehir, "Permanence of Inconsistency," 139; Northern and Pack, "Role of Outside Actors," 114.

244 Notes

32 "Remarks by the President on the Situation in Libya," March 18, 2011, accessed November 3, 2021, https://obamawhitehouse. archives.gov/the-press-office/2011/03/18/remarks-President-situation-libya.

33 Qaddafi quoted in Dan Bilefsky and Mark Landler, "As U.N. Backs Military Action in Libya, U.S. Role Is Unclear," *New York Times*, March 17, 2011; Qaddafi quoted in David D. Kirkpatrick, Steven Erlanger, and Elisabeth Bumiller, "Allies Open Air Assault on Qaddafi's Forces in Libya," *New York Times*, March 19, 2011.

34 Qaddafi quoted in Kirkpatrick et al., "Allies Open Air Assault."

35 Obama quoted in Kirkpatrick et al., "Allies Open Air Assault." See also Wehrey, *Burning Shores*, 38–39.

36 Alan J. Kuperman, "False Pretense for War in Libya?," *Boston Globe*, April 14, 2011.

37 Cameron statement to the House of Commons, March 18, 2011, accessed November 10, 2021https://www.bbc.com/news/uk-politics-12786225; French spokesman quoted in Steven Erlanger, "France and Britain Lead Military Push on Libya," *New York Times*, March 18, 2011; Frattini quoted in Steven Erlanger, "Confusion over Who Leads Libya Strikes, and for How Long," *New York Times*, March 21, 2011. See also Davidson, "France, Britain, and the Intervention in Libya," 310–29.

38 Gelvin, *Arab Uprisings*, 87–90; Steven Erlanger and Judy Dempsey, "Germany Steps Away from European Unity," *New York Times*, March 23, 2011.

39 Mullen quoted in David D. Kirkpatrick and Elisabeth Bumiller, "Allies Target Qaddafi's Ground Forces as Libyan Rebels Regroup," *New York Times*, March 20, 2011; Chorin, *Exit the Colonel*, 211.

40 Elisabeth Bumiller and David D. Kirkpatrick, "Allies Pressure Qaddafi Forces around Rebel Cities," *New York Times*, March 23, 2011; Kareem Fahim and David D. Kirkpatrick, "Airstrikes Clear Way for Libyan Rebels' First Major Advance," *New York Times*, March 26, 2011; David D. Kirkpatrick and Kareem Fahim, "Libyan Rebels March toward Qaddafi Stronghold," *New York Times*, March 27, 2011; C. J. Chivers and David D. Kirkpatrick, "Retreat for Rebels; Libyan Foreign Minister Quits," *New York Times*, March 30, 2011.

41 Ibrahim quoted in Kirkpatrick and Fahim, "Libyan Rebels."

42 Obama quoted in Elisabeth Bumiller and Kareem Fahim, "U.S.-Led Assault Nears Goal in Libya," *New York Times*, March 21, 2011; Clinton quoted in "Libya Military Action Will Continue until Gaddafi Bows to UN Demand—Clinton," *The Guardian*, March 29, 2011; Barack Obama, David Cameron, and Nicolas Sarkozy, "Libya's Pathway to Peace," *New York Times*, April 14, 2011.

43 Gortney quoted in Helene Cooper and David E. Sanger, "Target in Libya Is Clear; Intent Is Not," *New York Times*, March 20, 2011; Richards quoted in Noueihed and Warren, *Battle*, 183. See also Kirkpatrick and Bumiller, "Allies Target."

44 Pargeter, *Libya*, 234–47; Noueihed and Warren, *Battle*, 183–90; Wehrey, *Burning Shores*, 44–45.

45 "Remarks by the President on the Situation in Libya," March 18, 2011, accessed November 3, 2021, https://obamawhitehouse.archives.gov/the-press-office/2011/03/18/remarks-President-situation-libya; Clinton quoted in Steven Lee Myers and David D. Kirkpatrick, "Allies Are Split on Goal and Exit Strategy in Libya," *New York Times*, March 24, 2011.

46 Steven Erlanger, "Confusion over Who Leads Libya Strikes, and for How Long," *New York Times*, March 21, 2011; Mark Landler and Steven Erlanger, "Obama Seeks to Unify Allies as More Airstrikes Rock Tripoli," *New York Times*, March 22, 2011.

47 Rasmussen quoted in Kirkpatrick and Fahim, "Libyan Rebels." See also Elisabeth Bumiller and David D. Kirkpatrick, "NATO Agrees to Take Command of No-Fly Zone in Libya," *New York Times*, March 24, 2011; Daalder and Stavridis, "NATO's Victory in Libya," 2–7; Davidson, "France, Britain, and the Intervention in Libya," 310–29.

48 Qaddafi quoted in Pargeter, *Libya*, 240. See also Hilsum, *Sandstorm*, 212–21.

49 Qaddafi quoted in Weighill and Gaub, *Cauldron*, 119. See also Noueihed and Warren, *Battle*, 182–83; Wright, *History*, 236–40; Hilsum, *Sandstorm*, 163–64.

50 Pargeter, *Libya*, 234–42.

51 Wehrey, *Burning Shores*, 52–64.

52 David D. Kirkpatrick, "Qaddafi's Hold in Tripoli in Doubt as Rebels Advance," *New York Times*, August 19, 2011; Kareem Fahim and Mark Mazzetti, "Rebels' Assault on Tripoli Began with Careful Work Inside," *New York Times*, August 22, 2011.

246 Notes

53 Obama quoted in Kareem Fahim and David D. Kirkpatrick, "Jubilant Rebels Control Much of Tripoli," *New York Times*, August 21, 2011; Warren, *Battle*, 184–87; Pargeter, *Libya*, 238–42.

54 Qaddafi quoted in Hilsum, *Sandstorm*, 273.

55 Qaddafi quoted in Hilsum, *Sandstorm*, 3. See also Kareem Fahim, Anthony Shadid, and Rick Gladstone, "Violent End to an Era as Qaddafi Dies in Libya," *New York Times*, October 20, 2011.

56 Pargeter, *Libya*, 247.

57 Anderson, "Libya," 230. See also Kareem Fahim, "In His Last Days, Qaddafi Wearied of Fugitive's Life," *New York Times*, October 22, 2011; Robert Evans, "Gaddafi Wanted to Stage Last Stand in Desert—U.N. Report," *Reuters*, March 2, 2012, accessed November 1, 2021, https://www.reuters.com/article/libya-gadd afi-idINDEE8210HI20120302?edition-redirect=in.

58 Hilsum, *Sandstorm*, 272–76.

59 Anderson, "Libya," 229; Al-Turk, *Arab Awakening*, 117.

60 John Simpson, "Gaddafi's Legacy Continues to Haunt Libya," *BBC News*, January 20, 2015, accessed May 31, 2024, https://www.bbc.com/news/world-30876573.

61 Robert F. Worth, "In Libya, the Captors Have Become the Captive," *New York Times*, May 9, 2012.

62 Noueihed and Warren, *Battle*, 184–93.

63 "Remarks by the President on the Death of Muammar Qaddafi," October 20, 2011, accessed October 26, 2021, https://obam awhitehouse.archives.gov/the-press-office/2011/10/20/rema rks-president-death-muammar-qaddafi; Cameron quoted in "Gaddafi Death Hailed by David Cameron," *Independent*, October 24, 2011; Merkel quoted in "News of Gadhafi's Death Met with Relief," *VOA News*, October 19, 2011; Berlusconi quoted in "World Leaders React," *Foreign Policy*, October 20, 2011.

64 "Remarks by President Obama to the United Nations General Assembly," September 28, 2015, accessed October 28, 2021, https://obamawhitehouse.archives.gov/the-press-office/2015/09/28/remarks-president-Obama-united-nations-gene ral-assembly; Obama quoted in Jeffrey Goldberg, "The Obama Doctrine," *The Atlantic*, April 2016; Obama quoted in "President Barack Obama on 'Fox News Sunday,'" *Fox News*, April 10, 2016, accessed December 1, 2021, https://www.foxnews.com/transcr ipt/exclusive-president-barack-obama-on-fox-news-sunday.

See also Thomas L. Friedman, "Obama on the World," *New York Times*, August 8, 2014.

65 Gates, "Overmilitarization," 121–32.

66 House of Commons, Foreign Affairs Committee, "Libya: Examination of Intervention and Collapse and the UK's Future Policy Options," September 14, 2016, accessed December 3, 2021, https://publications.parliament.uk/pa/cm201617/cmselect/cmfaff/119/119.pdf.

67 Kuperman, "Model Humanitarian Intervention?," 105–36; Kuperman, "Obama's Libya Debacle," 66–77; Bannerman, "Libya."

68 Western and Goldstein, "Humanitarian Intervention," 54. See also Simon Sebag Montefiore, "Dictators Get the Deaths They Deserve," *New York Times*, October 26, 2011; Shadi Hamid, "Everyone Says the Libya Intervention Was a Failure. They're Wrong," *Brookings*, April 12, 2016, accessed December 4, 2021, https://www.brookings.edu/blog/markaz/2016/04/12/everyone-says-the-libya-intervention-was-a-failure-theyre-wrong/; Pape, "When Duty Calls"; Hehir, "Permanence of Inconsistency"; Chollet and Fishman, "Who Lost Libya?"; Chivvis, *Toppling Qaddafi*.

Chapter 7

1 Paul Salem and Amanda Kadlec, "Libya's Troubled Transition," June 14, 2012, accessed November 15, 2021, https://carnegie-mec.org/2012/06/14/libya-s-troubled-transition-pub-48511.

2 Pack and Cook, "July 2012 Libyan Election," 175–96.

3 Martin, "The United Nations' Role," 136.

4 Fitzgerald, "Finding Their Place," 185. See also Noueihed and Warren, *Battle*, 186–88.

5 Cretz quoted in Tara Bahrampour, "Battles in Libya Raise Specter of Insurgency," *Washington Post*, September 22, 2011.

6 David D. Kirkpatrick, "Libya Names an Engineer as Premier," *New York Times*, October 31, 2011. See also Wehrey, *Burning Shores*, 66–69, 100–3.

7 Wehrey, *Burning Shores*, 74–78.

8 US Senate Select Committee on Intelligence, "Review of the Terrorist Attacks," January 14, 2014.

9 Report of the US State Department Accountability Review Board for Benghazi, n.d. [December 2012], accessed November 19,

248 **Notes**

2021, https://2009-2017.state.gov/documents/organization/202 446.pdf.

10 Rachel Blade, "Final Benghazi Report Details Administration Failures," *Politico*, June 28, 2016; Trump quoted in Dana Milbank, "Nobody Brings the Crazy Quite like Trump," *Washington Post*, June 22, 2016.

11 David D. Kirkpatrick, "A Deadly Mix in Benghazi," *New York Times*, December 28, 2013; Baumgardner, "Barack, Benghazi, and Bungles," 1–6.

12 US Senate Select Committee on Intelligence, "Review of the Terrorist Attacks," January 14, 2014; Mark Mazzetti et al., "Benghazi Attack Called Avoidable in Senate Report," *New York Times*, January 15, 2014.

13 UN official quoted in Wehrey, *Burning Shores*, 73.

14 Kuperman, "Obama's Libya Debacle."

15 "Libya's Civil War," *The Economist*, January 10, 2015; Wehrey, *Burning Shores*, 85–88.

16 Wehrey, *Burning Shores*, 145–50.

17 Cameron quoted in Andrew Sparrow, "G-8 Summit—Day Two: Politics Live Blog," *The Guardian*, June 18, 2013. See also "Remarks with Libyan Prime Minister Ali Zeidan," March 13, 2013, accessed November 19, 2021, https://2009-2017.state.gov/secretary/remarks/2013/03/206147.htm; "G-8 Leaders Communique," June 18, 2013, accessed November 19, 2021, https://obamawhitehouse.archives.gov/the-press-office/2013/06/18/g-8-leaders-communique.

18 Chris Stephen and Ewen MacAskill, "Cameron's Plan to Train Libyan Soldiers Had Makings of Disaster from the Start," *The Guardian*, November 4, 2014; Missy Ryan, "Libyan Force Was Lesson in Limits of U.S. Power," *Washington Post*, August 5, 2015.

19 Haftar quoted in David D. Kirkpatrick, "In Libya, a Coup. Or Perhaps Not," *New York Times*, February 14, 2014.

20 Haftar and Zeidan quoted in Ghaith Shennib, "Libyan PM Dismisses Army Officer's Plot to 'Rescue' Country," *Reuters*, February 14, 2014, accessed November 19, 2021, https://www.reuters.com/article/us-libya-crisis/libyan-pm-dismisses-army-officers-plot-to-rescue-country-idUSBREA1D1JH20140214.

21 Obaid, *Failure of the Muslim Brotherhood*, 23; Hweio, "Muslim Brotherhood," 16–17.

22 Frederic Wehrey, "What's Behind Libya's Spiraling Violence?," *Washington Post*, July 28, 2014; "Libya's Civil War," *The Economist*, January 10, 2015.
23 David D. Kirkpatrick, "Strife in Libya Could Presage Long Civil War," *New York Times*, August 24, 2014.
24 Wehrey, *Burning Shores*, 52–56; "Libya's Civil War," *The Economist*, January 10, 2015; Declan Walsh, "A Libyan Strongman Looks to Washington," *New York Times*, April 12, 2018; Declan Walsh, Eric Schmitt, and John Ismay, "American Missiles Found in Libyan Rebel Compound," *New York Times*, June 28, 2019.
25 Wehrey, *Burning Shores*, 171–83.
26 Jones quoted in Wehrey, *Burning Shores*, 189–91. See also "Libya's Civil War," *The Economist*, January 10, 2015; "Italy Closes Libyan Embassy amid Mounting 'Instability,'" *Al-Jazeera*, February 15, 2015.
27 Leon quoted in "Libya's Civil War," *The Economist*, January 10, 2015.
28 Zelin, "Islamic State's First Colony"; Jack Moore, "5,000 Foreign Fighters Flock to Libya as ISIS Call for Jihadists," *Newsweek*, March 3, 2015.
29 Aaron Y. Zelin, "The Islamic State's Model," *Washington Post*, January 28, 2015; David S. Kirkpatrick, "ISIS Finds New Frontier in Chaotic Libya," *New York Times*, March 10, 2015.
30 Pinotti quoted in Jack Moore, "Italy Ready to Lead Coalition in Libya to Prevent 'Caliphate across the Sea,'" *Newsweek*, February 16, 2015. See also Tamer El-Ghobashy and Hassan Morajea, "Islamic State Tightens Grip on Libyan Stronghold of Sirte," *Wall Street Journal*, November 29, 2015.
31 Obama quoted in Eric Schmitt, "U.S. Scrambles to Contain Growing ISIS Threat in Libya," *New York Times*, February 21, 2016. See also Jack Moore, "5,000 Foreign Fighters Flock to Libya as ISIS Call for Jihadists," *Newsweek*, March 3, 2015; Helene Cooper, "U.S. Conducts Airstrikes against ISIS in Libya," *New York Times*, August 1, 2016.
32 Nathalie Guibert, "La France Mène des Opérations Secrètes en Libye," *Le Monde*, February 23, 2016; Chris Stephen, "Three French Special Forces Soldiers Die in Libya," *The Guardian*, July 20, 2016; Stephanie Kirchgaessner, "Italy to Allow US Drones to Fly Out of Sicily Air Base for Attacks on ISIS," *The Guardian*, February 22, 2016.

250 **Notes**

33 Eric Schmitt, "Obama Is Pressed to Open Military Front against ISIS in Libya," *New York Times*, February 4, 2016; Randeep Ramesh, "SAS Deployed in Libya since Start of Year, Says Leaked Memo," *The Guardian*, March 25, 2016; Missy Ryan and Sudarsan Raghavan, "U.S. Special Operations Troops Aiding Libyan Forces in Major Battle against Islamic State," *Washington Post*, August 9, 2016; Eric Schmitt, "ISIS Remains Threat in Libya Despite Defeat in Surt, U.S. Officials Say," *New York Times*, December 8, 2016.

34 Spokesman quoted in Eric Schmitt, "ISIS Leader in Libya Is Targeted in U.S. Airstrike," *New York Times*, November 14, 2015. See also Ahmed Elumami and Aidan Lewis, "U.S. Air Raid Hits Islamic State in Libya, 43 Dead," *Reuters*, February 19, 2016, accessed November 19, 2021, https://www.reuters.com/article/libya-security/u-s-air-raid-hits-islamic-state-in-libya-43-dead-idUSKCN0VS1A5; Guibert, "La France Mène"; Eric Schmitt and Michael R. Gordon, "U.S. Bombs ISIS Camps in Libya," *New York Times*, January 19, 2017.

35 Alexander Smith, "ISIS in Libya: Trump Orders First Airstrikes Near Sirte," NBC News, September 25, 2017, accessed November 30, 2021, https://www.nbcnews.com/storyline/isis-terror/isis-libya-trump-orders-first-airstrikes-near-sirte-n804461; Wehrey, "Islamic State."

36 Sudarsan Raghavan, "Libya's Civil War Creates Opening for ISIS Return as Counterterrorism Effort Falters," *Washington Post*, November 24, 2019.

37 Aziz El Yaakoubi, "Libyan Factions Sign U.N. Deal to Form Unity Government," *Reuters*, December 17, 2015, accessed November 22, 2021, https://www.reuters.com/article/us-libya-security-idUSKBN0U00WP20151217.

38 Lin Noueihed and Ahmed Mohammed Hassan, "Egypt Brokers Libya Peace Roadmap, but Key Figures Fail to Meet," *Reuters*, February 15, 2017, accessed November 22, 2021, https://www.reuters.com/article/us-egypt-libya-talks-idUSKBN15V01B.; "Fayez al-Sarraj Meets Khalifa Haftar in UAE for Talks," *Al-Jazeera*, May 2, 2017.

39 David D. Kirkpatrick, "In Libya, Militia Advances on Capital, Raising Prospect of Renewed Civil War," *New York Times*, April 4, 2019; Carole Nakhle, "Libya's Uphill Struggle to Attract Oil Investment," accessed on May 15, 2024, https://www.gisreportsonline.com/r/libyas-uphill-struggle-to-attract-oil-investment/.

Notes 251

40 Patrick Wintour, "Italy Mulls Temporary Humanitarian Visas to Aid Libyan Migrants," *The Guardian*, July 19, 2017; Patrick Wintour, "Libyan Factions Agree to Hold Elections on 10 December," *The Guardian*, May 29, 2018.

41 Vari, "Italy–Libya Memorandum of Understanding," 108–22.

42 "Italian Elections 2018—Full Results," *The Guardian*, March 5, 2018.

43 Karasapan, "Libya and Its Migrants"; "Relief as Italian Court Says Rescued Refugees Cannot Be Sent Back to Libya," *Al Jazeera*; February 27, 2024; European Council on Refugees and Exiles, "Italy: Prime Minister in Libya for Discussions on Further Migration Co-Operation," May 10, 2024, accessed May 16, 2024, https://ecre.org/italy-prime-minister-in-libya-for-discussi ons-on-further-migration-co-operation-%E2%80%95-joint-ital ian-finnish-proposal-on-migration-presented-to-eu-member-sta tes-%E2%80%95-ngo-monitoring-aircraft-b/.

44 Wintour, "Libyan Factions"; Patrick Wintour and Chris Stephen, "Libyan Rival Leaders Agree to Ceasefire after Macron-Hosted Talks," *The Guardian*, July 25, 2017; Aidan Lewis, "Johnson Visits Libyan Strongman, Backs Ceasefire," *Reuters*, August 24, 2017, accessed November 22, 2021, https://www.reuters.com/article/ uk-libya-security-britain-idUKKCN1B42TH.

45 De Maio, "Palermo Conference."

46 Glenn Thrush, "No U.S. Military Role in Libya, Trump Says, Rejecting Italy's Pleas," *New York Times*, April 20, 2017; Jo Becker and Eric Schmitt, "As Trump Wavers on Libya, an ISIS Haven, Russia Presses On," *New York Times*, February 7, 2018.

47 White House press release, December 1, 2017, accessed May 31, 2024, https://trumpwhitehouse.archives.gov/briefings-stateme nts/readout-president-donald-j-trumps-meeting-prime-minister- fayez-al-sarraj-libya/. See also Becker and Schmitt, "As Trump Wavers."

48 Walsh, "Libyan Strongman.".

49 Sarraj and militia leaders quoted in David D. Kirkpatrick, "In Libya, Militia Advances on Capital, Raising Prospect of Renewed Civil War," *New York Times*, April 4, 2019.

50 Joint statement on Fighting Near Gharyan, Libya, April 4, 2019, US Department of State, Global Public Affairs, accessed December 3, 2021, https://2017-2021-translations.state.gov/ 2019/04/05/joint-statement-on-fighting-near-gharyan-libya/

index.html; European Union quoted in David D. Kirkpatrick, "Thugs and Extremists Join Battle for Tripoli, Complicating Libyan Fray," *New York Times*, April 12, 2019. See also Jihâd Gillon, "France-Libya: Marshal Haftar, the Controversial Friend of the Élysée," *Africa Report*, March 20, 2020, accessed November 22, 2021, https://www.theafricareport.com/24823/france-libya-marshal-haftar-the-controversial-friend-of-the-elysee/.

51 Pompeo quoted in Sudarshan Raghavan, "American Troops in Libya Moved Out of Country as Violence Escalates Near Capital," *Washington Post*, April 8, 2019.

52 Press release quoted in David D. Kirkpatrick, "Trump Endorses an Aspiring Libyan Strongman, Reversing Policy," *New York Times*, April 19, 2019. See also Julian Borger and Patrick Wintour, "'No Coherent Policy': Trump's Scattergun Approach Plunges Libya Deeper into Peril," *The Guardian*, April 30, 2019; Feltman, "Trumpian Storm Clouds."

53 Prince quoted in Declan Walsh, "Erik Prince, Trump Ally, Denies Role in Libya Mercenary Operation," *New York Times*, February 21, 2021. See also Declan Walsh, "Erik Prince, Trump Ally, Violated Libya Arms Embargo, U.N. Report Says," *New York Times*, February 19, 2021.

54 Walsh et al., "American Missiles"; Eric Schmitt and Declan Walsh, "U.S. Missiles Found in Libyan Rebel Camp Were First Sold to France," *New York Times*, July 9, 2019.

55 Becker and Schmitt, "As Trump Wavers"; David D. Kirkpatrick, "Russian Snipers, Missiles and Warplanes Try to Tilt Libyan War," *New York Times*, November 5, 2019; Greg Miller, Missy Ryan, Sudarsan Raghavan, and Souad Mekhennet, "At the Mercy of Foreign Powers," *Washington Post*, February 25, 2021.

56 Declan Walsh, "In Stunning Reversal, Turkey Emerges as Libya Kingmaker," *New York Times*, May 21, 2020; Nick Cumming-Bruce and Declan Walsh, "Libya Cease-Fire Raises Hopes for Full Peace Deal," *New York Times*, October 23, 2020; Miller et al., "At the Mercy.".

57 UN Security Council Resolution 2473, June 10, 2019, accessed December 4, 2021, https://undocs.org/en/S/RES/2473(2019); Declan Walsh, "In Libya, Toothless U.N. Embargo Lets Foreign States Meddle with Impunity," *New York Times*, February 2, 2020.

58 Sudarsan Raghavan, "Pro-Government Forces in Libya Seize Warlord's Last Western Stronghold," *Washington Post*, June 5, 2020; Cumming-Bruce and Walsh, "Libya Cease-Fire."
59 Cumming-Bruce and Walsh, "Libya Cease-Fire."
60 Miller et al., "At the Mercy."
61 Vivian Yee and Mohammed Abdusamee, "After a Decade of Chaos, Can a Splintered Libya Be Made Whole?," *New York Times*, February 16, 2021.
62 Official quoted in Mona El-Naggar and Vivian Yee, "A Tense Libya Delays Its Presidential Election," *New York Times*, December 22, 2021. See also Vohra, "Elections Can't Fix."
63 Raja Abdulrahim and Russell Goldman, "Renewed Violence in Libya Reflects Power of Militias" *New York Times*, August 17, 2023; Raja Abdulrahim and Isabella Kwai, "After Libya Floods, a Chaotic Scramble for Rescuers," *New York Times*, September 14, 2023; "Libyan Leaders Agree to Form New Unified Government," *Reuters*, March 10, 2024, accessed May 15, 2024, https://www.reuters.com/world/middle-east/libyan-leaders-agree-form-new-unified-government-2024-03-10/.

BIBLIOGRAPHY

Published Primary Sources

Ansell, Meredith O., and Ibrahim Massaud al-Arif, eds. *The Libyan Revolution: A Sourcebook of Legal and Historical Documents*. Harrow, England: Oleander Press, 1972.

Brinkley, Douglas, ed. *The Reagan Diaries*. New York: Harper, 2007.

"The Libyan Revolution in the Words of Its Leaders: Proclamations, Statements, Addresses, Declarations, and Interviews." *Middle East Journal* 24, no. 2 (Spring 1970): 203–17.

Metz, Helen Chapin, ed. *Libya: A Country Study*. Washington: US Government Printing Office, 1989.

"Mussolini in Italy." Film. March 18, 1937. Accessed August 18, 2021. https://www.britishpathe.com/video/mussolini-in-libya

Obama, Barack. *A Promised Land*. New York: Crown, 2020.

Qadhafi, Muammar. *The Green Book*. Part 1: *The Solution of the Problem of Democracy: "The Authority of the People."* London: Martin, Brian, & O'Keefe, 1976.

Qadhafi, Muammar. *The Green Book*. Part 2: *The Solution of the Economic Problem: "Socialism."* London: Martin, Brian, & O'Keefe, 1978.

Rice, Condoleezza. "U.S. Diplomatic Relations with Libya." US Department of State. 2006/493. May 15, 2006. Accessed November 16, 2021. https://2001-2009.state.gov/secretary/rm/2006/66235.htm

Squassoni, Sharon A., and Andrew Feickert. "Disarming Libya: Weapons of Mass Destruction." US Library of Congress. Congressional Research Service. RS21823. 2004. https://www.eve rycrsreport.com/files/20040422_RS21823_9c2b81fe3a3385f6aa0d7 8a8ac41e3e8cd0cb7ad.pdf

256 Bibliography

US Department of State. *Foreign Relations of the United States.* Washington: Government Printing Office.

US Department of State. "U.S.–Libyan Relations since 1969." *Current Policy* No. 216 (1980).

US Senate. Senate Select Committee on Intelligence. "Review of the Terrorist Attacks on U.S. Facilities in Benghazi, Libya, September 11–12, 2012." January 14, 2014.

Newspapers and Periodicals

Associated Press
British Broadcasting Corporation
Chicago Tribune
Deutsche Welle
Glasgow Herald
Globe and Mail
Guardian
Herald
Independent
Le Monde
Los Angeles Times
Maclean's
New York Times
Reuters
Toronto Sun
Washington Post

Secondary Sources

Monographs and Edited Volumes

Abulafia, David. *The Great Sea: A Human History of the Mediterranean.* New York: Oxford University Press, 2011.

Abun-Nasr, Jamil M. *A History of the Maghrib in the Islamic Period.* Cambridge: Cambridge University Press, 1987.

Ahmida, Ali Abdullatif. *The Making of Modern Libya: State Formation, Colonization, and Resistance.* Albany: State University of New York Press, 2009.

Al-Turk, Akram, et al. *The Arab Awakening: America and the Transformation of the Middle East.* Washington: Brookings, 2011.

Baldinetti, Anna. *The Origins of the Libyan Nation: Colonial Legacy, Exile, and the Emergence of a New Nation State.* London: Routledge, 2010.

Bills, Scott L. *The Libyan Arena: The United States, Britain, and the Council of Foreign Ministers*. Kent, OH: Kent State University Press, 1995.

Bowen, Wyn Q. *Libya and Nuclear Proliferation: Stepping Back from the Brink*. London: Routledge, 2006.

Brett, Michael. "The Maghreb." In *The Cambridge History of Africa*, edited by A. D. Roberts, 7:267–328. Cambridge: Cambridge University Press, 1986.

Burton, Fred, and Samuel M. Katz. *Under Fire: The Untold Story of the Attack in Benghazi*. New York: St. Martin's, 2013.

Carver, Michael. *Dilemmas of the Desert War: A New Look at the Libyan Campaign of 1940–1942*. London: Batsford, 1986.

Childs, Timothy W. *Italo-Turkish Diplomacy and the War over Libya, 1911–1912*. Leiden: Brill, 1990.

Chivvis, Christopher S. *Toppling Qaddafi: Libya and the Limits of Liberal Intervention*. Cambridge: Cambridge University Press, 2013.

Chorin, Ethan. *Exit the Colonel: The Hidden History of the Libyan Revolution*. New York: Public Affairs, 2012.

Christides, Vassilios. *Byzantine Libya and the March of the Arabs towards the West of Africa*. Oxford: British Archeological Reports, 2000.

Dearden, Seth. *A Nest of Corsairs: The Fighting Karamanlis of Tripoli*. London: Murray, 1976.

DeCandole, E. A. V. *The Life and Times of King Idris of Libya*. N.p.: Ghalbon, 1990.

De Grazia, Victoria. *The Perfect Fascist: A Story of Love, Power, and Morality in Mussolini's Italy*. Cambridge, MA: Harvard University Press, 2020.

Dietrich, Christopher R. W. *Oil Revolution: Anticolonial Elites, Sovereign Rights, and the Economic Culture of Decolonization*. Cambridge: Cambridge University Press, 2017.

ElWarfally, Mahmoud G. *Imagery and Ideology in U.S. Policy toward Libya*. Pittsburgh, PA: University of Pittsburgh Press, 1988.

Freedman, Lawrence. *A Choice of Enemies: America Confronts the Middle East*. New York: Public Affairs, 2008.

Galaty, Michael L., and Charles Watkinson, eds. *Archaeology under Dictatorship*. New York: Kluwer/Plenum Publishers, 2004.

Gaub, Florence. *The North Atlantic Treaty Organization and Libya: Reviewing Operation Unified Protector*. Carlisle, PA: US Army War College Press, 2013.

Gelvin, James L. *The Arab Uprisings: What Everyone Needs to Know*. New York: Oxford University Press, 2012.

258 Bibliography

Gurney, Judith. *Libya: The Political Economy of Oil*. Oxford: Oxford University Press, 1996.

Haley, P. Edward. *Qaddafi and the United States since 1969*. New York: Praeger, 1984.

Hehir, Aidan. *The Responsibility to Protect: Rhetoric, Reality, and the Future of Humanitarian Intervention*. London: Palgrave Macmillan, 2012.

Hehir, Aidan, and Robert Murray, eds. *Libya: The Responsibility to Protect and the Future of Humanitarian Intervention*. New York: Palgrave Macmillan, 2013.

Hilsum, Lindsey. *Sandstorm: Libya in the Time of Revolution*. New York: Penguin Press, 2012.

Kelly, Saul. "Britain, the United States, and the End of the Italian Empire in Africa, 1940–1952." In *International Diplomacy and Colonial Retreat*, edited by Kent Fedorowich and Martin Thomas, 51–70. New York: Routledge, 2013.

Kelly, Saul. *Cold War in the Desert: Britain, the United States, and the Italian Colonies, 1945–52*. New York: St. Martin's, 2000.

Kelly, Saul. *The Lost Oasis: The True Story behind "The English Patient."* Boulder: Westview, 2002.

Kitzin, Michael L. S. *Tripoli and the United States at War: A History of American Relations with the Barbary States, 1785–1805*. Jefferson, NC: McFarland, 1993.

Kolinsky, Martin. *Britain's War in the Middle East*. New York: St. Martin's, 1999.

Laham, Nicholas. *The American Bombing of Libya: A Study of the Force of Miscalculation in Reagan Foreign Policy*. Jefferson, NC: McFarland, 2008.

Leiner, Frederick C. *The End of Barbary Terror: America's 1815 War against the Pirates of North Africa*. New York: Oxford University Press, 2007.

Liddell Hart, B. H. *History of the Second World War*. London: Cassell, 1970.

Louis, Wm. Roger. *The British Empire in the Middle East, 1945–1951: Arab Nationalism, the United States, and Postwar Imperialism*. New York: Oxford University Press, 1985.

Mann, James. *The Obamians: The Struggle inside the White House to Redefine American Power*. New York: Viking, 2012.

Matar, Khalil I., and Robert W. Thabit. *Lockerbie and Libya: A Study in International Relations*. Jefferson, NC: McFarland, 2004.

McLaren, Brian L. *Architecture and Tourism in Italian Colonial Libya: An Ambivalent Modernism*. Seattle: University of Washington Press, 2006.

Migdal, Joel S. *Shifting Sands: The United States in the Middle East*. New York: Columbia University Press, 2014.

Minawi, Mostafa. *The Ottoman Scramble for Africa: Empire and Diplomacy in the Sahara and the Hijaz*. Stanford, CA: Stanford University Press, 2016.

Moore, Martin. *Fourth Shore: Italy's Mass Colonization of Libya*. London: Routledge, 1940.

Mourani, Maurice M. *The Jews of Libya: Coexistence, Persecution, Resettlement*. Portland, OR: Sussex, 2008.

Muschik, Eva-Marie. *Building States: The United Nations, Development, and Decolonization, 1945–1965*. New York: Columbia University Press, 2022.

Murray, Williamson, and Allan R. Millett. *A War to Be Won: Fighting the Second World War*. Cambridge, MA: Harvard University Press, 2000.

Nolutshungu, Sam C. *Limits of Anarchy: Intervention and State Formation in Chad*. Charlottesville: University of Virginia Press, 1996.

Noueihed, Lin, and Alex Warren. *The Battle for the Arab Spring: Revolution, Counter-Revolution, and the Making of a New Era*. New Haven, CT: Yale University Press, 2012.

Obaid, Nawaf. *The Failure of the Muslim Brotherhood in the Arab World*. New York: Bloomsbury, 2020.

Paoletti, Emanuela. *The Migration of Power and North-South Inequalities: The Case of Libya and Italy*. London: Palgrave Macmillan, 2011.

Pargeter, Alison. *Libya: The Rise and Fall of Qaddafi*. New Haven, CT: Yale University Press, 2012.

Pelt, Adrian. *Libyan Independence and the United Nations: A Case of Planned Decolonization*. New Haven, CT: Yale University Press, 1970.

Pennell, C. R., ed. *Piracy and Diplomacy in Seventeenth Century North Africa: The Journal of Thomas Baker, English Consul in Tripoli, 1677–1685*. Rutherford, NJ: Farleigh Dickinson University Press, 1989.

Prashad, Vijay. *Arab Spring, Libyan Winter*. Edinburgh: AK Press, 2012.

Seale, Patrick, and Maureen McConville. *The Hilton Assignment*. London: Temple Smith, 1973.

Segrè, Claudio G. *Fourth Shore: The Italian Colonization of Libya*. Chicago: University of Chicago Press, 1974.

260 Bibliography

Simon, Rachel. *Libya between Ottamism and Nationalism: The Ottoman Involvement in Libya during the War with Italy (1911–1919).* Berlin: Klaus Schwartz Verlag, 1987.

Simons, Geoff. *Libya and the West: From Independence to Lockerbie.* New York: Oxford University Press, 2003.

Stanik, Joseph T. *El Dorado Canyon: Reagan's Undeclared War with Qaddafi.* Annapolis: Naval Institute Press, 2003.

St. John, Ronald Bruce. *Libya and the United States: Two Centuries of Strife.* Philadelphia: University of Pennsylvania Press, 2002.

Tinniswood, Adrian. *Pirates of Barbary: Corsairs, Conquests, and Captivity in the Seventeenth Century Mediterranean.* New York: Riverhead Books, 2010.

Toaldo, Mattia. *The Origins of the US War on Terror: Lebanon, Libya, and American Intervention in the Middle East.* New York: Routledge, 2013.

Uldricks, Teddy J. *The Second World War: A Global History.* New York: Rowman & Littlefield, 2024.

Vandewalle, Dirk J. *A History of Modern Libya.* New York: Cambridge University Press, 2006.

Weighill, Rob, and Florence Gaub. *The Cauldron: NATO's Campaign in Libya.* New York: Oxford, 2018.

Wehrey, Frederic. *The Burning Shores: Inside the Battle for the New Libya.* New York: Farrar, Straus, and Giroux, 2018.

Wheelan, Joseph. *Jefferson's War: America's First War on Terror, 1801–1805.* New York: Carroll & Graf, 2003.

Woodward, Bob. *Veil: The Secret Wars of the CIA, 1981–1987.* New York: Simon and Schuster, 1987.

Wright, John. *The Emergence of Libya.* London: Silphium Books, 2008.

Wright, John. *A History of Libya.* New York: Columbia University Press, 2010.

Scholarly Articles

Ahram, Ariel I. "On the Making and Unmaking of Arab States." *International Journal of Middle East Studies* 50, no. 2 (May 2018): 323–27.

Anderson, Lisa. "Demystifying the Arab Spring." *Foreign Affairs* 90, no. 3 (May/Jun 2011): 2–7.

Anderson, Lisa. "Libya: A Journey from Extraordinary to Ordinary." In *The 2011 Libyan Uprisings and the Struggle for the Post-Qadhafi Future,* edited by Jason Pack, 229–32. New York: Palgrave Macmillan, 2013.

Bibliography 261

Anderson, Lisa. "Ramadan al-Suwayhli: Hero of the Libyan Resistance." In *Struggle and Survival in the Modern Middle East*, edited by Edmund Burke III, 114–28. Berkeley: University of California Press, 1993.

Bannerman, Graeme. "Libya: A Costly Victory." *Politico*, October 21, 2011.

Baumgardner, Paul. "Barack, Benghazi, and Bungles: Tracing the Obama Administration's Handling of the Benghazi Attacks." *Cornell International Affairs Review* 5, no. 4 (2013): 1–8.

Bini, Elisabetta. "From Colony to Oil Producer: US Oil Companies and the Reshaping of Labor Relations in Libya during the Cold War." *Labor History* 60, no. 1 (2019): 44–56.

Bowlus, John V. "Shifting Energy-Security Priorities and the Iran-Turkey Pipeline Scheme, 1967–1971." *Diplomatic History* 45, no. 2 (April 2021): 356–82.

Chollet, Derek, and Ben Fishman. "Who Lost Libya? Obama's Intervention in Retrospect." *Foreign Affairs* 94, no. 3 (May/Jun 2015): 154–59.

Colafrancesco, Valentina. "A Case of Paradiplomacy? Italian-Libyan Diplomatic Relations from the Rise to Power of Gaddafi till the Beginning of the 'Arab Spring.'" *Studia Diplomatica* 65, no. 3 (2012): 93–118.

Collins, Carole. "Imperialism and Revolution in Libya." *MERIP Reports* 27 (April 1974): 3–22.

Craig, Malcolm M. "The 'Islamic Bomb': Perceptions of Middle Eastern Nuclear Proliferation, 1979–1989." *Diplomatic History* 44, no. 4 (September 2020): 580–608.

Daalder, Ivo H., and James G. Stavridis. "NATO's Victory in Libya: The Right Way to Run an Intervention." *Foreign Affairs* 91, no. 2 (March/ April 2012): 2–7.

Davidson, Jason W. "France, Britain, and the Intervention in Libya: An Integrated Analysis." *Cambridge Review of International Affairs* 26, no. 2 (June 2013): 310–29.

El-Khuwas, Mohamed A. "Qaddafi and Islam in Libya." *American Journal of Islam and Society* 1, no. 1 (April 1984): 61–81.

Fitzgerald, Mary. "Finding Their Place: Libya's Islamists during and after the Revolution." In *The Libyan Revolution and Its Aftermath*, edited by Peter Cole and Brian McQuinn, 177–206. New York: Oxford University Press, 2015.

262 Bibliography

Francis, Samuel T. "Libya's Empire of Terror." *Africa Insight* 12, no. 1 (1982): 4–10.

Garavini, Giuliano. "Completing Decolonization: The 1973 'Oil Shock' and the Struggle for Economic Rights." *International History Review* 33, no. 3 (2011): 473–87.

Gates, Robert M. "The Overmilitarization of American Foreign Policy." *Foreign Affairs* 99, no. 4 (July/August 2020): 121–32.

Graf, Rudiger. "Making Use of the 'Oil Weapon': Western Industrialized Countries and Arab Petropolitics in 1973–1974." *Diplomatic History* 36, no. 1 (January 2012): 185–208.

Heefner, Gretchen. "'A Slice of Their Sovereignty': Negotiating the U.S. Empire of Bases, Wheelus Field, Libya, 1950–1954." *Diplomatic History* 41, no. 1 (January 2017): 50–77.

Hehir, Aidan. "The Permanence of Inconsistency: Libya, the Security Council, and the Responsibility to Protect." *International Security* 38, no. 1 (Summer 2013): 137–59.

Hess, Robert L. "Italy and Africa: Colonial Ambitions in the First World War." *Journal of African History* 4, no. 1 (1963): 105–26.

Hweio, Haala. "The Muslim Brotherhood: Libya as the Last Resort for the Continued Existence of the Global Movement." *Middle East Law and Governance* 13 (2021): 5–21.

Jentleson, Bruce W., and Christopher A. Whytock. "Who 'Won' Libya? The Force-Diplomacy Debate and Its Implications for Theory and Policy." *International Security* 30, no. 3 (Winter 2005/2006): 47–86.

Joffé, George. "Civil Activism and the Roots of the 2011 Uprisings." In *The 2011 Libyan Uprisings and the Struggle for the Post-Qadhafi Era*, edited by Jason Pack, 23–51. New York: Palgrave Macmillan, 2013.

Judy, Michael E. "Benghazi: Deception, Denial and Fatal Diplomacy." *Global Security Studies* 5, no. 4 (Fall 2014): 1–17.

Kaplan, Fred. "Obama's Way: The President in Practice." *Foreign Affairs* 95, no. 1 (January/February 2016): 46–63.

Kemp, R. Scott. "The Nonproliferation Emperor Has No Clothes: The Gas Centrifuge, Supply-Side Controls, and the Future of Nuclear Proliferation." *International Security* 38, no. 4 (Spring 2014): 39–78.

Kuperman, Alan J. "A Model Humanitarian Intervention? Reassessing NATO's Libya Campaign." *International Security* 38, no. 1 (Summer 2013): 105–36.

Kuperman, Alan J. "Obama's Libyan Debacle: How a Well-Meaning Intervention Ended in Failure." *Foreign Affairs* 94, no. 2 (March/April 2015): 66–77.

Labbate, Silvio. "Italy and Its Oil Dealings with Libya. Limits and Obligations of a Dependency: The Difficult 1970s and 1980s." *Middle Eastern Studies* 56, no. 1 (2020): 84–99.

Landau-Wells, Marika. "High Stakes and Low Bars: How International Recognition Shapes the Conduct of Civil Wars." *International Security* 43, no. 1 (Summer 2018): 100–37.

Little, Douglas. "Mission Impossible: The CIA and the Cult of Covert Action in the Middle East." *Diplomatic History* 28, no. 5 (November 2004): 663–701.

Little, Douglas. "To the Shores of Tripoli: America, Qadhafi, and Libyan Revolution, 1969–89." *International History Review* 35, no. 1 (February 2013): 70–99.

Martin, Ian. "The United Nations' Role in the First Year of the Transition. In *The Libyan Revolution and Its Aftermath,* edited by Peter Cole and Brian McQuinn, 127–52. New York: Oxford University Press, 2015.

Meijer, Hugo, and Stephen G. Brooks. "Illusions of Autonomy: Why Europe Cannot Provide for Its Security If the United States Pulls Back." *International Security* 45, no. 4 (Spring 2021): 7–43.

Nincic, Miroslav. "Getting What You Want." *International Security* 35, no. 1 (Summer 2010): 138–83.

Northern, Richard, and Jason Pack. "The Role of Outside Actors." In *The 2011 Libyan Uprisings and the Struggle for the Post-Qadhafi Future,* edited by Jason Pack, 113–49. New York: Palgrave Macmillan, 2013.

Nutt, Cullen G., and Reid B. C. Pauly. "Caught Red-Handed: How States Wield Proof to Coerce Wrongdoers." *International Security* 46, no. 2 (Fall 2021): 7–50.

Ostrum, Nicholas. "Interdependency and Economic (Ir)rationality: West German–Libyan Petro-relations in 'Crisis.'" *International History Review* 43, no. 6 (2021): 1291–311.

Pack, Jason, and Haley Cook. "The July 2012 Libyan Election and the Origin of Post-Qadhafi Appeasement." *Middle East Journal* 69, no. 2 (2015): 171–98.

Pape, Robert A. "When Duty Calls: A Pragmatic Standard of Humanitarian Intervention." *International Security* 37, no. 1 (Summer 2012): 41–80.

Perroux, Jean-Louis Romanet. "The Deep Roots of Libya's Security Fragmentation." *Middle Eastern Studies* 55, no. 2 (2019): 200–24.

Philipps, Tracy. "Fourth Shore: Italy's Mass Colonisation of Libya." *Journal of the Royal African Society* 39 (April 1940): 129–33.

264 Bibliography

Ronen, Yehudit. "Britain's Return to Libya: From the Battle of al-Alamein in the Western Libyan Desert to the Military Intervention in the 'Arab Spring' Upheaval." *Middle Eastern Studies* 49, no. 5 (September 2013): 675–95.

Ronen, Yehudit. "Libya's Conflict with Britain: Analysis of a Diplomatic Rupture." *Middle Eastern Studies* 42, no. 2 (March 2006): 271–83.

Ronen, Yehudit. "Libya's Qadhafi and the Israeli-Palestinian Conflict, 1969–2002." *Middle Eastern Studies* 40, no. 1 (January 2004): 85–98.

Ronen, Yehudit. "Qadhafi and Militant Islamism: Unprecedented Conflict." *Middle Eastern Studies* 38, no. 4 (October 2002): 1–16.

Sawani, Youssef Mohammad. "Gaddafi's Legacy, Institutional Development, and National Reconciliation in Libya." *Contemporary Arab Affairs* 13, no. 1 (March 2020): 46–68.

Takeyh, Ray. "The Rogue Who Came In from the Cold." *Foreign Affairs* 80, no. 3 (May/June 2001): 62–72.

"The Secret Laval-Mussolini Agreement of 1935 on Ethiopia." *Middle East Journal* 15, no. 1 (Winter 1961): 69–78.

Toaldo, Mattia. "The Italo-Libyan Relationship between 1969 and 1976." *Libyan Studies* 44, no. 1 (January 2013): 85–94.

Utley, Rachel. "France and the Arab Upheavals: Beyond Sarkozy." *RUSI Journal* 158, no. 2 (2013): 68–79.

Vari, Elisa. "Italy–Libya Memorandum of Understanding: Italy's International Obligations." *Hastings International and Comparative Law Review* 43, no. 1 (Winter 2020): 1–31.

Western, Jon, and Joshua S. Goldstein. "Humanitarian Intervention Comes of Age: Lessons from Somalia to Libya." *Foreign Affairs* 90, no. 6 (December 2011): 48–59.

Vandewalle, Dirk. "Research Facilities and Document Collections in the Socialist People's Libyan Arab Jamahiriyah." *MESA Bulletin* 28 (1994): 9–13.

Wright, John. "Italian Fascism and Libyan Human Resources." In *Planning and Development in Modern Libya*, edited by M. M. Buru, S. M. Ghanem, and K. S. McLachlan, 46–56. London: Means Press, 1985.

Other Articles/Reports

Cordesman, Anthony H. "Weapons of Mass Destruction in the Middle East: Regional Trends, National Forces, Warfighting Capabilities, Delivery Options, and Weapon Effects." Center for Strategic and International Studies. Washington, DC: CSIS Press, September 2000.

De Maio, Giovanna. "The Palermo Conference on Libya: A Diplomatic Test for Italy's New Government." *The Brookings Institute*. November 2018. Accessed December 2, 2021. https://www.brookings.edu/blog/order-from-chaos/2018/11/19/the-palermo-conference-on-libya-a-diplomatic-test-for-italys-new-government/

Feltman, Jerry. "Trumpian Storm Clouds over Tripoli." *The Brookings Institute*. April 2019. Accessed December 2, 2021. https://www.brookings.edu/blog/order-from-chaos/2019/04/19/trumpian-storm-clouds-over-tripoli/

Gillon, Jihâd. "France-Libya: Marshal Haftar, the Controversial Friend of the Élysée." *The Africa Report*. March 20, 2020. Accessed November 16, 2021. https://www.theafricareport.com/24823/france-libya-marshal-haftar-the-controversial-friend-of-the-elysee/

Goldberg, Jeffrey. "The Obama Doctrine." *The Atlantic*. April 2016. Accessed December 1, 2021. https://www.theatlantic.com/magazine/archive/2016/04/the-obama-doctrine/471525/

Gwertzman, Bernard. "Libyan Expert: Qaddafi, Desperate to End Libya's Isolation, Sends a 'Gift' to President Bush." Interview with Lisa Anderson. December 22, 2003. Accessed December 11, 2024. https://www.cfr.org/interview/libyan-expert-qaddafi-desperate-end-libyas-isolation-sends-gift-president-bush

Indyk, Martin S. "The Iraq War Did Not Force Gadaffi's Hand." *The Financial Times*. March 9, 2004. Accessed November 16, 2021. https://www.brookings.edu/opinions/the-iraq-war-did-not-force-gadaffis-hand/

Karaspan, Omer. "Libya and Its Migrants Confront New Threats." *The Brookings Institute*. May 2020. Accessed December 1, 2021. https://www.brookings.edu/blog/future-development/2020/05/20/libya-and-its-migrants-confront-new-threats/

Lizza, Ryan. "The Consequentialist: How the Arab Spring Remade Obama's Foreign Policy." *The New Yorker*. April 25, 2011.

Pack, Jason. "Qaddafi's Legacy." *Foreign Policy*. October 20, 2011.

Packer, George. "Two Speeches and a Tragedy." *The New Yorker*. October 1, 2014. Accessed November 16, 2021. https://www.newyorker.com/news/daily-comment/obamas-two-speeches-tragedy

Rasmi, Farah. "Beyond the War: The History of French–Libyan Relations." *Atlantic Council*. April 8, 2021. Accessed November 16, 2021. https://www.atlanticcouncil.org/in-depth-research-reports/issue-brief/beyond-the-war-the-history-of-french-libyan-relations/

266 Bibliography

Salem, Paul, and Amanda Kadlec. "Libya's Troubled Transition." *The Carnegie Papers*. Carnegie Endowment for International Peace, Washington DC. June 14, 2012. Accessed November 16, 2021. https://carnegie-mec.org/2012/06/14/libya-s-troubled-transit ion-pub-48511

"That It Should Come to This." *The Economist*. January 10, 2015. Accessed November 16, 2021. https://www.economist.com/brief ing/2015/01/10/that-it-should-come-to-this

Vohra, Anchal. "Elections Can't Fix What's Wrong with Libya." *Foreign Policy*. January 4, 2022. Accessed December 11, 2024. https://foreig npolicy.com/2022/01/04/libya-elections-not-solution-haftar-qadd afi-dbeibah/

Wehrey, Frederic. "When the Islamic State Came to Libya." *The Atlantic*. February 2018. Accessed December 1, 2021. https://www.theatlan tic.com/international/archive/2018/02/isis-libya-hiftar-al-qaeda-syria/552419/

Zelin, Aaron Y. "The Islamic State's First Colony in Libya." *Washington Institute for Near East Policy*. October 10, 2014. Accessed November 30, 2021. https://www.washingtoninstitute.org/policy-analysis/islamic-states-first-colony-libya

Zelin, Aaron Y. "The Islamic State's Model." *Washington Institute for Near East Policy*. January 28, 2015. Accessed November 22, 2021. https://www.washingtoninstitute.org/policy-analysis/islamic-sta tes-model

INDEX

For the benefit of digital users, indexed terms that span two pages (e.g., 52–53) may, on occasion, appear on only one of those pages.

9/11 (September 11, 2001 attacks), 147–48, 204

Abu Salim prison, 137, 161, 165–66
Abushagur, Mustapha, 201–2
Abu-Shuawayrib, Saad al-Din, 68
Achille Lauro hijacking, 120
Adams, John, 6–7
Adowa, Battle of, 10
Afghanistan, 136–37, 147, 178–79, 183–85, 203, 209
Africa, 9–10, 97–100
  Europe trade partnership with, 173
  Italian-German expulsion from North, 41–43
  Italy and, 31–32, 46, 157
  shift to pan-Africanism and, 140
  treatment of migrants from, 156
  2011 Revolution and, 174–75, 185, 190–91
  World War I and, 16–17
agriculture, 25–27
  economic reform and, 80
  Italy and, 29

airbases. *See* military bases
Al-Fateh University protests, 81–82
Algeria, 8
  War for Independence in, 56–57
Al-Ghad media company, 161
Algiers, 6
  Barbary Wars and, 8
Ali, Hajj, 8
Allah, Ansar, 136–37
Allies (World War I), 15–16
Allies (World War II), 43–45, 47
  Italian Peace Treaty and, 46
Alliot-Marie, Michele, 173
Amazigh tribes, 14, 162
Amin, Idi, 100
Anderson, Lisa, 193, 194
Ansar al-Sharia, 210, 214–15
Aouzou Strip, 32, 97–100, 111
  ICJ ruling on, 142
  international arbitration over, 111–12
A. Q. Khan network, 134, 151–52, 154
Arabia, 33–34

268 Index

Arabic, 73, 162
  source material and, 5
Arab-Israeli conflict, 1, 146–47
  Reagan administration and, 112
  weapons of mass destruction
    and, 152–53
Arab-Israeli War (1973), 92
  oil exports to United States and,
    103
Arab-Israeli War of 1967, 64–65
  Qaddafi and, 67
Arab League, 100, 140, 176, 178,
    179
  intervention effects and, 198
  Libyan Civil War and, 212–13
  2011 Revolution and, 180, 181–82,
    188–89, 190–91
Arab oil embargo (1973-1974), 103
Arabs, 28, 96. *See also* Arab states;
  pan-Arabism
Arab Socialist Union, 75
Arab Spring, 1, 164–65
  intervention effects and, 198–99
  Qaddafi reaction to, 168
  Saif Qaddafi and, 230
  2011 Revolution and, 185
  United States and, 172
  US policies and, 166–67
Arab states, 49–50
  air operations and, 189
  Libyan Civil War and, 219
  Libyan coup and, 70–71
  Libya's pro-Western orientation
    and, 57–58
  post-Qaddafi government and,
    202
  post-Qaddafi power vacuum
    and, 198
  2011 Revolution and, 178,
    181–82
Arafat, Yasser, 93, 142
  Billy Carter and, 104–5
Arundell, R. D. H., 42–43
al-Assad, Hafez, 91–92
  pan-Arabism and, 93

assassination plots, 118–19
Atlantic Charter, 43–44
Axis of Evil, 151
Axis powers, 46
  Aouzou Strip and, 98
  Azienda Generale Italiana Petroli
    (AGIP), 89–90, 101–2, 134–35

Badoglio, Pietro, 22
al-Bakkush, Abdel Hamid, 65
Balbo, Italo, 24, 26, 30–31
  African expansion and, 31–32
  Italian expansionism and, 33–34
  Italian Muslims and, 28
Balkans, 13
Bannon, Stephen K., 222–23
Barbary States, 6–8
Baruni, Sulaiman, 17–18
Basic People's Congress, 77–78, 82
  election-fixing and, 82
Battle of Tripoli, 224–28
  ceasefire talks and, 228–30
  Libyan Civil War and, 224
Bedouin culture, 66–67, 77–78,
    114, 159, 161–62
Belgium, 94–95
Ben Ali, Zine El Abidine, 165, 173
  Arab Spring and, 168
Benghazi, 168–69, 170–71
  2011 uprising in, 165–66
  intervention effects in, 197
  post-Qaddafi government and,
    201
  2011 Revolution and, 175, 179,
    180, 182–83, 185–86
  US Consulate attack and, 203–6,
    208–9
Berlin bombing, 123–24
Berlin Conference of 1884-1885, 9
Berlin Crisis, 48–49
Berlusconi, Silvio, 156–57
  Qaddafi's fall and, 196
  2011 Revolution and, 174–76
Bevin, Ernest, 45, 49
  Bevin-Sforza plan and, 51–52

Index   269

Bidault, Georges, 49
Biden, Joseph R., 228–29
Bills, Scott L., 41, 44–45
bin Laden, Osama, 136, 146–47
  US domestic politics and, 205
Black September group, 94–95
Blair, Tony, 151–52
  weapons of mass destruction
    and, 154–55
Bolton, John, 225
Bongiovanni, Luigi, 21
Bouchard, Charles, 189
Bourguiba, Habib, 93, 105
Britain, 1, 2
  air operations and, 189
  Arab-Israeli War and, 64–65
  Arab states and, 49–50
  Barbary Wars and, 6, 8
  Benghazi Consulate attack and,
    203–4, 208
  Cyrenaica and, 43–44
  embassy killing in, 118
  independence and, 38
  intervention effects and, 197–98
  Iraq invasion and, 153
  ISIS and, 216
  Islamism and, 136–37
  Italian expansionism and, 31–34
  Italian expulsion and, 42
  Italian-German expulsion from
    North Africa and, 41–43
  Italian-Ottoman War and, 13
  Libyan Civil War and, 213
  Libyan exiles fighting with,
    38–39
  Lockerbie and, 131–32, 139–41,
    144
  London embassy shooting and,
    146
  military bases and, 48–49
  Nasser and, 57–58
  Nasser criticism of, 62
  oil and, 58–59, 79–80
  Ottoman Cyrenaica and, 15
  Qaddafi and, 67

Qaddafi's Cold War policies
    and, 83
  restoration of King Idris and, 71
  Revolutionary Command
    Council and, 70
  Senussi and, 16
  statehood and, 52–53
  20-year mutual defense policy
    with, 55
  2011 Revolution and, 174, 176,
    185
  US air strikes and, 126–29
  weapons of mass destruction
    and, 150–52, 154–55
  World War I and, 16–17
  World War II and, 34–37
  See also Allies
British Military Administration
    (BMA), 41–43
British Petroleum (BP), 89–90
Brittan, Leon, 118
Brothers of Italy, 221
Burns, William, 148, 154
Bush, George H. W., 121
Bush, George W., 147
  credibility of, 167
  diplomatic recognition and, 158
  freedom agenda initiative and,
    166–67
  Iraq invasion and, 153
  lifting sanctions and, 150
  weapons of mass destruction
    and, 151–52, 154–55
Byrnes, James, 45

Calderoli, Roberto, 157
Cameron, David, 174, 175–77
  Benghazi Consulate attack and,
    208–9
  intervention effects and, 197–98
  Qaddafi's fall and, 196
  regime change and, 187
  2011 Revolution and, 178,
    183–85
Cameroon, 31–32

270 Index

Camp David Accords, 92–93, 103
Carlos the Jackal, 96
Carter, Billy, 104–5
Carter, James Earl, 103, 104–7
  Reagan campaign against, 112
Casey, William J., 113, 119
Central Intelligence Agency
    (CIA), 119–20, 129
  Libyan Civil War and, 213
  RCC and, 71
  Soviet Union and, 113
  US anti-terrorism strategy and,
    121
Central Powers (World War I), 15
Chad, 31, 32, 34, 97–100, 110–12
  ICJ ruling and, 142
  Qaddafi international
    interventions and, 117
  relations with France and, 101
  Soviet Union and, 113
  2011 Revolution and, 185
  World War I and, 16–17
Chemical Weapons Convention,
    150–51, 154
Cherbisc, Yusuf, 28
Chernobyl nuclear reactor
    disaster, 133–34
China, 140
  anti-Qaddafi movement and,
    172–73
  Battle of Tripoli and, 226
  2011 Revolution and, 176, 181,
    190–91
Chirac, Jacques, 149
Chorin, Ethan, 185–86
Chouchane, Noureddine, 216–17
Christianity, 21–22
  conversion to, 29–30
  slave trade and, 8
Church, Frank, 104
Churchill, Winston, 43–44, 154–55
Clinton, Bill, 146–47, 153
Clinton, Hillary, 158, 176–77, 178,
    179, 180

airstrikes and, 188–89
regime change and, 187
US domestic politics and,
    205–6
Cold War, 1, 2–3, 47–49
  base treaties and, 55–56
  Libya's permanent status and,
    45
  neutralism and, 62, 73
  Qaddafi and, 82–84
  trusteeship and, 47
colonialism, 2–3, 9–11, 24–25
  "crusader aggression" and,
    182–83
  Fourth Shore and, 25–26
  Italian Peace Treaty and, 46
  permanent status and, 43–45
  Qaddafi opposition to, 95–96
  reparations for, 157
  2011 Revolution and, 190
  United Nations and, 49–50
  World War I and, 16–17
  World War II and, 34, 39–40
  See also Italy
Committee of Twenty-One,
    52–53
communism, 83–84
Comprehensive Test Ban Treaty,
    151, 154
Congo, 142
constitution, 52–53
  federalism and, 61
Conte, Giuseppe, 220, 222
corruption, 163–64, 194, 206–7
Council of Foreign Ministers
    (CFM), 44–45
  Italian Peace Treaty and, 46
Covid-19 pandemic, 221
Craxi, Bettino, 128
Cretz, Gene, 202
Crispi, Francesco, 10–11
Crowley, Philip J., 173–74
cultural revolution of 1973, 77
Cumming, Duncan C., 42–43

Cyrenaica, 3
British Military Administration in, 41–42
Executive Committee of Tripolitanian and Cyrenaican Communities and, 30–31
Idris and, 48
Idris favoritism toward, 54–55
Italian colonization and, 22–23
Italian conquest and, 21
Italian-Ottoman War and, 13, 14, 15
Italian rule and, 18–19
Italy and, 43–44
Libya's permanent status and, 45
loss of authority of, 164
modernization and, 24–25
oil-based socioeconomic development and, 61
post-Qaddafi autonomy and, 207
protests in, 170
regional schisms and, 51
Revolutionary Command Council and, 69
statehood and, 52–53
World War I and, 16
World War II and, 35, 37–39
Cyrenaican National Front, 51–52

D'Alema, Massimo, 145–46
Day of Revenge (October 7), 86–87
Days of Rage, 165–66
Dbeiba, Abdul Mamid, 229–30
de Bono, Emilio, 25–26
democracy, 2–3
intervention effects and, 198–99
post-Qaddafi government and, 201, 202
Qaddafi's fall and, 195, 197
Democratic Party (US), 205–6
Derna flood, 230

development, 1
de Villepin, Dominique, 149
Dini, Lamberto, 140–41, 145–46
Dodecanese Islands, 13

East Africa, 33–34
economic development, 60–64, 80, 109–10, 164
domestic reforms and, 161
impact of sanctions and, 134–36
oil-based development and, 60–62
socialism and, 79–80
US sanctions and, 125
Eden, Anthony, 43–44
Egypt, 31
Arab Spring and, 164–65, 168
Battle of Tripoli and, 227
British penetration of, 10
Chad and, 110–12
exile repatriation from, 41–42
Italian expansionism and, 31–32, 33
Libyan Civil War and, 212–13, 219
Muslim Brotherhood and, 74
Nasser and, 57–58
oil and, 58–59
oil exports to United States and, 103
Operation Rose and, 119–20
pan-Arabism and, 92
Qaddafi's Cold War policies and, 83–84
Qaddafi's pan-Arabism and, 91–93
recognizing legitimacy of Israel and, 103–4
Sudan and, 100
2011 Revolution and, 179
World War I and, 15–16
World War II and, 34–37
Eid, Guy, 94–95
Eilts, Herman, 103–4

272 Index

elections, 82, 201, 229–30
  Islamist militias and, 210–11
  United Kingdom of Libya and, 54
Ente Nazionale Idrocarburi (ENI),
    85–86, 145–46, 157, 174–75
Erdogan, Recep Tayyip, 227
Eritrea, 9, 31
al-Esawi, Ali, 177–78
Esso Corporation, 59
Ethiopia, 9–10, 31, 32–33
  conquest of, 28
  Qaddafi agreement with,
    116–17
ethnography, 76f
Euro-Mediterranean Partnership,
    155
Europe, 117–18, 203
  response to US pressure on
    Qaddafi in, 125–26
  US air strikes and, 126–29
European Union, 146
  Battle of Tripoli and, 224–25
  2011 Revolution and, 176–77,
    178, 181–82, 185
Executive Committee of
    Tripolitanian and Cyrenaican
    Communities, 30–31
exiles, 30–31
  Qaddafi and, 81
  repatriation and, 41–42
  royalist movements by, 87
  settler communities as, 73
  World War II and, 38–39
extradition, 139–41, 145–46

Falklands War, 127
fascism, 19, 26, 27–28, 30
federalism, 61
Federation of Arab Republics
    (FAR), 91–92
Fezzan, The, 3
  Aouzou Strip and, 98
  coup against revolutionary
    government in, 74

France and, 49
French withdrawal from, 56–57
Italian colonization and, 22–23
Italian conquest and, 20–21
Italian expulsion and, 41–42
Italy and, 29
Libya's permanent status and,
    45
regional schisms and, 51
Revolutionary Command
    Council and, 69
Fhimah, Al-Amin Kalifa, 131–32,
    141, 143–44
First Barbary War, 7–8
Fitzgerald, Mary, 201–2
Five Star Movement (FSM), 220
"Five Year Economic and Social
    Transformation Plan" (1976-
    1980), 80
Five-Year Plan (1963), 61–62
Fletcher, Yvonne, 118
food supply, 110
Fourth Shore, The *(la Quarta
    Sponda)*, 23, 25–26
France, 8, 49, 189, 226
  air space denials by, 126, 128
  anti-Qaddafi movement and,
    173–74
  Aouzou Strip and, 98–100
  Chad and, 110–12
  early treaties with, 6
  embassy closings and, 105
  Italian expansionism and,
    32–34
  Italian expulsion and, 41–42
  Italian-Ottoman War and, 13
  Kingdom of Libya and, 56–57
  Libyan Civil War and, 213
  Libyan Civil War settlement
    and, 221–22
  Libyan coup and, 72
  lifting sanctions and, 149–50,
    155–56
  Lockerbie and, 148–49

Morocco colonized by, 11
Nasser and, 57–58
policies towards Qaddafi
and, 85
relations with, 101
Tunisia seized by, 10
2011 Revolution and, 176–78,
183–85, 191
UTA bombing and, 131, 146
World War I and, 16–17
World War II and, 37
See also Allies; Free French
Frattini, Franco, 183–85
Free French, 37, 41
Aouzou Strip and, 98
See also France
Fundamental Law (1919), 17–18
second issue (October 1919) of,
18–19

Gates, Robert M., 178–79, 197
General Directorate for External
Security (DGSE), 216
General National Congress
(GNC), 200–2
Islamist militias and, 209–11
Libyan Civil War and, 212,
217–18
Political Isolation Law
and, 208
General People's Committee
(Qaddafi cabinet), 160–61
General People's Congress (GPC),
77–79, 108–9
national liberation movements
and, 113
General Purpose Force, 208
Geneva Convention on
the Territorial Sea and
Contiguous Zone, 106
genocide, 176, 179, 183, 198
2011 Revolution and, 179–80
Gentiloni, Paolo, 220, 222–23
Georgia (US state), 104

Germany, 13, 41–43, 189
Italian expansionism and, 32,
33, 34
land purchase rumors by, 12
Nazism and, 30
resistance to French by, 11
2011 Revolution and, 176–77,
181, 183–85
World War I and, 15–17
World War II and, 35–36, 37,
38–39
Ghanem, Shukri, 161
al-Ghwell, Khalifa, 212
Giolitti, Giovanni, 12
global recession (1970s), 90
Goldstein, Joshua S., 198–99
Gorbachev, Mikhail, 133–34
Gortney, William E., 187–88
Government of National Accord
(GNA), 215–16, 217–19
Battle of Tripoli postwar
settlement and, 228
Haftar and, 226–28
Libyan Civil War and, 224
Libyan Civil War settlement
and, 221
Macron and, 224–25
Trump policy and, 223
Government of National
Salvation (GNS), 212
Grant, Mark Lyall, 180–81
Graziani, Rodolfo, 22
Italian conquest and, 20–21
Great Depression, 25–26
Great Man-Made River, 109–10
Greece, 35–36
NATO and, 47–48
Green Book, The (Qaddafi), 77–78,
79, 160–61
Group of Eight (G-8), 178, 208
Group of Seven (G-7), 128
Gulf of Sidra, 106–7, 114–17, 123
European powers and, 117–18
Guterres, António, 224

Habré, Hissène, 99–100, 110–12
al-Hadawi, Bashir, 81
Haftar, Khalifa, 224–28
  Civil War settlement and, 221–22,
    228, 229–30
  ISIS and, 216, 217
  Islamist militias and, 209–11
  Libyan Civil War and, 211,
    212–13, 218–19, 224
  Trump policy and, 223
Hague Convention, 41
Haig, Alexander, 110–11
Ham, Carter F., 188–89
Hamid II, Sultan Abdul, 11–12
Hasan, Crown Prince, 66
  abolition of monarchy and, 68
  Revolutionary Command
    Council and, 69–70
  revolutionary government
    and, 75
High State Council (HSC), 217–18
Hitler, Adolf, 34–35, 36
  Amin praise of, 100
Hollande, Francois, 215
House of Representatives (Libya),
  210–12, 217–18
House of Representatives (United
  Kingdom of Libya), 53
human rights, 157–58, 185
  2011 Revolution and, 175–76
Hussein, King (King of Jordan),
  57–58

Ibrahim, Musa, 186–87
Idaho, 104
Idris, Mohammed (King Idris), 16,
  18–19, 38–39
  abolition of monarchy and, 68
  Aouzou Strip and, 98
  Arab-Israeli War and, 65
  Britain and, 48, 71
  exile of, 69–70
  foreign policy of, 55–57
  Italian expulsion and, 42–43
  as king, 54–58

Kissinger on, 70–71
  Nasser criticism of, 62
  nuclear policy and, 132–33
  oil-based socioeconomic
    development and, 60–62
  Petroleum Law of 1955
    and, 60
  pro-Western orientation and,
    57–58
  Qaddafi and, 66–68
  regional schisms and, 51
  revolution and, 65–66
  statehood and, 52–53
  trial in absentia of, 75
  World War II and, 37–38
Imazighen community, 162, 164
imperialism, 82–83, 94, 95. *See also*
  colonialism
independence, 43–45, 50
India, 2011 Revolution and, 176
Indyk, Martin, 153
International Atomic Energy
  Agency (IAEA), 132–33, 154
International Code of Conduct
  Against Ballistic Missile
  Proliferation, 151
International Court of Justice
  (ICJ), 111–12, 140, 142
International Criminal Court
  (ICC), 176
  Saif Qaddafi and, 230
International Monetary Fund, 161
Iran, 58–59, 105–7, 136
Iran and Libya Sanctions Act
  (1996), 132, 147
Iran-Iraq War, 93
Iraq, 57–58
  Benghazi Consulate attack and,
    209
  cultural cohesiveness of, 202
  invasion of, 153, 155
  Israeli nuclear reactor airstrike
    and, 133
  Qaddafi UN address and, 159
  2011 Revolution and, 178–79

Irish Republican Army (IRA), 97, 127

Islam, 29–30
anti-Islamic cartoons and, 165–66
Christian republican triumph over, 8–9
confinement of extremism and, 2–3
constitution and, 53
Italian conquest and, 21–22
Italian-Ottoman War and, 14
Italy and, 29–30
Qaddafi and, 66–67
Qaddafi's Third Universal Theory and, 77
radical union of, 95
reforms contrary to, 81
revolutionary government and, 73–74
2011 Revolution and, 190

Islamic Pan-African Brigade, 168–69

Islamic State in Iraq and Syria (ISIS), 197–98, 214–17, 228–29
Haftar and, 218
Trump and, 222–23

Islamic Youth Shura Council (MSSI-*Majlis Shura Shaba al-Islam*), 214

Islamism, 147, 164
assassinations of former Qaddafi officials, 203–4
Battle of Tripoli and, 225–27
Benghazi Consulate attack and, 206
domestic reforms and, 162
Erdogan and, 227
ISIS and, 214–15
Libyan Civil War and, 211–14, 224
Libyan Civil War settlement and, 222
Lockerbie and, 139
normalization and, 146–47

post-Qaddafi government and, 201–2, 209–11
protests blamed on, 169, 170
Qaddafi and, 136–38
Qaddafi's fall and, 195
2011 Revolution and, 191
weapons of mass destruction and, 151, 152–53

Israel, 1
Amin and, 100
French arms and, 85
Libyan coup and, 70–71
Munich Olympic incident and, 103–4
Nasser and, 57–58
nuclear reactor air raids by, 133
opposition to, 51
Oslo accords and, 142
Palestine and, 158–59
Palestinian liberation and, 95–96
pan-Arabism and, 94
Qaddafi's policy towards, 94–95
recognizing legitimacy of, 103
Sadat's moderation towards, 92–93
See also Arab-Israeli conflict

Italianization, 26–27

Italian-Ottoman War (1911-1912), 11–15

Italian-Senussi War of 1914-1917, 14–15

Italo-Libyan Joint Communication (1998), 140–41

Italy, 2–3, 28–32
1923 military operations and, 19–20
1947 peace treaty with, 46
African colonization and, 9–10
air operations and, 189
Aouzou Strip and, 98
Benghazi consulate attack and, 165–66
Berlusconi and, 156–57

276 Index

Italy (*cont.*)
  colonization by, 10–11, 22–27
  conquest by, 20–22
  Cyrenaica and, 43–44
  emergence of, 6
  expulsion of, 41–43
  Franco-British policy
    and, 33–34
  ISIS and, 215, 216
  Kingdom of Libya and, 56
  Libyan Civil War and, 213
  Libyan Civil War settlement
    and, 221–22
  Libyan coup and, 71
  loss of colonies by, 43–45
  migration and, 219–21
  normalization and, 145–46
  policies towards Qaddafi and,
    85–87
  Qaddafi and, 101–2
  settler exile and, 73
  2011 Revolution and, 174–75,
    176–77, 185, 191
  United Nations and, 49–50
  US airstrikes and, 128
  World War I and, 16–19
  World War II and, 34–40

al-Jahm, Fathi, 158
Jalil, Mustafa Abdel, 144
Jalil, Mustafa Mohammed Abdul,
  172
Jamahiriya (state of the masses),
  77–78, 81–82, 170, 180
Japan, 33
Jefferson, Thomas, 6–7
Jewish population, 64, 86–87
  compensation for expulsion
    of, 156
  exile of, 73
Jibril, Mahmoud, 177–78, 200, 201
  Qaddafi's fall and, 195
John Paul II, Pope, 140
Johnson, Boris, 221–22

Jones, Deborah, 213
Juppé, Alain, 180–81
Justice and Construction Party,
  201

Karamanli, Yusef, 7–8
al-Keeb, Abdel Rahim, 200,
  207–8
Khan, A. Q., 134, 151–52, 154
Ki-Moon, 181
Kissinger, Henry, 70–71
Kusa, Musa, 148, 150

labor, 61, 62
Latin America, 49–50
  Reagan administration
    and, 112
Lausanne, Treaty of (Treaty of
  Ouchy), 14, 19–20
Laval, Pierre, 32–33
League, the, 220
League of Nations, 33
Lebanon, 93
  2011 Revolution and, 180, 181
Leon, Bernardino, 213–14
Libya, United Kingdom of, 50, 53,
  54–58
  foreign policy of, 55–57
Libya Dawn, 211–12
  Civil War settlement and,
    217–18
  ISIS and, 214–16
Libya-Italy Memorandum of
  Understanding on Migration
  (LIMUM), 220, 221
Libyan Arab Force, 42–43
Libyan Arab Republic, 68
Libyan Civil War, 211–14,
  217–21
  Battle of Tripoli and, 224–28
  migration and, 219–21
Libyan Colonization Society, 26
Libyan Free Unionist Officers'
  Movement, 67–68

Libyan Islamic Fighting Group
(LIFG), 136–37
Libyan Labor Law of 1957, 61
Libyan Liberation Committee,
51–52
Libyan National Army (LNA),
210, 221–22
Libyan National Army, Battle of
Tripoli postwar settlement
and, 228
Libyan National Oil Company,
145–46
Libyan Patriots Movement,
136–37
Libyan People's Bureaus
(embassies), 105–6, 113–14
British police officer killed
outside, 118
London shooting and, 146
Libyan Political Agreement (LPA),
217–18
Lockerbie bombing (Scotland),
131–32
9/11 and, 148
lifting sanctions and, 150
normalization and, 145–47
Qaddafi and, 159–60
sanctions and, 151–52
sanctions impact after,
139–41
trial verdict of, 143–45
UTA bombing and, 148–49

al-Mabruk, Izz al-Din, 88
Macron, Emmanuel, 221–22,
224–25
Madison, James, 8
Magarha (tribe), 168–69
al-Magariaf, Mohammed Yousef,
201
al-Maghrabi, Mahmoud
Sulayman, 73, 88
Malta, 132, 140
Mandela, Nelson, 141, 144

Mann, James, 2011 Revolution
and, 179–80
Margerie, Emmanuel de, 128
Mathaba [World Center] to Resist
Imperialism, Racism, and
Reactionary Forces, 113–14
Mattis, James, 222–23
McMaster, H. R., 222–23
Mediterranean Union, 156
Medvedev, Dmitry, 222
al-Megrahi, Abdelbaset, 131–32,
141, 143–45
Meheisi, Omar Abdullah, 81, 96
Meloni, Giorgia, 221
mercenaries, 168–69
Merkel, Angela, 178, 183–85
Qaddafi's fall and, 196
Middle East, 89, 90, 136
Soviet Union and, 47–48
Migdal, Joel S., 165
migration, 2–3
human rights and, 156
ISIS and, 215
Italianization and, 26
Italy and, 157
Libyan Civil War and, 219–21
Libyan Civil War settlement
and, 222
2011 Revolution and, 174–75, 185
military bases, 47–49, 55–57
Arab-Israeli War and, 64
Nasser and, 57–58
Nasser criticism of, 62
Qaddafi's Cold War policies
and, 83
See also Wheelus Field
militias, 201
Benghazi Consulate attack and,
203–4
Libyan Civil War and, 211–14
post-Qaddafi government and,
203, 207–8, 209–11
See also Islamism; terrorism
al-Mishri, Khaled, 221–22

278 Index

Misrata, 166, 168–69, 171
  Qaddafi's fall and, 195
  2011 Revolution and, 185–86,
    188, 190
modernization, 24–25
Molotov, V. I., 45
monarchy, 48, 53, 54–55
  abolition of, 68
  Arab-Israeli War and, 65
  See also royalists
Montgomery, Bernard, 36–37
Montreal Convention of 1971,
  139, 140
Moore, George C., 94–95
Moro, Aldo, 72, 85–87, 101–2
Morocco, 6
  colonization of, 11
Moussa, Amr, 190–91
Mubarak, Hosni, 165
  Arab Spring and, 168
mujahedeen, 136–37
Mukhtar, Umar al, 21–22
Mullen, Mike, 185–86
Munich Olympic Games, 94–95,
  96, 103–4
al-Muntasser, Omar, 140–41
Muslim Brotherhood, 136, 164
  Lockerbie sanctions and, 139
  post-Qaddafi government and,
    201, 209, 210–11
  revolutionary government and,
    74
Muslims, Italy and, 28
Mussolini, Benito, 19–20
  1937 Libya visit by, 27–28
  Africa and, 31–32
  Fourth Shore and, 23, 25
  Islam and, 29–30
  Italian expansionism and, 32,
    33–34
  Libyan conquest and, 20–21
  World War II and, 34–37

Nabil, Abu, 216–17
Napoleonic Wars, 8

Nasser, Gamal Abdel, 57–58
  Arab-Israeli War and, 64–65
  influence on Qaddafi of, 66–68
  neutralism and, 62, 82–83
  Qaddafi and, 90–91
  revolution and, 65–66
Nasserism, 61–62
  Qaddafi and, 66–67
National Conference for the
  Libyan Opposition, 165
National Congress of Tripolitania
  (NCP), 54
National Constituent Assembly of
  Libya (NCAL), 52–53
National Forces Alliance, 201
National Front for the Salvation of
  Libya, 119
nationalism, 30–31, 75
  liberation movements and, 113
  Muslim Brotherhood and, 74
  Qaddafi's Third Universal
    Theory and, 77
  revolution and, 65–66
  See also pan-Arabism
nationalization, 85, 88–90
National Oil Corporation (NOC),
  219
National Security Decision
  Directives (NSDD), 115–16,
  121–22
National Transitional Council
  (NTC), 171–72, 177–78, 190–
  91, 200–1
  Qaddafi's fall and, 195–96
  2011 Revolution and, 191–93
Netherlands (Holland), 141
  Algiers shelling by, 8
  early treaties with, 6
neutralism, 73
  anti-imperialism and, 82–83
  revolution and, 65–66
Newsom, David D., 96
New York City, 158–60
New York Times, 158–59, 221–22
Nicaragua, 112, 118–19

Nidal, Abu, 96, 120, 142
al-Nimeiri, Jaafar, 91, 100
Noel, Cleo, 94–95
No-Fly Zone (NFZ), 178–80, 184*f*
  Libyan Civil War and, 212–13
  2011 Revolution and, 176
nomadic lifestyle, Italy and, 29
non-Arab states, 97–100
non-state actors, 95
normalization, 145–47, 157–60
North Atlantic Council, 189
North Atlantic Treaty
  Organization (NATO), 47–48,
  140–41, 189–93
  airstrikes and, 186–89
  post-Qaddafi government and,
  203
Northern, Richard, 181
North Korea, 134, 151
Norway, air operations and, 189
Nouheid, Lin, 163–64
nuclear capability, 83–84, 151, 154
  intervention effects and, 198
  weapons development and,
  132–34
Nuclear Non-Proliferation Treaty
  (1968), 132–33

Obama, Barack, 158–59
  airstrikes and, 187
  Benghazi Consulate attack and,
  203, 205, 208
  Cairo address by, 167
  European leadership and, 203
  intervention and, 196–98
  ISIS and, 215–17
  "leading from behind" policy
  of, 179–80
  Libyan Civil War and, 213
  Lockerbie and, 144
  2011 Revolution and, 173–74,
  175–76, 178–80, 181–83
Occidental Petroleum, 88–89
oil, 2–5
  Aouzou Strip and, 97–98

Arab-Israeli War and, 64, 65
  British reliance on, 127
  discovery of, 58–60
  economic instability and,
  109–10
  economic reform and, 80
  European powers and, 117–18
  impact of sanctions and, 134–35
  Italy and, 101–2, 157
  Libyan Civil War and, 211–12,
  219
  Libyan coup and, 70–71
  Lockerbie sanctions and, 139
  map of infrastructure for, 58*f*
  normalization and, 145–47,
  159–60
  policies towards Qaddafi and,
  85–86
  post-Qaddafi government and,
  202
  RCC and, 71
  Reagan sanctions and, 122
  relations with France and, 101
  revolution and, 65–66
  socioeconomic development
  and, 60–62
  standards of living and, 81
  2011 Revolution and, 178, 185,
  196
  United States and, 102–3
  US embargos on, 115–16
  US sanctions and, 125
  weapons of mass destruction
  deal and, 155
  Western corporate interests
  and, 87–90
oligopoly, 88–89. *See also* oil
Omar Agha (Dey Omar), 8
One September Agreement, 88–89
Operation Dignity, 210, 211–13
  Civil War settlement and,
  217–18
  ISIS and, 214–16
Operations Tulip and Rose,
  119–20

280 Index

Organization for the Prohibition of Chemical Weapons (OPCW), 154
Organization of African States, 140
Organization of African Unity, 99–100, 140
Organization of Petroleum Exporting Countries (OPEC), 89, 90, 116
Oslo accords, 142
Ottoman Empire, 8, 10
  Italian-Ottoman War and, 11–15
  World War I and, 15–16
Oueddei, Goukouni, 99–100, 110
Own, Ahmed, 148

Pack, Jason, 163–64, 181
Palestine, 93
  Arab-Israeli War and, 64–65
  arming of, 94–95
  Israel and, 158–59
  liberation of, 95–96
  recognition of, 142
  statehood for, 125
  weapons stockpiled for, 170
Palestinian Liberation Organization (PLO), 133
Palmer, Joseph, 103
Pan Am Flight 103 bombing, 131. *See also* Lockerbie bombing (Scotland)
pan-Arabism, 30–31, 51, 72
  foreign policy moderation and, 142
  Italian Peace Treaty and, 46
  Muslim Brotherhood and, 74
  Qaddafi policies towards, 90–94
  Qaddafi's Israel policy and, 94
  Qaddafi's Third Universal Theory and, 77
  shift to pan-Africanism and, 140
  socioeconomic instability and, 62
  tribal cultures and, 164

Pargeter, Alison, 193
Paris Peace Conference (1919), 16–17
Paris Peace Forum (2018), 221–22
Pelt, Adrian, 52–53
perestroika, 133–34
Petroleum Law of 1955, 60
Philosophy of the Revolution (Nasser), 66–67
Pinotti, Roberta, 215
piracy, 6, 8–9
Political Isolation Law, 208
Pompeo, Mike, 223, 225–26
Potsdam Conference (1945), 44
poverty, oil and, 60–62
Power, Samantha, 179
Presidency Council (PC), 217–18
Prigozhin, Yevgeniy, 226–27
Prince, Erik, 226
Prodi, Roman, 155
Putin, Vladimir, 226–27

Qadaffa (tribe), 168–69
al-Qaddafi, Hanna, 124
al-Qaddafi, Khami, 194
al-Qaddafi, Moatassim, 158, 194
  domestic reforms and, 161–62
al-Qaddafi, Muammar, 1, 66
  9/11 and, 147–48
  airstrikes and, 186–89
  Aouzou Strip and, 97–100
  Arab-Israeli War and, 64–65
  Arab Spring and, 166–67
  Berlusconi and, 156–57
  Carter administration and, 104–7
  Chad and, 110–12
  civilian airliner bombings and, 131
  Cold War and, 82–84
  consolidation of power and, 69–70
  corporate oil interests and, 87–90

deteriorating US relations and, 118–20

diplomatic recognition and, 157–58

domestic opposition to, 81–82

domestic reforms and, 160–62

economic instability and, 109–10

economic reform and, 79–80

Europe and, 125–26

European powers and, 117–18

fall of, 192–96

foreign policy moderation by, 141–43

France and, 72

Gulf of Sidra and, 114–17

human rights and, 175–76

impact of sanctions and, 134–36

Iraq invasion and, 153

Islamism and, 136–38

Israel policy of, 94–95

Italy and, 101–2

Lockerbie bombing and, 131–32

Lockerbie sanctions and, 139–41

Lockerbie trial and, 143–45

migration and, 219–20

National Transition Council and, 171–72

1980s revolutionary reforms and, 108–9

non-Arab African states and, 97–100

normalization and, 145–47

nuclear weapons development and, 132–34

oil exports to United States and, 102–3

political reformation by, 75–79

post-Qaddafi transition and, 200–2

psychological assessments of, 114

Qaddafi UN address and, 158–60

reaction to mass protests by, 168–71

Reagan administration and, 112–14

Reagan and, 129–31

relations with France, 101

Revolutionary Command Council and, 70

revolutionary government and, 72–75

Revolution of 2011 origins and, 163–64

Sarkozy and, 155–56

seizure of power by, 66–68

significance of, 3–5

terrorism and, 121–23

terrorism objectives of, 95–97

2011 Revolution and, 163–64, 168–71, 177–80, 183–86, 190–92, 196–99

United Nations Security Council and, 176–77, 180–83

US air strikes and, 126–29

US anti-terrorism strategy and, 121

UTA bombing and, 148–49

weapons of mass destruction and, 150–52, 154–55

Western policies towards, 84–87

al-Qaddafi, Saad, 194

al-Qaddafi, Saif al-Arab, 188, 194

al-Qaddafi, Saif al-Islam, 143, 149, 169

Battle of Tripoli postwar settlement and, 230

capture of, 194

death of, 188

domestic reforms and, 161–62

intervention effects regarding, 198

2011 Revolution and, 190

weapons of mass destruction and, 151

Qaddafi International Foundation for Charitable Associations, 143

282 Index

al-Qaida, 136, 146–47, 154–55
  Biden and, 228–29
  US domestic politics and,
    205–6
  Qatar, 181–83, 188, 189, 202,
    212–13

Rabb, Maxwell, 115
Rabta chemical weapons plant,
  130–31
Rajma Agreement, 18–19
Rasmussen, Anders Fogh, 189,
  203
Reagan, Ronald, 2, 107
  air strikes and, 126–29
  anti-terrorism strategy of,
    123–25
  Chad and, 111
  civilian airliner bombings and,
    131
  Gulf of Sidra engagements and,
    114–17
  military options and, 125–26
  Qaddafi and, 129–31
  terrorism and, 119–20, 121–23
  US anti-terrorism strategy and,
    121
Red Brigades, 97
reform, 79–80, 81
  Qaddafi's five stages of, 75–79
regime change, 186–87, 197
  intervention effects and, 198
Renzi, Matteo, 215
Republican Party (US), 205–6
Responsibility to Protect doctrine
  (RtoP), 175–76, 179, 183
  intervention effects and, 198–99
Revolutionary Command Council
  (RCC), 68, 72–75
  CIA and, 71
  consolidation of power and,
    69–70
  corporate oil interests and, 88
  GPC replacement of, 77–78
  Italy and, 86–87

revolutionary committees, 77–78,
  108–9
Revolutionary Committees
  Movement, 82
revolutionary movements, 108–9
  1973 cultural revolution
    and, 77
  globalization of, 95
  terrorism and, 96–97
Revolution of 1969, 65–66
  Qaddafi and, 66–68
  Western reactions to, 70–72
Revolution of 2011, 163–64, 168–
  71, 177–80, 183–86, 190–92,
  196–99
  airstrikes and, 186–89
  Arab Spring and, 166–67
  fall of Qaddafi and, 192–96
  human rights and, 175–76
  National Transition Council
    and, 171–72
  No Fly Zones and, 184f
  triggers of, 164–66
  United Nations and, 176–77,
    180–83
  Western governments and,
    172–75
Rice, Condoleezza, 158, 160,
  166–67
Rice, Susan, 179, 180–81
Richards, David, 187–88
al-Rida, Hasan, 54–55
Rogers, William P., 70–71
Roman Empire, 23, 24–25
Rome airport attack, 120, 121–23
Rommel, Erwin, 35–37
Romney, Mitt, 205
Roosevelt, Franklin D., 44
  permanent status and, 43–44
Royal Dutch Shell, 155
royalists, 69–70
  exile movements by, 87
  revolutionary government and,
    74
  See also monarchy

Russia, 140, 154
anti-Qaddafi movement and, 172–73
Battle of Tripoli and, 226–29
intervention effects and, 197
post-Qaddafi power vacuum and, 198
2011 Revolution and, 176, 181, 190–91
See also Soviet Union
Rutte, Mark, 178

al-Sadat, Anwar, 91–93
oil exports to United States and, 103
al-Sadawi, Bashir, 54
Sadr, Imam Musa, 93
Sahara Desert, 3
Saint-Lot, Emile, 50
Salame, Ghassan, 227–28
Saleh, Aguila, 221–22
Saraa Triangle, 32
Sarkozy, Nicolas, 155–56
anti-Qaddafi movement and, 173–74
regime change and, 187
2011 Revolution and, 175–76, 177–78, 182, 185, 191
al-Sarraj, Fayez, 217–18, 221–22
criticism of France and, 224–25
Libyan Civil War and, 224
Libyan Civil War settlement and, 222
Trump policy and, 223
Saudi Arabia, 31, 47–48, 65, 102, 157
Sayf-al-Nasr tribe, 51
Scotland, 131–32, 139–41
Lockerbie court and, 143–45
See also Lockerbie bombing (Scotland)
Second Barbary War, 8
Second Italian-Senussi War (1923-1931), 21
Security Brigades, 137–38

segregation, 30
al-Senussi, Abdullah, 146
Senussi Order, 14, 25–26, 164
abolishment of, 75
Italy and, 29
revolutionary suppression of, 74
Second Italian War and, 21–22
statehood and, 52–53
World War I and, 15–16
World War II and, 37–39
settlement, 25–27
nomadic lifestyle and, 29
revolutionary government and, 73
World War II and, 39–40
Sforza, Carlo, 49
Bevin-Sforza plan and, 51–52
Shalgam, Abdel Rahman, 144, 149, 152
2011 Revolution and, 176
al-Shalhi family, 63–64, 66
Sharia law, 29–30
ISIS and, 214
revolutionary government and, 73–74
al-Sharif, Sayed Ahmed, World War I and, 15–16
Simpson, John, 194–95
Sirte, 192–93
Sirtica, The (desert region), 3
al-Sisi, Abdel Fattah, 209–10, 211
Battle of Tripoli and, 225–26
Libyan Civil War settlement and, 222
Trump policy and, 223
slave trade, 8
socialism, 72
economic reform and, 79–80
Muslim Brotherhood and, 74
Socialist People's Libyan Arab *Jamahiriya*, 77–78
social media, 164, 204
Arab Spring and, 164–65
Somalia, 9

284 Index

Somaliland, 31, 32–33
  World War I and, 16–17
source material, 5
Soviet Union, 36, 57
  anti-Soviet security issues and, 47–49
  arms for terrorists and, 95
  Cold War and, 46
  collapse of, 135–36, 141–42
  containment of, 2–3
  European powers and, 117
  Italian Peace Treaty and, 46
  nuclear weapons development and, 132–34
  Qaddafi's Cold War policies and, 83–84
  Reagan administration and, 112–13
  Sadat expulsion of, 92
  Sudan and, 100
  threat of alliance with, 115
  US-Libyan relations and, 103
  See also Allies; Russia
Spain, 6, 126
Spanish Civil War, 33–34
Stalin, Joseph, 43–44
state-building, 194–95
  failure of, 197, 198
statehood, 52–53
  delay of, 49–50
  oil and, 58–60
Steadfastness and Confrontation Front, 92–93
Stevens, Christopher, 203–4, 213
  US domestic politics and, 205–6
Stewart, Michael, 71
strada litoranea (coastal highway), 24, 27–28, 36–37
Sudan, 31, 32, 100
  British penetration of, 10
  Chad and, 110–12
  Libyan Civil War and, 212–13
  pan-Arabism and, 91

Suez Canal, 1, 9
  Italian expansionism and, 31–32, 33
  oil and, 58–59
  World War II and, 34–35, 36–37
Suez War (1956), 63
al-Suwayhli, Ramadan, 15, 17–18
Switzerland, 159–60
Syria, 92
  cultural cohesiveness of, 202
  Egypt merger with, 91
  intervention effects and, 198–99
  ISIS and, 214
  pan-Arabism and, 93
  post-Qaddafi power vacuum and, 198

Tajoura Nuclear Research Center, 132–33, 134, 154
Taliban, Qaddafi UN address and, 159
Tanzania, 100
Tawergha community, 168–69
Tehran Agreement (1971), 89
Terbil, Fathi, 165–66, 170
terrorism, 2
  civilian airliner bombings and, 131
  deteriorating US relations and, 118–20
  ISIS and, 214–15, 217
  labeled state sponsor of, 106
  Libyan Civil War and, 213
  Lockerbie bombing and, 131–32
  post-Qaddafi power vacuum and, 198
  Qaddafi's foreign policy objectives and, 95–97
  Reagan administration and, 113
  Reagan and, 129–30
  removal from state-sponsored list and, 148
  Sadat reaction to, 92
  Saif Qaddafi moderation on, 143

US airstrikes and, 126–29
US-Libyan relations and, 103–4
US relations restored and, 157–58
US sanctions and, 125
US strategy and, 121, 123–25
See also Islamism; militias
Thatcher, Margaret, 118, 127
al-Thinni, Abdullah, 210, 215–16
Third Universal Theory (of Qaddafi), 77
Three Year Economic and Social Development Plan (1973-1975), 80
Tindemans, Leo, 126
Tobruk, 36
Toyota War, 111
Treaty of Friendship, Cooperation, and Good Neighbor Policy, 156, 157
Treaty of Lausanne (Treaty of Ouchy), 13
Treaty of London (1915), 16–17
tribal cultures, 12, 14, 17–18, 22, 41–43, 54
  Italy and, 29
  mass protests and, 168–69
  pan-Arabism and, 164
  Qaddafi and, 137–38
  unitary state and, 75
tribute system, 8
Tripoli, 6
  Barbary Wars and, 7–8
  Green Square demonstrations in, 166
  Italian-Ottoman War and, 13
  protests in, 169, 170–71
  Qaddafi's fall and, 195
  2011 Revolution and, 185–86, 187–88, 191–93
  United States evacuation from, 174
Tripolitania, 3, 17–18, 19

British Military Administration in, 41
Executive Committee of Tripolitanian and Cyrenaican Communities and, 30–31
Italian colonization and, 22–23
Italian conquest and, 20–21
Italian-Ottoman War and, 14
Libya's permanent status and, 45
modernization and, 24–25
post-Qaddafi government and, 201
regional schisms and, 51
statehood and, 52–53
United Nations and, 50
World War II and, 37–38
Tripolitania National United Front, 51–52
Truman Doctrine, 47–48
Trump, Donald J., 205–6, 217, 222–23, 225–26
trusteeship, 43–45
  Cold War and, 47
  division of, 49
  United Nations and, 48
Tuareg (tribe), 41
Tunis, 6
Tunisia, 34
  Arab Spring and, 164–65, 168
  backing armed insurgency in, 105
  Israeli airstrikes and, 133
  Qaddafi provoking revolts in, 93
  2011 Revolution and, 179, 191–92
  World War II and, 37
al-Turk, Akram, 194
Turkey, 19–20
  air operations and, 189
  Battle of Tripoli and, 227–28
  Libyan Civil War and, 212–13
  NATO and, 47–48
  post-Qaddafi power vacuum and, 198
  2011 Revolution and, 190–91

286 Index

UAE, Battle of Tripoli and, 227
Uganda, 100, 104, 142
UNESCO (United Nations
  Educational, Scientific and
  Cultural Organization), 156
Union de Transports Aériens, Flight
  772 (UTA), 144, 146, 155–56
  lifting sanctions and, 150
  Lockerbie settlement and,
  148–49
unitary state, declaration of, 63–64
United Arab Emirates (UAE), 202,
  212–13
  Battle of Tripoli and, 227–28
  French arm sales to, 226
  Libyan Civil War and, 219
United Arab Republic, 91
United Nations, 45, 51–52, 228–30
  airstrikes and, 186–88
  Battle of Tripoli and, 225–26,
  227–28
  Battle of Tripoli postwar
  settlement and, 228–30
  Chad and, 111–12
  European leadership and, 203
  impact of sanctions and, 134–36
  Italian colonialism and, 49–50
  Italian Peace Treaty and, 46, 47
  Kingdom of Libya and, 56–57
  Libyan Civil War and, 212–14,
  217–19
  Libya's permanent status and,
  43–44
  lifting sanctions and, 149–50
  Lockerbie and, 131–32, 139–41,
  144, 148–49, 151–52
  normalization and, 145–47
  Qaddafi address to, 158–60
  Qaddafi seeking US
  condemnation by, 130–31
  Qaddafi's fall and, 195, 196
  Qaddafi UN address and, 159

Resolution 1973 of, 163–83,
  186–88
Responsibility to Protect
  doctrine and, 175–76, 179
sanctions and, 139, 141,
  148–50
sanctions lifted by, 160–61
self-defense clause of, 127
Soviet Union membership veto
  in, 57
statehood and, 52–53
trusteeships and, 48
2011 Revolution and, 174–78,
  180–83, 190–91, 198
United States, 1, 2
  9/11 and, 147–48
  airstrikes and, 133, 187
  air strikes by, 126–29
  anti-terrorism strategy of, 121,
  123–25
  Arab-Israeli War and, 64–65
  Arab Spring and, 166–67
  Arab states and, 49–50
  Barbary Wars and, 6–9
  Battle of Tripoli and, 224–26
  Benghazi Consulate attack and,
  203–6, 208–9
  Camp David Accords and,
  92–93
  Carter administration and,
  104–5
  Chad and, 99–100, 110–12
  civilian airliner bombings and,
  131
  deteriorating relations with,
  118–20
  diplomatic recognition and,
  157–58
  Europe and, 125–26
  Gulf of Sidra air engagements
  with, 114–17
  intervention and, 196–98

Iran hostage crisis and, 105–7
Iraq invasion and, 153
ISIS and, 215–17
Libyan Civil War and, 213
Libyan coup and, 70–72
lifting sanctions and, 149–50
Lockerbie and, 131–32, 139–41, 144
military bases and, 48–49
Nasser and, 57–58
Nasser criticism of, 62
normalization and, 145–47, 157–60
oil and, 58–59, 102–3
oil embargo by, 117–18
pan-Arabism and, 94
protests against, 135
Qaddafi policy of, 85
Qaddafi's Cold War policies and, 83
Qaddafi's Israel policy and, 94–95
Reagan administration and, 112–14
Reagan and, 129–31
Revolutionary Command Council and, 70
revolutionary struggles in, 96
statehood and, 52–53
strike-breaking and, 62
Sudan and, 100
terrorism and, 121–23
Truman Doctrine and, 47–48
Trump Libya policy in, 222–23
2011 Revolution and, 173–74, 175–76, 178–80, 181–83
weapons of mass destruction and, 150–52, 154–55
Wheelus Field and, 55–56
World War II and, 37
See also Allies

United States House of Representatives Benghazi Committee, 205–6
United States Senate Select Committee on Intelligence (SSCI), 206
UN Support Mission in Libya (UNSMIL), 203
USS Philadelphia, 7–9

Vatican, 140
Victor Emmanuel (King of Italy), 12
Victor Emmanuel III, King, 19–20
Vienna airport attack, 120, 121–23
Vitelleschi, Nobili, 9
Volpi, Giuseppe, 19–20
Libyan conquest and, 20–21

Wagner Group, The, 226–27
Walters, Vernon L., 126, 127, 128
Warfalla (tribe), 168–69
Warfalla Conspiracy, 137–38
War of 1812, 8
Warren, Alex, 163–64
Warsaw Pact, 103, 113
Washington, George, 6–7
Washington Post, 107
Wavell, Archibald, 35, 38–39
weapons of mass destruction (WMD), 150–52, 154–55
Iraq invasion and, 153
Western, Jon, 198–99
Western Libya Gas Project, 145–46
Westerwelle, Guido, 178, 181
Wheelus Field, 48–49, 55–56, 63
Qaddafi's Cold War policies and, 83
Revolutionary Command Council and, 70
Whitehead, John, 125–26

Williams, Stephanie, ceasefire talks and, 228–29
Wilson, Harold, 71
Wilson, Woodrow, 17
Woodward, Bob, 119
World Trade Organization, 155
World War I, 15–19
  French-German colonization tensions and, 11
  Italian-Ottoman War and, 13
World War II, 2, 37–40
  colonialism and, 34
  Libya's strategic significance in, 34–37
  permanent status after, 43–45

Yalta Conference (1945), 43–44
Yemen, Qaddafi agreement with, 116–17
Younes, Abdel Fattah, 195
Young Turks, 11–12

Zeidan, Ali, 201–2
  Benghazi Consulate attack and, 208–10
  Libyan Civil War and, 213
Zenga Zenga videos, 169–70
Zintani militias, 210, 211–12
Zionism, 94–95, 141–42
  revolution and, 65–66
Zuma, Jacob, 190–91